ISBN 978-1-332-31027-2
PIBN 10312317

1 MONTH OF
FREE
READING

at

www.ForgottenBooks.com

By purchasing this book you are eligible for one month membership to ForgottenBooks.com, giving you unlimited access to our entire collection of over 700,000 titles via our web site and mobile apps.

To claim your free month visit: www.forgottenbooks.com/free312317

Similar Books Are Available from
www.forgottenbooks.com

The Christian Mythology
by Brigham Leatherbee

Jesus and What He Said
by Arthur Salter Burrows

Reincarnation in the New Testament
by James Morgan Pryse

Dictionary of the Holy Bible
by William Wilberforce Rand

Being a Christian
by Jas A. Duncan

Heaven
by Dwight Lyman Moody

How to Pray
by R. A. Torrey

The Bible and Evolution
by W. H. Sparshott

The Aquarian Gospel of Jesus the Christ
by Levi

Christ and His Church in the Book of Psalms
by Andrew A. Bonar

Christian Healing
A Sermon Delivered at Boston, by Mary Baker Eddy

Church History Through All Ages
by Thomas Timpson

The Life of Jesus, Vol. 1 of 2
For the People, by David Friedrich Strauss

The Serpent, Satan and False Prophet
Or the Trinity of Evil, by Unknown Author

The Christian Faith and the Old Testament
by John M. Thomas

Christianity and Sex Problems
by Hugh Northcote

The Evolution of Spiritual Man
by William McIntire Lisle

The Beacon of Truth
Or Testimony of the Coran to the Truth of the Christian Religion, by William Muir

A Biblical View of the Church
by Josiah Goodman Bishop

Muhammad and Christ
by Moulvi Muhammad Ali

ante festum 23 vi 16

To Joe,

If you *really* can't do the math (or are looking for something more profound), you could do worse than try this.

Paul Beattie

CHAPTERS ON THE BOOK OF MULLING

Paul Beattie
St Molin's Cottage
(nistioge
Thomastown.

Printed by Neill & Company, Edinburgh

FOR

DAVID DOUGLAS

LONDON	SIMPKIN, MARSHALL, HAMILTON, KENT, AND CO., LIM.
CAMBRIDGE	MACMILLAN AND BOWES.
GLASGOW .	JAMES MACLEHOSE AND SONS.

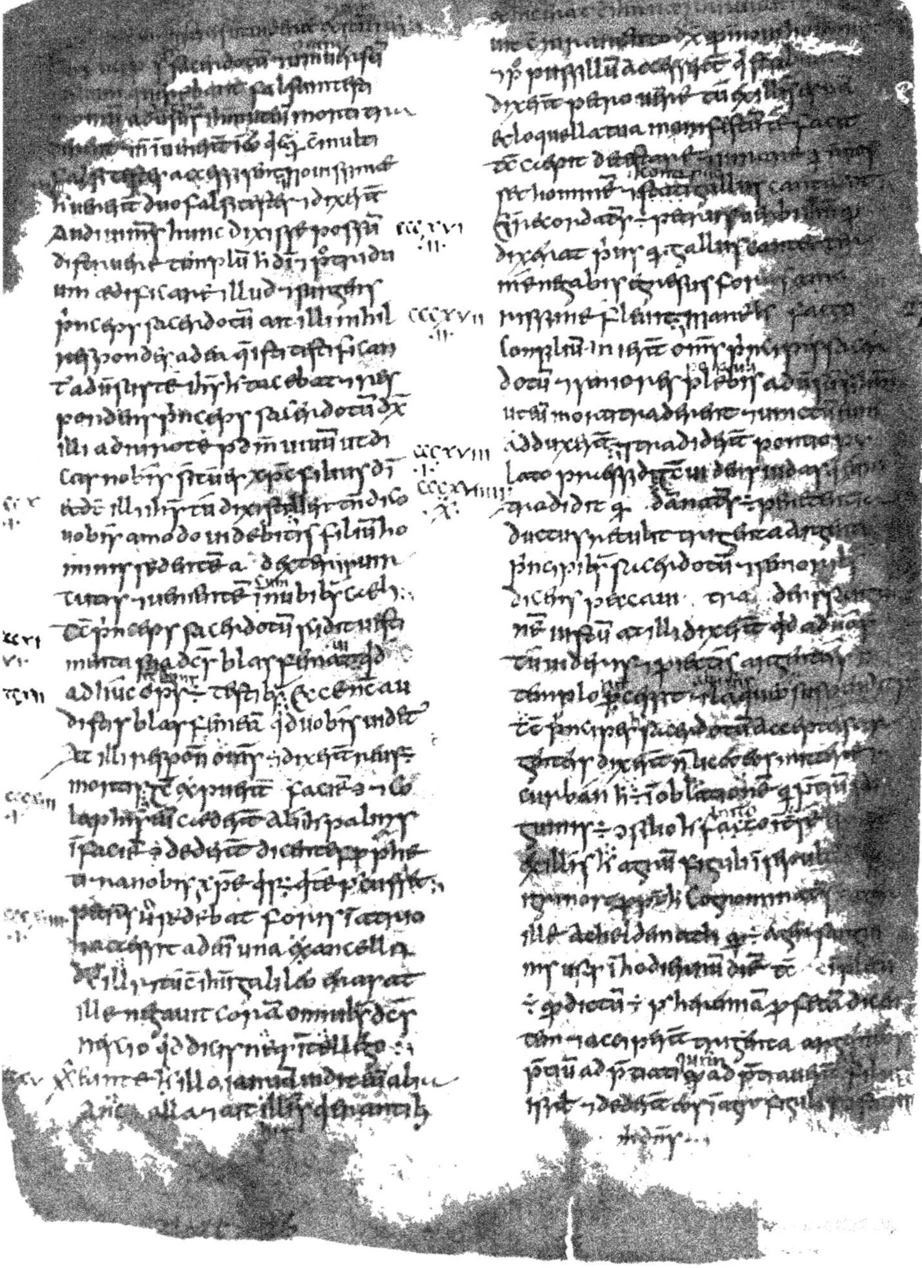

Book of Mulling, f. 48 r. (S. Matt. xxvi. 58–xxvii. 10).

D.

CHAPTERS

ON THE

BOOK OF MULLING

BY

H. J. LAWLOR, B.D.

SENIOR CHAPLAIN OF ST MARY'S CATHEDRAL, EDINBURGH, AND
EXAMINING CHAPLAIN TO THE BISHOP OF EDINBURGH

EDINBURGH: DAVID DOUGLAS

1897

IN PIAM MEMORIAM
CARISSIMORUM

K. A. H. L.

J. H. L.

A. S.   K. S.

CONTENTS.

THE BOOK OF MULLING.

CHAPTER I.

INTRODUCTORY.

M. BERGER, in his account of the early Irish Biblical Texts,[1] gives special prominence to two manuscripts which he describes as among the most important of the national manuscripts of Ireland. The first of these is the celebrated Book of Armagh, the other is that which is the subject of this essay, the Book of Mulling. The principal contents of this book are the four Gospels in Latin, but it has also the prefaces of Jerome, the table of the Eusebian Canons, an Office for the Visitation of the Sick, and other matter of which some account will be given in succeeding chapters. The book can scarcely be dated later than the third quarter of the ninth century, for an incidental notice in the *Annals of the Four Masters*[2] of the monastery in which it was beyond doubt written, proves that shortly after that time it had become a Danish settlement. Palæographers, judging from the character of the script, assign it to that, or the previous century.

Notwithstanding the interest and importance of our manuscript it has received but little attention from students of the ancient lore of Ireland. To Archbishop Ussher it appears to have been unknown. There is no reference to it, so far as I can discover, in the many volumes of his works.

The first author in whose writings I have found a notice of the book is the well-known Irish antiquary General Vallancey. For him, however, that which was of main interest was not the book, which he seems to have examined in the most cursory fashion, but its ancient case or cumdach, of which, under the name of the Liath

---

[1] *L'Histoire de la Vulgate pendant les premiers siècles du Moyen Age*, par Samuel Berger, Paris, 1893, p. 31.

[2] A.D. 888. "A battle was gained by Riagan, son of Dunghal, over the foreigners of . . . . Tech-moling."

Meisicith, he gives a lengthy description.[1] All that is really known of this shrine is that it was in existence—possibly even then a venerable relic—in the year 1402.[2] Vallancey ascribed to it a much greater antiquity, and was persuaded that it had come down from the ancient Druids. Of its contents he briefly and not very correctly writes :—

"It contains a number of loose sheets of vellum, on which are written extracts of the gospel and prayers for the sick, in the Latin language, and in the Irish character. There are also some drawings in water colours of the apostles, not ill executed ; these are supposed to be the work of Saint Moling, the patron of that part of the country." [3]

When Vallancey wrote (1783[4]), the Book of Mulling was still, as it had been for many centuries, in the charge of the family of Kavanagh, and was seen by him at their family seat at Borris Idrone, only a few miles from the site of the monastery founded by St Molling of Ferns, known as Tech Moling, or in its anglicised form, St Mullins. But a few years later it was deposited, with its cumdach, and the Charter Horn of the Kavanaghs, in Trinity College, Dublin. It thus became more accessible to scholars.

Among those who subsequently inspected it in its new resting place was the indefatigable entomologist and student of ancient manuscripts, Mr J. O. Westwood, to whom Trinity College owes so much for making generally known many of the priceless literary treasures which it possesses. Westwood's *Palæographia Sacra Pictoria* appeared between 1843 and 1845, and in it[5] a description (unfortunately not very accurate) of the Book of Mulling,[6] together with facsimiles of a few lines of its writing.

Some years later our manuscript was incidentally mentioned by Professor O'Curry in his *Manuscript Materials*, and the Appendix to that work was enriched with two facsimiles of its script, one being taken from Jerome's Preface to St John's Gospel, the other from Matt. vi. 9 *sqq.* (the Lord's Prayer), accompanied by a brief description.[7]

But about this time the attention of liturgical students was drawn

[1] Vallancey, *Collectanea de Rebus Hibernicis*, Dublin, 1786, vol. iv. no. xiii. pp. 13–21.

[2] See Professor Abbott's "Note on the Book of Mulling" in *Hermathena*, viii 89.

[3] The Rev. J. F. M. ffrench, in his article entitled "St Mullins, Co. Carlow," in the *Journal of the Royal Society of Antiquaries of Ireland*, 5th series, part iv. vol. ii. p. 379, repeats almost verbatim this description of Vallancey.

[4] This is the date appended to the dedication of his thirteenth number, which is inscribed to the Society of Antiquaries of Scotland.

[5] "Irish Biblical MSS.," Plate II. (Letterpress, p. 4 *sq.*). Some account of the book is given also in his later work, *Facsimiles of the Miniatures and Ornaments of Anglo-Saxon and Irish Manuscripts*, London, 1868, p. 93.

[6] Westwood's descriptions are the basis of that given by Miss M. Stokes in *Early Christian Art in Ireland*, p. 24 *sq.*

[7] O'Curry's *Lectures on the Manuscript Materials of Ancient Irish History*, Dublin, 1861, pp 28, 335 *sq.*, App., pl. 5, p. 653.

to the Office for the Visitation of the Sick which is found at the
close of St Matthew's Gospel. The late Dr William Reeves, Bishop
of Down, Connor, and Dromore, whose loss Irish antiquarians still
mourn, supplied a transcript of this Office to Bishop A. P. Forbes of
Brechin, by whom it was printed in the preface to his edition of the
Arbuthnott Missal.[1] The Visitation Office was again printed by
Mr F. E. Warren in 1881.[2]

After an interval of five years from the publication of the
Arbuthnott Missal (in 1869) two works appeared almost simultan-
eously, in which attention was called to the character of the Biblical
text contained in our manuscript. The first in order of time was
the first volume of Haddan and Stubbs' *Councils*.[3] In an appendix
to this work the attempt was made to prove the existence of a distinct Irish recension of the Latin Scriptures, and to trace the general
history of the text of the Bible in that country in the centuries
following the introduction of Christianity. Among other codices
collated for this purpose was the Book of Mulling; and once more
the hand of Dr Reeves was engaged in the task. Later in the same
year Dr John Stuart edited for the Spalding Club the remarkable
relic of the early Scottish Church which had been discovered in the
Cambridge University Library, twelve years before, by Mr Henry
Bradshaw.[4] At the end of his preface,[5] Dr Stuart printed, in parallel
columns, collations of the fourth chapter of the Gospel according to
St John as given in the principal Irish codices—and one of the
columns is assigned to our book.

In the Introduction to the first part of Gilbert's great collection
of *Facsimiles of National Manuscripts of Ireland*, published in 1874,
our manuscript is once more described,[6] unfortunately in the most
meagre fashion. But what specially distinguishes this notice of the
book is the fact that three complete pages are given in facsimile,
together with one of the drawings of the evangelists alluded to by
Vallancey and Westwood. The reproduced pages are f. 42 *r* and
v (Matt. xviii. 8—xix. 16), and f. 94 *r* (John xxi. 13–25 and
colophon).[7] On the opposite pages of Gilbert's work the text of
these passages is printed line for line, contractions being expanded.
It is strange that, with Westwood's *Palæographia* before him, Gilbert
has read only fourteen words of the colophon, and of these, at
least two incorrectly.

Finally, in 1893, was published the epoch-making work of M.

[1] *Liber Ecclesie Beati Terrenani de Arbuthnott. Missale secundum usum
Ecclesiæ Sancti Andreæ in Scotia*, Burntisland, 1864, pp. x, *sq.*, xx, *sqq.*
[2] *Liturgy and Ritual of the Celtic Church*, Oxford, 1881, p. 171 *sqq.*
[3] *Councils and Ecclesiastical Documents relating to Great Britain and Ireland*,
vol. i., Oxford, 1869, Appendix G. (pp. 170-198).
[4] G. W. Prothero, *Memoir of Henry Bradshaw*, London, 1888, p. 69.
[5] *The Book of Deer, edited for the Spalding Club*, by John Stuart, LL.D.,
Edinburgh, 1869, p. xxxiv, *sqq.*
[6] *National MSS. of Ireland*, i. p. xiii.
[7] *Ib.*, pl. xx., xxi.

Berger, to which reference was made at the beginning of this chapter.
It gives a description of our manuscript, with some interesting obser-
vations on its text.[1]

This is an enumeration as complete as I have been able to make
it—though doubtless the learned reader will observe some omissions—
of the principal notices of the Book of Mulling up to the present
time.

The latest event in its history is the satisfactory settlement of a
controversy which had been for some time pending between the
representatives of its former owners and the authorities of Trinity
College.   The point in dispute was whether, when towards the close
of the last century it was deposited in the College, it was placed there
merely for safe keeping during the troublous times preceding the
Union, or was conveyed to the University of Dublin as a gift by the
then head of the family of Kavanagh.   In accordance with the
agreement finally reached, the manuscript has been definitely acknowledged to be the property of the College, while its ancient shrine has
been restored to Walter Kavanagh, Esq., D.L., and now once more
rests in Borris House.

It remains to pen a few words about the purpose and aim of the
present essay.   Let it be at once said that the design of the writer is
not to give an exhaustive account of the book.   He is quite conscious
that many things have been left unsaid upon which students might
desire to have information.   He is conscious also that the subjects
upon which, in the pages now offered to the public, he has touched
have been but imperfectly treated.   But his aim throughout has been
rather to stimulate the interest of others far more competent than
himself for such investigations, than to give a complete account of
the manuscript.   He has, therefore, contented himself with selecting
one or two features of the book which had been scarcely noticed by
previous writers, and discussing them as best he could.   Much
remains for other better equipped workers in the same field.

It is a pleasant task to enumerate here those to whose kind assistance I have been most beholden while conducting the researches, the
results of which are now set forth.   Professor Gwynn first introduced
me to the study which has proved a constant source of pleasure.
Abundant help and encouragement have been given by him, by his
colleague, Professor Bernard, and by the Rev. Thomas Olden.   It is
scarcely likely that, without the help of these three friends, this
book would have been undertaken.   But not to these alone must
gratitude be expressed.   The Rev. J. M. Harden has spent much
valuable time in examining, with care and accuracy, many of the
manuscripts preserved in the libraries of Trinity College and the
Royal Irish Academy, a change in my residence having made it
impossible for me to consult them, except at rare intervals ; and the

---

[1] *Op. cit.*, pp. 33, 380.

Rev. J. A. MacCulloch has performed the wearisome task of reading the proofs. To them it is due that the errors in these pages are much fewer than they would otherwise have been. Mr J. H. Cunningham, F.S.A. Scot., has also given me valuable help, which is acknowledged at p. 183. I take this opportunity of thanking the Provost and Senior Fellows of Trinity College, Dublin, for their kind assistance in defraying the cost of publication.

Chapters IV. and VI. have already appeared in the *Proceedings of the Society of Antiquaries of Scotland*, and Chapters VII. and VIII. are founded on a communication to the same Society.

CHAPTER II.

THE COLOPHON.

The colophon of the Book of Mulling is written on the concluding page of St John's Gospel (f. 94 *r*). It occupies the four last lines of the first column, and the first few lines of the second. Several attempts have been made to read it, and a portion has been reproduced in facsimile by Westwood in his *Palæographia Sacra*. But as mistakes have crept into all the published transcripts which I have seen, I give it here in full, so far as I have been able to decipher the faded letters.

col. a. ɸINIT   amen   ɸINIT
    ó tv quicūq: Scripseris
    ĩ scrutatus fueris ĩ etıa
    uideris ħ uolumin dm̄ orá
             a

col. b. – – – – – – – – *p* – – – – –
    – – – – – – – [mi]ssericordiā sua
    – – – – – *s* ᵱ cliuosū mondi in
    *d*usq: altissimum :—
    [N]omen ħ scriptoris mulling
    dicitur Finiunt quatuor euan
    gelia

This colophon is to form the text of our discourse in the present chapter. If the discourse does not always adhere very strictly to the limits suggested by the text, it does no more than many other discourses have done. My excuse must be that there are some things which I feel ought to be said about our book, and that I know of no place more fitting for saying them than the present.

§ 1. *The Form of the Book.*

"O tu quicumque scripseris uel scrutatus fneris uel etiam uideris hæc uolumina." Such is the opening address of the colophon of Mulling. Incidentally, it presents us with a description of the book, meagre but worth noting, "hæc uolumina." These two words have not, indeed, so far as I am aware, been hitherto so read. Mr Westwood printed them "ħ (=hæc) uolumen," others, more grammatically, but less correctly, "hoc volumen." There can, I believe, be no doubt that "hæc uolumina" is correct, though the final letter easily escapes notice, being much faded and written below the line.

The author of the colophon then describes his book as consisting of several distinct fasciculi or volumina. That this is true of the Book of Mulling as we have it I now propose to show. It is not applicable, be it observed, to what is handed to the student who asks for our manuscript in the library of Trinity College, Dublin. This is a large quarto volume of paper leaves, in each of which is inserted, with all the skill which marks the work of the binders employed by the British Museum, a leaf of vellum. The volume is duly described on the back, " Book of Mulling," and its contents are arranged in the following order : (1) ff. 1–17, Gospel according to St Mark ; (2) ff. 18–28, Jerome's Epistle to Damasus, the Arguments of the Gospels, and the Eusebian Canons ; (3) ff. 29–50, Gospel according to St Matthew, and other matter ; (4) ff. 51–53, three portraits ; (5) ff. 54–81, Gospel according to St Luke ; (6) ff. 82–94, Gospel according to St John, colophon and other matter ; (7) ff. 95–98, fragments of St Matthew and St Mark ; (9) f. 99, blank. It may perhaps be a relief to learn that some of the folios here brought together do not belong to our book, and that for the rest the peculiar arrangement indicated above has no other source than the ingenuity of the binder.

In the year 1892 I undertook to make a collation of the Biblical text of the so-called " Book of Mulling," now included in this volume. I will describe the condition in which it was on the 18th of February 1893, the day on which my collation was completed. In doing so, I am obliged to depend on notes made without any intention of publication, and much less complete and satisfactory than they might have been had I known that I should have no opportunity in the future of revising them by comparison with the manuscript in the state in which it then was.[1]

There lay, in February 1893, in the library of Trinity College, where it had rested for more than a century, an ancient cumdach, inscribed with the name of " Arthurus rex dominus lagenie," better known as Art MacMurrough Kavanagh († 1417), the opponent of Richard II.,[2] and containing, unstitched and unbound, five fasciculi of vellum leaves, six loose leaves, and one pair of conjugate leaves, the contents and arrangement of which will, I trust, be made clear by the accompanying diagrams and the following description. In the diagrams each leaf is indicated by a line, those which have been lost by dotted lines, and each is connected with its conjugate by a line. Where conjugates had been dismembered when I examined the manuscript, a

[1] I may note that my reconstruction does not seem to agree with that of M. Berger, who must have examined the manuscript some little time before it fell to my lot to do so. He notes (L'Histoire, p. 380), " Cahiers de 12, 22, 17, 1, 28, 14 et 4 ff. ; 98 ff. Les 4 ff. de la fin contiennent un fragment de Matth. xxvi. et xxvii., et de Marc. i.–vi. ; ils sont étrangers au ms. " He had already remarked (p. 34), " Les feuillets étant détachés, il a été quelque peu difficile de reconstituer les cahiers." If I understand his figures they must involve some error. The actual number of leaves now bound together is 99, not 98. If he includes lost leaves (as he seems to do in at least the first gathering), the total would be increased.
[2] See Professor Abbott in Hermathena, viii. p. 90.

row of dots is substituted for the connecting line. The figures in thick type indicate the numbers given to the folios by the British Museum binders; those in ordinary type, numbers which correspond more nearly with the intention of the scribes.

I. The first "volumen," or gathering, at present consists of five pairs of conjugate leaves and one single leaf. There are from twenty-three to twenty-six lines on each page, written all across the page, and about forty letters in each line.[1] It contains (1) f. 18 *r*, Jerome's Epistle to Damasus (the earlier part); (2) f. 19, the arguments of the several Gospels (the first portion of that of St Matthew being lost), ending in the middle of f. 21 *v* with the rubricated subscription, partly retraced in black, "finit [argum]en-[tum euangeliorum]"; and (3) f. 22, the Eusebian Canons (part of the 10th Canon being lost). The hand appears to be the same as that in which the Gospels are written, if indeed we may assume that they were penned throughout by a single scribe. Vermilion appears in the headings to the arguments of the several Gospels (" *de iohanne*," etc.), in the subscription to that of St John, and in the Eusebian Canons. Large ornamental initials (uncoloured) are prefixed to the epistle and the several arguments. The leaves measure about 16·5 × 11·8 cent.

The original contents of this gathering may be inferred from the following considerations. The portion of the epistle (" Novum Opus") contained in f. 18 ends with the words " quod in," p. 3, l. 9, of Bishop Wordsworth's edition of the Vulgate, and is thus represented by 37 lines of that work. The lost portion of the epistle is therefore the equivalent of 24 of Bishop Wordsworth's lines. The earlier portion of the argument of St Matthew, also lost (all before " resurgens," Wordsworth, p. 16, l. 9), = 13 lines. The two together would therefore make 37 lines, or exactly the same amount as f. 18 of our MS. From this we may infer that one leaf intervened between the present ff. 18 and 19, and that it contained the remainder of the epistle and the opening part of the first argument. It is more difficult to determine the contents of the pages which have disappeared at the end. If neither the first nor second (lost) leaf was without conjugate, there must have been at least two of them, as represented in the diagram. On the recto of the first of these was the second half of Canon 10 (all after § 94), which may have filled about one-third of the page. The remainder of these two leaves would have sufficed for the " Prologus Quattuor Evangeliorum" (Wordsworth, p. 11, where it fills 64 lines = nearly 3½ pp. of our book). This fact in itself, in the absence of conflicting evidence, justifies the assumption that both f. 18 and the lost leaf following it had conjugates, as represented in the diagram. Fol. 18 has no marks of stitching, but its inner edge is much worn. Its present width is 11·35 cent. That this gathering was written by the same scribe as those that follow appears to be the opinion of all palæographers who have examined the book. It is one which it seems safe to accept. The hand no doubt differs in some respects from that found in the Gospels, as may be seen from Professor O'Curry's facsimile (*Lectures on the Manuscript Materials of Irish History*, Appendix, pl. 5). But it differs no more from the writing of any part of the Gospels than the writing of one of their pages frequently differs from another. Any one who will compare the exquisite script of the early chapters of St Matthew or St Luke with that of the last pages of St John, will

---

[1] This, of course, does not apply to the Canons.

be sufficiently impressed with this fact. Indeed, a glance at two consecutive pages will sometimes enable us to detect striking variations in the character of the hand. Thus the writing of f. 62 *r* (Luke vii. 4–27) is manifestly inferior to that of f. 61 *v* (Luke vi. 36—vii. 4), and in passing from the latter to the former we meet with several changes in the form of the letters, etc.—*e.g.*, ᵶ is used for ÷ (=est), 5 for ꝫ (*g*), *dīx̄* for *dx̄* (=dixit), etc., and the form of the letter t (that which is commonly used throughout the MS.) differs from that found in the immediately preceding pages. It will be evident to the student who compares them together, that the writing of this leaf closely resembles that of the first fasciculus. The peculiarities now mentioned are gradually dropped on the verso of the leaf, and the normal type of writing reappears on f. 63.

II. The second gathering consisted, as the diagram shows, of eleven pairs of conjugate leaves. Two, originally conjugate, afterwards became dismembered (ff. 29, 50). This quire contained St Matthew's Gospel, ending in the middle of the second column of f. 49 *v*, with the subscription "finit amen finit." The remainder of this column and the following leaf were left blank. On the vacant portion of f. 49 *v*, and on f. 50 *r*, was subsequently written by another scribe[1] the Office for the Communion of the Sick,[2] f. 50 *v* still remaining blank. The writing is bi-columnar, and better executed than that of the preceding fasciculus. The number of lines in a column varies from 25 to 41, being greater towards the end of the Gospel. The average size of a page in this and the three succeeding gatherings is at present $16 \cdot 4 \times 11 \cdot 9$ cent. Elaborate initials, finely drawn and coloured, are found at the beginnings of the Gospels, and at St Matt. i. 18. They have the usual rows of red dots, double in St Matthew and St Mark, single (apparently) in St Luke and St John.

An examination of the Office for the Communion of the Sick (ff. 49 *v*, 50 *r*) appears to justify the statement just made that it is by a different hand from the Gospel. (1) The writing is neater here than anywhere else in the manuscript. (2) The use of large and carefully formed initial letters is much more frequent than usual. (3) Here—one might almost say here alone—the page is divided by lines ruled with a pointed instrument for the guidance of the scribe. Elsewhere, the points at which the lines of writing are intended to begin are occasionally marked, but these marks are but little attended to in practice. (4) Here alone the margins are ruled with two parallel lines, one to serve as a boundary for the ordinary writing, the other for the large initials which stand outside it. It seems improbable that a scribe would expend so much more care on a liturgical office, which is evidently only an addendum to his real work, than on the sacred text itself. (5) The form of several of the letters is peculiar to this part of the book. Such, for example, are *d*, *r*, *g*, and the diphthong *œ*, elsewhere represented commonly by *ę*, here by *ę*. And lastly (6) some of the *compendia scribendi* used by the writer of these pages are very rare in the manuscript, if they occur elsewhere at all. As instances, we may refer to *û* for *ut* or *usque*, the symbols for *per* (ꝑ, else-

---

[1] Westwood (*Pal. Sac.*, "Irish Biblical MSS.," ii. p. 4) says emphatically: "The *original scribe* had" written this Office (the italics are his). But emphasis does not necessarily imply accuracy. In the very next line he declares, with a like use of italics, that the ornamental initials at the beginnings of the Gospels are "*not coloured.*" This is an extraordinary mis-statement. But, indeed, Mr Westwood's account of the Book of Mulling is very inexact throughout.

[2] Printed in Warren's *Liturgy and Ritual of the Celtic Church*, p. 171 *sqq.*, and Forbes' *Arbuthnott Missal*, p. x, *sq.*

where þ) and *pro* (p : elsewhere ꝑ), and the abbreviations *oia* for *omnia*, and *sclā* for *sæcula.* The page is ruled for 33 lines of writing.

III. The third "volumen" contains St Mark's Gospel, and consists of at least six (ff. 8, 9 probably once formed a seventh) conjugate pairs of leaves, and three (or five) single leaves (ff. 4, 15, 16), two of which, it will be noticed, immediately precede the final leaf of the gathering—in all 17 leaves. The writing is again bi-columnar, and there are from 26 to 32 lines in a column. The subscription "finit" is written at f. 17*va*, l. 19, the remainder of the page being left blank.

IV. Here, for St Luke's Gospel, as the diagram again shows us, we have 13 conjugate pairs, and two single leaves (ff. 76, 79) inserted near the end of the quire—altogether 28 leaves. There are from 27 to 39 lines in a column. The Gospel ends on f. 81*vb*, with the subscription "finit amen finit," the part of the column following this being left blank.

V. St John's Gospel is written in a gathering of 13 leaves, the last of which (f. 94) had no conjugate. The remainder of the fasciculus consists of six pairs of leaves, five of which, and probably the sixth (ff. 83, 92), were conjugates. The inner edges of ff. 84, 91 are quite fresh, so that these leaves must have been recently parted from one another. The Gospel ends on f. 94 *r a*, and is immediately followed by the colophon. The greater part of the second column of this page is blank. The verso of the leaf is occupied with matter which will be considered at some length in subsequent chapters. The writing of this gathering is distinctly inferior to that of those which have been already described. It is bi-columnar, except in f. 93, both recto and verso of which have three columns.[1] Towards the end the writing becomes smaller, and the number of lines in a column much greater. The number of lines ranges from 26 on the recto of f. 82, to 50 on f. 93 *r.*

We have now come to the end of the matter which, as I believe, has a clearly established claim to have formed part of the Book of Mulling in its final shape. We have gone far enough also to see that the expression of the colophon is absolutely accurate—"hæe volumina." These "volumina" were never (till these later days) bound together: but that each was separately stitched was, if my memory does not deceive me,[2] vouched for by holes made for the purpose, in such of the sheets (making pairs of leaves) as time and rough usage had left in anything approaching their original condition. They may still be seen in at least three of the six inserted leaves (ff. 4, 16, 79, and perhaps 15, 76). Where these holes are found their distance from the outer edge of the leaf is about the width of an ordinary page. We may remark that the scribe was evidently most anxious to confine each Gospel to its own fasciculus, though he makes grievous

---

[1] This temporary lapse into tri-columnar writing finds a parallel in the Book of Armagh : Stokes, *Tripartite Life,* p. xc.

[2] Even now enough can be discerned to convince me that my recollection is not altogether at fault.

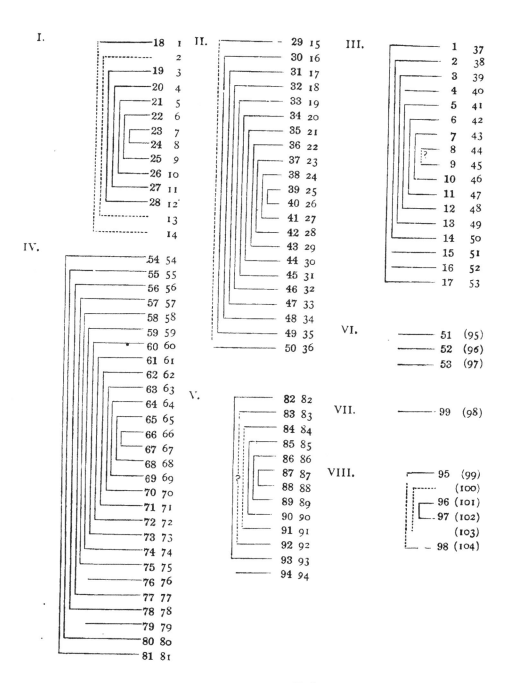

I. II. III. IV. V. VI. VII. VIII.

To face page 10.

miscalculations as to the space required. Thus in St Matthew, he begins in a fine bold hand with 26 lines to a page. As the work advances he seems to become afraid that the quire is too small for what he had designed that it should contain. He accordingly writes more closely, lengthens the lines, and increases the number of lines in each column to 35 or 40, finally ending the Gospel with more than a leaf in hand. In St Mark he miscalculates again, and is obliged to insert two leaves at the end. The same fate awaits him in St Luke. In St John, write as small and as closely as he will, the Gospel runs over its allotted space, and the last thirteen verses demand a special leaf for themselves.

This appears to be the best place to remark that the method of writing here exemplified, each Gospel having a separate gathering, seems not to have been uncommon in the early Celtic Churches. The same arrangement is found in the manuscript known as "St Patrick's Gospels" (*Royal Irish Academy*, 24. Q. 23).[1] The familiar portraits of the evangelists again, each holding a book (of which the drawings formerly preserved in the cumdach of the Book of Mulling are a specimen), indicate that the Gospels were usually regarded as consisting of *four* volumes, and not one. In later times the several Gospels were sometimes provided with separate shrines or cumdachs. Witness the pictures of the evangelists in the Book of Deer, depicted with books, *in cases*, suspended from their shoulders.[2] So again at Banchory-Ternan was preserved, in the early part of the sixteenth century, the Gospel according to St Matthew, written by St Ternan. Both it and the remaining Gospels, written by his hand, were said to have been enclosed in metal cases, adorned with gold and silver.[3] And in like manner St Patrick is represented as bestowing, in one instance,[4] the "*libri* æuanguelii"; in another, the "likeness of the case of the Book of John,"[5] upon churches founded by him, while he and St Brigid are spoken of as "sowing the *four books* of the Gospel with a sowing of faith, and belief, and piety."[6] A further illustration will be found in the next chapter, where it is proved that the Gospels of our book are copied from at least three different exemplars. And indeed, several examples are known of single Gospels being copied apart.[7]

---

[1] J. H. Bernard, *Trans. R.I.A.*, xxx. 307 *sq.*

[2] Such at least seems to be the probable explanation. See Stuart, *Book of Deer*, p. xx.

[3] Martyrology of Aberdeen (*Proceedings of Society of Antiquaries of Scotland*, ii. p. 264): "Fridie Idus Junij.—In Scotia natalis sancti Terrenani Pictorum archipresulis apud ecclesiam de Banquorefterny sepultus. . . Euuangelistarum quoque *quatuor voluminibus* metallo inclusis argento auro texto in superficie fabricatis remuneraretur quorum Mathei euuangeliste volumen adhuc apud Banquory."

[4] Muirchu Maccu-Mactheni's notes in the *Book of Armagh*, f. 8 *b*. 2. *Cf.* Whitley Stokes, *Tripartite Life*, i. p. cxcvii.

[5] Stokes, *Tripartite Life*, i. p. 87.

[6] Stokes, *Lives of Saints from Book of Lismore*, p. 193.

[7] The Stonyhurst St John (Berger, *L'Histoire*, p. 39), the St Gall St John

We must now examine the remaining leaves formerly preserved in the cumdach of our book, and now bound up with it. To begin with the set numbered VIII. in our diagram. This contains St Matt. xxvi. 42—xxvii. 35 *mittentes* (f. 95); St Mark i. 1—iv. 8 *dabit* (ff. 96, 97); and St Mark v. 18 *nauem*—vi. 35 *eius* (f. 98). These leaves appear to have formed part of a single manuscript, and, if so, they may have been two sheets of a quire as shown in the diagram. The writing is not columnar. The size of the leaves varies slightly, the length being from 15·4 to 15·9 cent., and the breadth from 12 to 12·3 cent.; ff. 95, 96, 98 have 36 lines in a page; f. 97 has 33. These fragments, of course, formed no part of our book.

It is scarcely worth while to discuss the blank leaf (f. 99), numbered here VII. It is smaller (15·2 × 11·8 cent.) than any of the four leaves just mentioned, and considerably smaller also than the leaves of the Book of Mulling. It is possibly an accidental intruder.

Of more importance is VI. (ff. 51, 52, 53), the three leaves on the rectos of which we find portraits, presumably of evangelists. They have been described by Mr Westwood in his *Palæographia*; and by him, as well as by others, are regarded as having formed part of our book.[1] This has, perhaps, been too hastily assumed. Their connection with our book is not proved by the fact that they were kept in the same case with it; for the fragments of St Matthew and St Mark, which we have just examined, were enshrined in St Mulling's cumdach also. And this is not the only instance of a manuscript having found its way into a shrine that was not meant for it.[2] Nor is their claim established by the near coincidence in the size of these pictorial leaves with those which undoubtedly belong to our book, for they agree in measurement even more closely with the leaves of St Matthew and St Mark already referred to. They measure, in fact, about 16 × 12·2 cent. In other words, they fall short of the average height of the pages of Mulling's book by nearly half a centimetre, while they exceed the average breadth by more than a quarter of a centimetre. The difference in breadth may indeed have been less originally than it is now, but for similar reasons the difference in height was probably greater.

(*ib.*, 56), and apparently at least one other copy of the same Gospel, which was in the St Gall Library in the ninth century (Keller, *Bilder u. Schriftzüge*, p. 61), and (this, of course, is not a Celtic MS.) the Chartres St John (Berger, p. 89). Not, however, the Stowe St John (Bernard, *Trans. R.I.A.*, xxx. 314). A copy of St Matthew's Gospel, apart from the others, is mentioned in the story of the invention of St Barnabas, written in the sixth century. See *AA. SS.*, Jun. 11, ii. pp. 422, 450. Whatever may be thought of the historical character of the narrative, the reference seems to prove that the writer was aware that such a manuscript existed. M. Berger remarks (*ib.*, 69) that St John was the only Gospel so copied in the early Middle Ages. But the statement seems to need some modification.

[1] Westwood, *Pal. Soc.*, "Irish Manuscripts," pl. ii. p. 5. Of other writers who accept this view I shall mention only one, M. Berger (*op. cit.*, p. 380). His knowledge of the Book of Mulling stands in striking contrast to that of some others who have written about it. It has been derived at first hand from an inspection of the manuscript itself.

[2] J. H. Bernard, *Trans. R.I.A.*, xxx. 305 *sq.*, 313.

On the other hand, they are in exact agreement as to size with one
of the leaves of the fragment—f. 98. But what makes the supposition that they belonged to our book specially doubtful is this. They
have evidently no conjugates among the genuine pages of our book.
Now the inserted leaves, which have the appearance of having
suffered little injury, are, as we might expect, wider than the ordinary
leaves of the manuscript;[1] and, moreover, they have, at a little
distance from the inner edge, the marks of the stitching by which
they were attached to their respective Gospels. This is not true of
the leaves now under consideration. It seems, then, that if these
pictures really belonged to our book, they must have lain loose in
the case in which it was kept, without any mark to indicate the
Gospels to which they severally belonged. When we add that
analogy points to the belief that the Book of Mulling had no metal
box such as that in which it was in later centuries preserved, for a
considerable time after it was written, the improbability of the supposition becomes manifest.[2] It seems, on the whole, likely that
these three pictures (connected quite possibly with some unknown
manuscript) were put for safe keeping into the cumdach of the Book
of Mulling. They were put there, we may suppose, for no better
reason than that, being nearly of the same size and shape as the
inside of the box, they fitted it easily ; just as, for the same reason
no doubt, some other odd leaves of a Gospel book found their way
into the same shrine, and as, owing to a similar agreement in size,
the Stowe St John and the Stowe Missal were placed together in a
single cumdach, and ultimately bound together in one volume.[3]

§ 2. The Date.

What data have we for determining the period at which our
manuscript was written ?

Many scholars have been content to answer that question by
quoting the words of the colophon, "[N]omen hautem scriptoris mulling dicitur." The Mulling here mentioned, it has been urged, can be
no other than Molling, Bishop of Ferns, who died in the year 696.[4]
The book is therefore expressly stated to have been penned by him,
and must be dated in the latter part of the seventh century.

Let me at once say that I believe there is much force in this

[1] The average width is about 12·2 cent., which is identical with that of the
pictorial pages.

[2] All that is certain about the date of the cumdach of the Book of Mulling, as
has been already remarked, is that it existed before A.D. 1402. Whether it was
originally made as a shrine for our book we can never know, though its size and
shape agree with this supposition (inside measurement, 18·2 × 13·3 cent.). The
Book of Durrow (not later than the eighth century) was not enshrined till the end
of the ninth ; the Book of Armagh, written in 807, not until the following century.
The shrine of the Cathach of St Columba, though the Psalter itself certainly
belongs to a much earlier period, is dated 1084 (Miss M. Stokes' *Early Christian
Art in Ireland*, p. 89 sqq.). That of the Stowe Missal may be contemporary
with the later writing of the manuscript enclosed in it.

[3] Bernard, *Trans. R.I.A.*, xxx. 313.

[4] *Annals of Four Masters, Annals of Ulster*, A.D. 696 ; *Annals of Clonmacnoise*, 692 ; *Trip.*, p. 519, A.D. 693.

argument. In the first place, Molling is a name of extreme rarity. The seventh century bishop is the only person mentioned by it, so far as I have been able to discover, in the Irish annals.[1] This is the more remarkable on account of his celebrity. He was reckoned as one of the four prophets of Ireland. Now it is very common to find the names of great saints adopted by others of lesser note. Columba, for example, is very frequently met with. That Molling occurs but once appears to be accounted for by the fact that it is not in the strict sense a " name " at all. The true name of the saint was Daircell, and he was called " Molling," the leaper, on account of his athletic prowess.[2] It is as much, therefore, a descriptive epithet as " Cœur de Lion " applied to Richard I. of England, or " le Chauve " applied to Charles II. of France. It is unlikely that it should be given to another. It may thus be regarded as highly probable that our " scriptor " was the famous Molling of Ferns.

And this probability becomes greater when we recall the history of the manuscript which bears the name. It was, until the end of the eighteenth century,[3] in the custody of the family of Kavanagh, of which St Molling was a member, and whose family seat at Borris Idrone is within a few miles of Tech Moling or St Mullins, the site of the monastery over which he presided. This fact leaves little room for doubt that, by whomsoever penned, every part of our book was written in the monastery of St Molling at St Mullins.[4]

But a further confirmation is found in the fact that St Molling was actually famed as a scribe. Keating, writing in 1630,[5] tells us that " when the Senchas had been purified, the Irish nobles decreed that it should be given into the charge of the prelates of the Irish Church. These prelates gave orders to have it copied out in their principal churches. Some of the old books so written, or rescripts of them, survive to the present day, such as the Book of Armagh, the Psalter of Cashel, the Book of Glendaloch, the Book of Ua Congbala, the Book of Clonmacnois, the Book of Fintann of Cluain Aidnech, the Yellow Book of Moling, and the Black Book of Molaga."

The " Yellow Book of Moling " to which he refers, appears, indeed, to have contained a collection of historical documents, and he does not mention a copy of the Gospels as transcribed by him. But it is almost incredible that an eminent Irish scribe of the seventh century should not have written at least one Gospel book, or that Gospels written by the hand of a saint of great renown would not be among the treasures of his own monastery.

[1] An earlier Molling, however, is mentioned in the Book of Leinster, Molling Luath (the swift), son of Fiacha, as distinguished from our Molling Luachra (of Luachair), son of Faelan, *Revue Celtique*, xiii. pp. 45, 101.
[2] *Dict. of National Biog*, xiii. p. 380.
[3] Vallancey's words, quoted above, p. 2, are sufficient to prove that the contents of the cumdach were the same in 1783 as in 1893.
[4] Mr Warren appears to overlook the importance of this consideration when he writes in the *Academy*, Jan. 26th, 1893, p. 83 : " But who is the ' Mulling Scriptor ' of this volume ? and where was his *civitas* ? The proposal to identify him with St Mulling of Ferns (who died 697) . . . must now be finally abandoned."
[5] *History of Ireland*, O'Mahony's translation, p. 412.

It seems, therefore, almost beyond question, that the assertion of the colophon is that the book to which it belonged was written by Daircell or Molling, the celebrated bishop and scribe of the seventh century.

On the other hand, the almost unanimous testimony of palæographers ascribes our manuscript to a later period. M. Berger,[1] than whom no one is more competent to give judgment, refers it to the ninth, and apparently not to the beginning of the ninth century. Others assign to it a slightly earlier date ;[2] but all agree in placing it at least a century after the time of St Molling.

It may, of course, be urged that one of the most difficult problems of palæography is the determination of the dates of Irish manuscripts.[3] Irish scribes appear to have been strongly conservative, and to have closely imitated older forms of writing and ornament. But, though this fact may move us to push back the date of the manuscript by a few decades, we can hardly place it within the lifetime of Molling if we are to be guided by palæography at all.

The evidence, therefore, of palæography and that of the colophon appear at first sight to be directly opposed. Is it possible to reconcile them? Or is the problem of our manuscript insoluble? What appears to me to be its true solution is suggested by a paper contributed by Professor T. K. Abbott to *Hermathena* on the colophon of the Book of Durrow.[4] The colophon of this copy of the Gospels states that it was written by one Columba, who has been identified with the Apostle of the Picts († 597).[5] Palæography, on the contrary, pleads for the seventh century.[6] Here is Dr Abbott's way of reconciling the two. The colophon, he says, was copied from the archetype. It contains, therefore, the name of the scribe of the archetype, not of the scribe of the manuscript at the end of which it is now found. The archetype, to which it was originally appended, was therefore written, as the colophon states, in the space of twelve days [and therefore probably " in smaller and more cursive characters " than the Book of Durrow] by a scribe named Columba, who may very well have been the founder of Hy.

It is unnecessary to recapitulate here the arguments by which Professor Abbott seeks to establish this conclusion. To prevent misconception, however, it may be well to say how far, as it appears to me, the inference from them is justified.

The state of the case seems to be this. Reasons of some weight have been given for believing that St Columba could not have written a codex with errors so numerous and of such a kind as are

[1] *L'Histoire de la Vulgate*, p. 34.
[2] Scrivener's *Introduction*. 4th ed., ii. p. 78.
[3] Thompson, *Greek and Latin Palæography*, p. 236 *sq.*
[4] Vol. viii. p. 199 *sqq.*
[5] The colophon is given in full in the paper referred to in the text, and also in Professor Abbott's *Evang. Versio*, p. xix.
[6] Berger, *op cit.*, p. 41. In Scrivener's *Introduction*, 4th ed., ii. 78, it is still described "[end of vi]" ; but in an earlier work (*Old Latin Biblical Texts*, iii. p. viii) Mr White had dated it " seventh or eighth century."

found in the Book of Durrow. It has been proved, moreover, that the copy to which the colophon refers must have been written in less elaborate style and in a more cursive character, and that the writer of that copy was named Columba. And finally, arguments falling little short of demonstration have been adduced to show that the colophon was transcribed from another document, which we may reasonably assume to have been that which served as the model for the Gospel text. All this is matter of practical certainty.

But what about the further and most interesting question, Was St Columba the scribe of the archetype to which the colophon belonged? As Dr Abbott truly remarks, there is nothing against this supposition in the fact that the text of the Book of Durrow is Vulgate. St Columba, as he says, may have habitually used an old Latin version, and yet have come across a copy of Jerome's translation and transcribed it for the purposes of private study.[1] We may, in fact, go further, and assert that there is absolutely no direct evidence as to what the version may have been from which St Columba habitually made his quotations. For all that can be proved it may have been just such a text as we find in the Durrow Gospels.

But Professor Abbott really gives us no evidence in favour of the archetype having been penned by St Columba, except the words, " Columbae scriptoris qui hoc scripsi himet (?) euangelium." And he warns us that Columba is a very common name. Thus, as he leaves it, the thesis is "not proven."

Now there is one piece of evidence which he has not mentioned, and which may be thought to tell against the supposition that the Book of Durrow was copied from an autograph of the great saint. It is the wording of the colophon itself : " Rogo beatitudinem tuam sancte praesbiter patriei." Here is a direct invocation of a departed saint. Is it possible that St Columba should have made use of it? It does not seem probable. Less than a century after his death, indeed, such a colophon would not have been surprising. It may be illustrated by several parallels from Adamnan.[2] But if we may judge from the evidence before us, the practice of invoking the departed did not come into vogue till after St Columba had passed away.

Our conclusion then is that the Book of Durrow, including its colophon, is a copy from an earlier codex written by one Columba,[3] whose date cannot with probability be placed earlier than the opening years of the seventh century.

Now, it will be seen that the Book of Mulling presents a problem very similar to that which arises in the case of the Book of Durrow. Palæography and the colophon are much more certainly at variance

---

[1] This supposition is confirmed by the very interesting remarks on St Finnian of Movilla and the introduction of the Latin Bible into Ireland, which will be found in Miss M. Stokes' *Six Months in the Apennines*, London, 1892, p. 25 *sqq.*
[2] Dowden's *The Celtic Church in Scotland*, pp. 225, 233.
[3] If so, Bishop Reeves' assertion (*Life of St Columba*, p. xiv), "that the colophon in Irish manuscripts is always peculiar to the actual scribe, and likely to be omitted in transcription," is scarcely justified by the facts.

here than in the Durrow Gospels. May not a similar solution be found? True, in our book the colophon bears no mark, on the face of it, that it is not original. But analogy has made it possible that it may have been transcribed from an earlier exemplar. The possibility is converted by palæographical considerations into a strong probability. And if it be once conceded that this is a fact, few will be found to question the identity of Mulling. Our manuscript, in short, will be admitted to have been transcribed, or at least ultimately derived, from an autograph of St Molling of Ferns. St Molling, we may suppose, wrote a copy of the Gospels; a century or more after his death an anonymous scribe made a transcript of this book, including the colophon; and this transcript is the "Book of Mulling" which has survived to the present day.

To this hypothesis I can think of only one objection. It scarcely indeed deserves to be so described, but I must not altogether pass it over. The colophon, as we have already seen, speaks of Mulling's book as consisting of several "volumina." This description applies accurately to the five fasciculi of the present book. If our theory is correct the later scribe must have, in this matter, imitated the *form* of his exemplar as well as copied its text. This in itself presents no difficulty. For we shall find that in the much less striking feature of the division into sections he has strictly adhered to the model of his archetype. But what is here in point is the further fact that he has had some difficulty in confining each Gospel to a single "volumen," and has miscalculated in every case the number of leaves required. What could be easier, it may be urged, if he had before him a manuscript arranged in this particular way, than to estimate beforehand how many sheets of vellum he should assign to each gathering? The answer is, first, that we have no measure of the stupidity, or of the incapacity for arithmetical calculation, of Irish scribes; and, secondly, that the requisite calculation was not very much more difficult if his exemplar was constructed on a different principle. A difference in the size of the pages might, perhaps, confuse him in one case; it may equally have done so in the other. His very determination, notwithstanding all mistakes, to adhere to his design may possibly rather indicate that the arrangement was commended to him, not merely by his own sense of fitness, but by some authority whom he desired to imitate closely. Such an authority would be the founder of his monastery.

§ 3. *The Order of the Gospels.*

It has been already remarked that the colophon is found at the end of St John's Gospel. This furnishes conclusive proof that in the conception of the scribe, St John was, as we are accustomed to regard it, the fourth Gospel. Hereafter reasons will be given for the further belief that the order of the Gospels in his view was identical with that of our modern Bibles, Matthew, Mark, Luke,

John. For the present I content myself with remarking that this fact is one which we have no right to assume without evidence.

It is true, indeed, that only one Irish manuscript is at present known in which the sequence is different. I refer, of course, to the Codex Usserianus, edited by Professor Abbott.[1] This copy exhibits the usual "Western" order, Matthew, John, Luke, Mark. This arrangement appears to have been superseded by the introduction of the Vulgate into Ireland. But there is ground for holding that the older tradition did not give way at once, but that, on the contrary, it exercised considerable influence centuries after the version of St Jerome had gained currency.

This influence comes out very clearly with reference to the evangelical symbols. A little space may be given to the examination of this subject.

The first Christian writer who explains the four forms of the Cherubim in the vision of Ezekiel (i. 10) or the four living creatures of the Apocalypse (iv. 7) as referring to the fourfold Gospel is Irenæus.[2] Each Gospel presents a different aspect of the life of Christ; and accordingly St Matthew is symbolised by the Man, proclaiming as he does the human descent of the Saviour and the humility of his human life; St Mark by the Eagle, which signifies the descent of the Holy Spirit upon the Church, on account of his opening quotation from the prophets, and his prophetic style of writing; St Luke, who begins his narrative with the story of Zacharias the Priest, by the Calf—the sacrificial victim; St John by the Lion, because he dwells upon the kingdom of Christ and opens his record with the statement of His divine generation.

For two centuries we hear no more of speculations of this kind, and then we come upon evidence which appears to show that the exegesis of Irenæus was not generally received. In the fourth and fifth centuries the assignment of the symbols to the several Gospels is discussed by several writers, the most important of whom was Jerome. He accepts the view of Irenæus as to the symbols of the first and third Gospels, but gives the Lion to St Mark and the Eagle to St John. It is worthy of special remark that in this he claims no originality. He discusses no rival theory. He professes to have derived his opinion on this subject from older writers.[3] And these

---

[1] *Evangeliorum Versio Antehieronymiana ex Codice Usseriano (Dublinensi)* etc., Dublin, 1884.

[2] Irenæus, *Adv. Hær.*, III. xi. 8 (Harvey, ii. p. 48).

[3] "Quidam quattuor evangelia, quos nos quoque in prooemio commentariorum Matthæi sequuti sumus, horum animalium putant nominibus designari," Vallarsius, v. 9, 10. This sentence is sufficient to disprove the statement made in the *Dictionary of Christian Antiquities*, s.v. "Evangelists," i. p. 633: "Nor was it till long after the four creatures had been taken as prefiguring the four evangelists, that a special application was made of each symbol to each writer. This may be referred to St Jerome on Ezekiel i." It is strange that the writer of the article should have overlooked, not only the words which we have quoted, but the evidence of Irenæus and that of Ambrose and Augustine.

writers, he tells us, had stated their views quite definitely.[1] St Matthew is denoted by the Man, because he commences his Gospel with the human genealogy of Christ; St Mark is symbolised by the Lion, because at the beginning of his Gospel he speaks of the voice crying in the wilderness (in quo vox leonis in eremo rugientis auditur : " Vox clamantis in deserto," etc.); St Luke brings us back to Zachariah the priest, and accordingly to him the Calf is appropriate; St John, taking a higher flight than the rest, proclaims " In the beginning was the Word," he, therefore, is the Eagle (qui assumtis pennis aquilæ, et ad altiora festinans, de Verbo Dei disputat). In the age preceding Jerome and the Vulgate we see that the four symbols were allotted, one to each of the evangelists, and that in the manner to which Jerome himself gave the weight of his authority.

But the witness of Jerome does not stand alone. The language of his contemporary, Ambrose of Milan,[2] is not indeed free from ambiguity, except when he speaks of St Matthew and St Luke, about whom we have hitherto found no difference of opinion. Having expressed his own belief as to the symbols of these Gospels, he goes on to state the accepted opinion.[3] And here it is that his meaning is less clear. His language with reference to the Gospel to which the Lion is to be assigned suggests rather St John than St Mark. " Alius," he says, " a potentiæ cœpit expressione divinæ, quod ex Rege Rex, fortis ex forti, verus ex vero, vivida mortem virtute contempserit." But that St Mark and not St John is intended, is made sufficiently plain by what he says about the meaning of the Eagle. Christ, according to most interpreters, he declares, is the Eagle, because He is the resurrection. And then he proceeds, " Quartus (sc. liber) copiosius cæteris divinæ miracula resurrectionis expressit." These words apply to the Gospel according to St John, and to it alone of the four.[4]

Jerome, then, and others whom he followed, Ambrose and the majority of interpreters known to him, were of one mind. The Man belonged to St Matthew, the Lion to St Mark, the Calf to St Luke, and the Eagle to St John. This was, it would seem, the prevalent view in the middle of the fourth century.[5]

It is not necessary to cite more than one other literary witness. That witness is Augustine of Hippo. He writes as follows[6] :—

[1] Com. in Ezek., i. (Vallarsius, v. 9, 10, 13); Com. in Matt. Prœm. (Vallarsius, vii. 5, 6); Adv. Jovinianum, i. 26 (Vallarsius, ii. 280).

[2] Expositio Evang. Sec. Lucam, Præf., 7, 8 (Migne, xv. 1532).

[3] Plerique tamen putant, etc.

[4] It ought, however, to be mentioned that in later times St Mark was regarded as especially the evangelist of the resurrection, and that this was one of the reasons given for the appropriateness to him of the symbol of the Lion. Durandus, Rationale, vii. 44, 4.

[5] Juvencus, the Spanish Presbyter, has indeed been cited as adhering to the opinion of Irenæus. But the verses in which his views have been supposed to be expressed, and of which more hereafter, are spurious. This is shown by Marold in his edition of Juvencus (Leipzig, 1886), p. vii. sq., and by Huemer in the twenty-fourth volume of the Vienna Corpus, p. xxiv sq.

[6] De Consensu Evangelistarum, I. vi. (9) (Migne, xxxiv. 1046).

" Unde mihi videntur, qui ex Apocalypsi illa quatuor animalia ad intelligendos quatuor Evangelistas interpretati sunt, probabilius aliquid attendisse illi qui leonem in Matthæo, hominem in Marco, vitulum in Luca, aquilam in Joanne intellexerunt, quam illi qui hominem Matthæo, aquilam Marco, leonem Joanni tribuerunt. De principiis enim librorum quamdam conjecturam capere voluerunt, non de tota intentione Evangelistarum, quæ magis fuerat persern-tanda," etc.

St Augustine here mentions two views of the symbols—his own, which agrees with that of Jerome as regards the third and fourth Gospels, and another which is identical with that of Irenæus.[1] Taken literally, his language implies that each of these opinions had supporters in his own or a previous age. But the forms of literary speech must not be pressed too strictly. It seems at least as likely that he was simply controverting (and, we must add, not very fairly [2]) the interpretation of Irenæus, and maintaining his own private gloss.[3] If he had meant to review the main opinions current on the subject, it is inconceivable that he should have passed over that held by Ambrose and Jerome, of which he cannot have been ignorant.

On the whole, the evidence before us is sufficient to convince us that the majority of fourth-century divines were, in this matter, in agreement with Jerome. And our conclusion is corroborated from an unexpected quarter. A small bronze coin, of uncertain *provèn-ance*, which has been assigned to the time of Justinian, is described and figured by various writers.[4] On one side it has, to the left, the head of a man ; on the right, that of an eagle, each surmounted by a star, the two figures being separated by a cross. Underneath are the words, in characters half Greek, half Latin :—

ΝΑΘΕΟC ΙΟΗΑΝΝΙS

On the other side, similarly disposed, are the heads of a lion and

[1] It is curious to find Mr J. R. Allen, in a passage in which he actually refers to St Augustine (*Christian Symbolism*, p. 265), affirming : " In the first instance the application of the symbolic beasts to the Four Evangelists was general . . . . but we have evidence in the Fathers of the fourth century of their being individualised. There appears, however, to have been a difference of opinion as to the appropriation of the symbols of St Matthew and St Mark, *although there is none with regard to the other two Evangelists.*" Like some other writers on the sub-ject, he appears to have been unaware of the passage in which Irenæus discusses the symbols.

[2] For Irenæus does not confine himself to observing the opening words of the Gospels. Of St Matthew he writes : "Propter hoc et per totum euangelium humiliter sentiens et mitis homo seruatus est"; and of St Mark, διὰ τοῦτο δὲ καὶ σύντομον καὶ παρατρέχουσαν τὴν καταγγελίαν πεποίηται· προφητικὸς γὰρ ὁ χαρακ-τὴρ οὗτος.

[3] So Westcott appears to understand him, *Introduction to the Study of the Gospels*, 4th ed., p. 245, note 2.

[4] P. M. Faciaudi, *De Cultu S. Johannis Baptistae*, etc., Rome, 1755, p. 162 ; Münter, *Sinnbilder d. Alten Christen*, Altona, 1825, i. p. 45 and pl. i. fig. 15. See also Louisa Twining, *Symbols and Emblems of Early and Mediæval Christian Art*, London, 1852, p. 92 (pl. xlv. fig. 10) ; *Dict. of Christ. Ant.*, i. 634.

an ox, and beneath them $\frac{\text{N A P C}}{\text{L V C A}^s}$, while to the left of the lion's
head is the letter V, and to the right of the ox's head the letter S.
The designer of the coin, whoever he may have been, had not come
under the influence of the great Italian doctor : his semi-Greek
letters, and his adoption of the " Western " order of the Gospels, may
suffice to produce conviction on that point. It is no less clear that
he allotted the symbols to the evangelists in the way which received
the imprimatur of Jerome and the later Western Church.

This, then, was probably the tradition which was imported into
Ireland when St Patrick and his successors brought thither the
pre-hieronymian Latin version of the Holy Scriptures. We shall
not be held to make a very violent assumption if we suppose that
in Ireland, in the days when this Old Latin version was still current,
the symbols were represented in the Gospel books, placed each in
immediate connection with its own Gospel. But since the order of
the Gospels was then Matthew, John, Luke, Mark, the order of the
symbols must have been Man, Eagle, Ox, Lion. Let us suggest
another hypothesis, which may, perhaps, seem a little more daring.
Suppose that a scribe copied his text from a Vulgate, and the illuminator who completed his work copied his symbols (and it is certainly
unlikely that they were, in the majority of cases, altogether original
compositions) from an Old Latin exemplar, without observing the
transposition in the text of the second and fourth Gospels. In such
a case the result would be a manuscript in which the following
order was presented ·—

1. Miniature of a Man.
2. Gospel of St Matthew.
3. Miniature of an Eagle.
4. Gospel of St Mark.
5. Miniature of an Ox.
6. Gospel of St Luke.
7. Miniature of a Lion.
8. Gospel of St John.

The hypothesis, after all, scarcely deserves to be so called. This
is, in fact, the order which obtains in the Book of Durrow.[1] And I
do not know what explanation of the fact can be given, except the
one which I have ventured to suggest—that the text was taken from
a manuscript with a Vulgate text (as it certainly was), and the

---

[1] "These emblems of the evangelists," writes Bishop Westcott (*Introduction
to Study of Gospels*, p. 245), "are not found [*i.e.*, apparently in artistic repre-
sentation] before the Mosaics of the 15th century." Can "15th" be a misprint
for "5th"? Otherwise the statement is incomprehensible. Representations are
found in Biblical manuscripts such as the Book of Durrow, in metal work (*e.g.*,
the shrine of St Molaise's Gospels in the Museum of the Royal Irish Academy),
and in architectural ornament from the seventh century onwards, and perhaps
from an earlier period. See Mrs Jameson, *Sacred and Legendary Art*, 7th ed.
(1874), vol. i. p. 133; L. Twining, *Symbols and Emblems*, pp. 90, 92 ; Garrucci,
Storia dell' Arte Cristiana, vi. pl. 425.

illuminated pages from one with an Old Latin text. It might
perhaps be thought that the explanation is rather to be found in
the vagaries of a binder who has misplaced some of the leaves. But
this is easily put out of court. The scribe has left sufficient guidance for the binder, and it has been followed. On the recto of the
leaf, the verso of which is occupied with the Lion, the words are
written in vermilion : "Explicit euangelium saecundum Lueam,
incipit saecundum iohannem." One thing is clear, and it
strongly confirms our theory, that if the archetype of the Durrow
text was an autograph of St Columba (or, indeed, of anyone else),
executed in twelve days,[1] that archetype could not have been adorned
with elaborate pictorial representations. The illuminator must have
gone elsewhere for suggestions. And why not to what may well
have been near at hand, an Old Latin manuscript?[2]

It seems, moreover, quite clear that the Book of Durrow was no
solitary example of the confusion between the symbols of St Mark
and St John. It became, in the course of time, so common to place
the Eagle before St Mark's Gospel, and the Lion before St John,
that men forgot that this collocation had its root in a confusion. It
came to be the accepted arrangement, with some at least, and reasons
were given (quite as good, one doubts not, as those of Jerome for
the other view) why the Lion was appropriate to St John, and the
Eagle to St Mark.

Before giving proof of this assertion, we may remind our readers
that in early Latin manuscripts are sometimes found verses in which
the evangelists are commemorated in connection with their symbols.
Not the least common of these are the following, which were composed by Sedulius[3] in the fifth century :—

> Hoc Mattheus agens hominem generaliter implet,
> Marcus ut alta fremit uox per deserta leonis,
> Jura sacerdotis Lucas tenet ore iuuenci,
> More nolans aquilæ uerbo petit astra Ioannes.

---

[1] See Abbott, "On the Colophon of the Book of Durrow" (*Hermathena*, viii.
199), above, p. 15.

[2] A patriotic Scotsman, named John Forrest, published in the year 1701 an
edition of the works of Sedulius, moved thereto apparently by the supposition
that the author of the *Carmen Paschale* was Sedulius *Scotus*, and that the latter
cognomen proved him to be a native of North Britain ! In one of his notes
(p. 20) he declares, "Græci Marco aquilam, Ioanni Leonem tribuunt," a statement which may suggest to those who are fond of referring everything in the
early Irish Church to an Eastern source a different origin for the phenomena
of the Book of Durrow from that which I have proposed. But no proof of the
assertion is given, nor have I succeeded in finding any.

[3] *Carmen Paschale*, i. 355-358. The lines are found in at least two British
Museum MSS., Add. 11,848 (9th century) ; Cott. Tib., A. II. (early 10th century).
We shall shortly have occasion to quote a similar set of verses from an Irish
codex. Compare also those cited from the "Gospels of Beneventum" below,
p. 26. The verses are also inscribed on scrolls on an ancient baptistery at
Cividale, in Frioul (Garrucci, *ubi sup.*). See also Ciampini, *Vetera Monimenta*,
Rome, 1690, i. p. 135.

It is quite obvious to remark that such verses are not likely to be found in any considerable number of manuscripts unless the tradition which they embody was of old standing and widespread.

And now, this inference being accepted, for our proof of the statement made on the last page. The verses just cited connect the evangelists and the symbols in the orthodox and approved fashion. But there are rival lines. About the same time that some of the manuscripts containing the verses of Sedulius just cited were written, an Irish scribe, MacRegol by name (said to have been an abbot of Birr, King's County, Ireland, †820), wrote a book which now rests on the shelves of the Bodleian Library (Auct. D. 2, 19). It is known as the Rushworth Gospels. MacRegol also gives us mnemonic lines on the symbols.[1]

> Matheus instituit uirtutum tramite moras
> bene uiuendi iusto dedit ordine leges
>
> Marcus amat terras inter celumque uolare
> et uehymens aquila stricto sceat omnia labsu
>
> Lucas uberius descripsit proelia christi
> iure sacrato uitulus quia uatum moenia fatur
>
> Johannis fremit ore leo similisque rudenti
> intonat intonate terne pandens misteria uite

We recognise at once a faulty transcript of lines, by some editors attributed to Juvencus, and printed as a first preface to his *Historia Evangelica*.[2] St Mark appears as the Eagle, St John as the Lion, in full agreement with the Book of Durrow. The lines can scarcely have been introduced in this Gospel book merely as an idle embellishment. They point rather to an actual tradition as to the arrangement of the symbols in ancient Irish manuscripts. And this tradition must have been of long standing in the early years of the ninth century. For let us notice that the tradition was, as far as MacRegol was concerned, already dead. There is nothing in the Rushworth Gospels which corresponds to the lines, or which could have suggested their use. The portrait of St Mark is surmounted by a winged Lion,[3] that of St John by an Eagle,[4] and in the latter case, to make assurance doubly sure, the word "iohannis" is written across the figure. The Eagle appears once more in the decoration of the opening page of the fourth Gospel.

It was impossible that these verses should remain long unaltered in such alien surroundings. A century later we find their form slightly, but significantly, changed. The tenth century Irish Gospels

---

[1] Gilbert, *National MSS. of Ireland*, Pt. i. pl. xxiv.
[2] See above, p. 19, note 5.
[3] Westwood, *Anglo-Saxon Manuscripts*, p. 54.
[4] *Ib.*, pl. xvi.

of MacDurnan are one of the treasures of Lambeth Palace Library. Here again the conventional symbols are represented. The first page of St Mark has an unmistakable Lion's head in the top right-hand corner of the decorated border,[1] and another in the centre of the page, while on the verso of the last leaf of St Matthew "is the winged Lion, with head not unlike that of a sheep," as Mr Westwood informs us.[2] These facts are conclusive, both as to the order of the Gospels, and as to the symbol assigned to each. Now over what was originally the outside leaf of the manuscript, another leaf is pasted, on which are written the following lines in a modern hand :—

> Hoc Mattheus agens hominem generaliter implet
> Marcus ut alta fremit vox per deserta leonis
> Jura sacerdotis Lucas tenet ore juventi
> More volans aquile verbo petit astra Johannes
> Mattheus instituit virtutum tramite mores
> Et bene vivendi justo dedit ordine legem
> Marcus amat terras inter cœlumque volare
> Atque volans aquila stricto sceat omnia lapsu
> Lucas uberius describit prelia Christi
> Jure sacer vitulus qui menia fatur auita.

These verses Mr Westwood supposes to have been copied from the page over which they are pasted. And this seems highly probable, the more so as on the verso are found the four symbols to which they refer. Now let us look at them more closely. In the first four lines we have another copy of the verses of Sedulius. The last six are old friends. They are the lines ascribed to Juvencus which we have just now found in the Rushworth Gospels. But we observe one important difference. The final lines on St John have disappeared. What has become of them? They were illegible, says Mr Westwood, in the exemplar from which our modern scribe copied, and which he has so carefully concealed from us.[3] One is tempted to offer a different account of the matter. They were not written, we should say, by the seventeenth-century scribe, because they did not exist in the writing of his tenth-century predecessor. And why omitted by him? Because they were distinctly at variance with the tradition which he held. When they were withdrawn, the lines, with a little forcing, were easily squared with the accepted view. Lions, as we know them, are not, it is true, accustomed "terras inter cœlumque volare": but what may not a winged lion of the very rare species found in Irish manuscripts do? Line 7, therefore, applies well enough to St Mark and his lion. Line 8 is excellent for St John. And so, by the omission of lines 11, 12, all is made right.

It may be urged that we have done violence to the seventh and

---

[1] Westwood, *Anglo-Saxon MSS.*, pl. xxii.
[2] *Pal. Sac.*, "Gospels of Mæiel Brith MacDurnan," p. 12.
[3] *Anglo-Saxon MSS.*, p. 69 ; *Pal. Sac.*, "Gospels of Mæiel Brith MacDurnan,' p. 8.

eighth lines by giving them this strained interpretation. No doubt we have. But it is plain that, if the verses relating to St John were omitted, some strange method of interpretation must have been used by those who regarded the remainder as a description of the four symbols. And that MacDurnan was not singular in giving them in this incomplete form we have sufficient proof. Witness the eighth century manuscript[1] known as the Gospels of St Boniface, preserved at Fulda, in which they run as follows[2] :—

> Mathius instituit virtutum tramite mores,
> Et bene vivendi justo dedit ordine leges.
> Marcus amat terras inter coelumque volare.
> Et vehemens aquila stricto secat omnia laphsu.
> Jure sacer vitulus, qui habitat moenia Patris ;
> Lucas uberius describit proelia Christi.

It will not be maintained that in this manuscript, as well as in the Gospels of MacDurnan, the last two lines were omitted because they were illegible in the exemplar.

We may refer briefly, in the last place, to another manuscript, which contains the lines of Ps.-Juvencus, the celebrated Codex Sangermanensis.[3] This Bible was not penned by an Irish scribe. It is French in origin, having been written, according to M. Berger, in the neighbourhood of Lyons. But manifold traces exist, in its Gospel text, of Irish influence. Possibly from an Irish source came the lines in question, which were, in all likelihood, in the exemplar, accompanied by drawings of the evangelical symbols. The manuscript itself is almost entirely devoid of ornament. The first four of our verses are found immediately before the opening words of St Mark's Gospel, the fifth and sixth before St Luke, the remaining two before St John. As in most of the other cases which we have examined, they are altered in such a way as to adapt them to the customary allocation of the symbols. But the process by which this

---

[1] Mr H. J. White kindly informs me that, judging from Schannat's facsimile, this was probably the date of the codex. The scribe, Vidrug by name, was apparently a companion of St Boniface († 755).

[2] Schannat, *Vindemiae Literariae* Fuldæ et Lipsiæ 1723 p. 224 sqq. Westwood (*Anglo Saxon MSS.* p. 55), who does not appear to have seen the manuscript, commits a curious blunder with reference to these lines. He implies that they occur twice in the Fulda Gospels, in slightly different forms. But the first set of verses which he quotes, are simply a mis-reading of the lines by Brower, which Schannat cites for the purpose of correcting it. Brower's punctuation (as Schannat represents it) is a proof that strained exegesis was not confined to Irish scribes :

> Matheus, instituit virtutum tramite mores.
> Et bene vivendi justo dedit ordine leges
> Marcus. Amat terras inter coelumque volantem
> Joannes aquilam. Sancto regit omnia lapsu
> Lucas, uberius describit proelia Christi

[3] My knowledge of this manuscript (g_1 : Paris, B.N. 11,553) is derived from Bishop Wordsworth's *Old Latin Biblical Texts*, No. I., and from Berger's *Histoire de la Vulgate*, pp. 65-72.

is accomplished is different from that which we have observed elsewhere.   The names of the second and fourth evangelists are inter-
changed, and the lines referring to them transposed, the verses being
otherwise unaltered except by mistakes of the transcriber.   These
facts point to the inference that one of the Irish ancestors of the
codex was a manuscript with the symbols arranged as in the Book
of Durrow.   That is to say, either its Gospels followed the Vulgate
order, while the symbols adhered to that of the Old Latin, or, more
probably, the order of the Gospels was "Western," that of the
symbols Vulgate.   The lines in the Saint Germain manuscript run
as follows ·—

> Mattheus instituit uirtutum tramite mores
> Et bene uiuendi iusto dedit ordine legis
>
> Marcus fremit ore leo similisque rudenti
> Intonaet eternae pandens misteria uitae
>
> Lucas uberius describit proelia xpi
> Iure sacer uitulus quia uatum munia fatur
>
> Ioannes amat terras intra caelumque uolare.
> Et uehemens aquila stricto secat omnia lapsu.[1]

The evidence passed under review will have demonstrated, if I
mistake not, that at one time there must have existed a large number
of Irish manuscripts in which, while the text followed the Vulgate
order, the symbols adhered to that of the older versions.   The old
and the new sequence were thus brought into direct conflict.   The
conflict could only issue in one or other of three results.

1. The tradition as to the connection between the evangelists and
their symbols might give way, and the accidental juxtaposition of St
John with the Lion and St Mark with the Eagle become permanent,
and be transformed into a new tradition.   This, as we have seen, did
to a certain extent actually happen.

---

[1] I think it better to give in a footnote than in the text the apparently unique
verses found in the so-called Gospels of Beneventum (century viii. or ix., Brit.
Mus., Add. 5463).   Whether or not M. Berger is right in his contention
(*L'Histoire*, p. 91 *sq.*) that this is a French codex, it is certain that it bears
marks, in its readings, of Irish influence.   The following lines, extracted from
it, are plainly founded on those of Sedulius.   But some of the words (I have
printed them in italics) are not derived from this source.   They are inappropriate
as they stand, and bear witness, as I cannot doubt, to the influence of the rival
theory of the symbols upon the scribe :—

> Primus Mattheus hominem generaliter implens
> Marcus leonis uocem rugiens intonans *celse*
> Iure Lucas tenet sacerdotii simulque more iuvenci
> Iohannes instar aquilæ uolans in principio *intonans* uerbum.

"Rugiens intonans" in line 2 may, perhaps, recall "rugienti intonat" in Ps.
Juvencus ; the more readily since neither verb occurs in the lines of Sedulius.

2. The older tradition as to the appropriation of the symbols might remain. In this case it is natural to suppose that the order of the symbols would give way to that of the Gospels themselves, and so there would ensue a complete victory for the Vulgate. This we know to have taken place in the great majority of Irish Gospel manuscripts now remaining. But another alternative is possible, though less probable. For

3. The order of the Gospels might have been altered to suit that of the symbols, and thus, so far as arrangement is concerned, the victory would lie with the Old Latin. This possibility is sufficient to make us pause before assuming without examination that the order of the Gospels in a given Irish manuscript is identical with that of Jerome's Vulgate.

But an objection may be made. ˙ If the arrangement of the Book of Durrow was not altogether exceptional, why is this copy the only one now known in which it is found? And if the possibility just suggested is one that ought seriously to be reckoned with, why has no single Irish Vulgate manuscript been reported in which the Gospels follow the older sequence?

In answering these questions, let us call to mind that very few indeed of the extant Irish manuscripts date further back than the ninth or perhaps the eighth century. The Book of Durrow is the earliest which we possess, and can scarcely be put later than the closing years of the seventh century.[1] In other words, all other copies belong to a period when the victory for the Vulgate had been practically won. The strange thing really is, that traces of the contest should remain in their pages even so late as the tenth century. Had we a few more Vulgate manuscripts ranging from the sixth to the eighth century, we should probably find others exhibiting the same phenomenon in the matter of the symbols as the Book of Durrow.

But even late copies are not without traces of the older arrangement in their illuminations. We may be allowed to mention two cases in point. Wattenbach describes a copy of the Gospels now deposited in the German museum at Nuremberg, but belonging to the library of the Princes of Oettingen-Wallerstein at Möttingen.[2] It is written in half-uncials of unmistakably Irish character, and is ascribed by Wattenbach to the seventh, if not to the sixth, century.[3] Now the last page of this manuscript has, above the versified colophon, a rude miniature of a lion, surmounted by the words (probably a more recent addition), " Ecce leo stat super euangelium." It does not appear from the description whether St John's Gospel ends on this or the preceding page. But in either case the picture

---

[1] Scrivener, *Introduction to Criticism of N. T.*, 4th ed., ii. 78 ; Berger, *Histoire de la Vulgate*, p. 41.

[2] Wattenbach's account of this manuscript appeared in the *Anzeiger für Kunde des Deutschen Vorzeit* (Oct. 1869), and in the *Revue Celtique*, i, p. 27 *sqq.*

[3] The reader may perhaps suspect that this date is somewhat too early.

may be assumed to be connected with that Gospel, and to be a
reminiscence of the days when the lion was regarded as the appropriate symbol of St John.   And this, although in the Möttingen
MS. the Gospels follow the now usual order, and although inscribed
on the verso of the first leaf it has verses which begin thus :—

> Quam in speciosa quadriga,
> Homo, leo, vitulus et aquila.

Our second example shall be an early ninth-century manuscript
first made known to students of the Vulgate by M. Samuel Berger,[1]
the Book of the Confraternities of Pfäffers.   It contains extracts
from the Gospels, for reading in the ecclesiastical offices, in an Irish
text.   The ornamentation is also in part Irish.   Each Gospel has its
symbol, but the Lion of St Mark is distinguished by having two
eagles below it.   It is right to add, however, that the origin of
these eagles may be merely the fancy of an illuminator desirous of
producing a page more richly adorned than usual.   The Calf of St
Luke, for example, has in like manner below it two lions ; and the
symbols of all four evangelists are surmounted by figures of animals
which have no appearance of being symbolic.

But further, if most of our copies were probably *written* not
before the eighth century, they have certainly all been *bound* at a
more recent date.[2]   And binders have little scruple in following
their own whims as to the arrangement of the leaves of the books
which are left to their mercy.   The binders of our Irish codices
knew no order of the Gospels, and no system of arranging the
symbols, but one : and we need scarcely doubt that in their hands
the manuscripts would, as far as possible, be made to suit it.   Not
much ingenuity would be required if the several Gospels were
written in separate fasciculi and the symbols on detached leaves, one
side of which was left blank.   This may possibly have been not so
uncommon as one might imagine.[3]

And finally, if scribes and binders were biassed by the tradition
of later centuries, no less so are modern palæographers.   There is
scarcely any instance in which the "make-up" of Irish manuscripts,
of which descriptions have been published, has been examined with
care, in order to discover whether the binder has adhered to the
intention of the original scribe as to the order of the books and the
position of the illuminated symbols.   And even where the arrangement as it now exists is exceptional, the prevailing tradition has been
strong enough to blind the eyes of observers to the anomaly.
To take but one instance.   Mr Westwood no doubt examined the
Book of Durrow with much care.   Yet in his *Palæographia Sacra*,
though he refers to the symbols, he never mentions that they are

---

[1] *L'Histoire de la Vulgate*, pp. 57 *sq.*, 419.

[2] "Les anciens Irlandais ne paraissent pas avoir connu l'art de la reliure,"
Berger, *Histoire de la Vulgate*, p. 34.

[3] See above, p. 13.

misplaced. In his *Anglo-Saxon Manuscripts* he goes further. The symbol which in the manuscript precedes St John is spoken of (p. 21) as the "Lion of St Mark," [1] and when (pls. iv., v.) reproductions are given of the Man, the Lion, the Ox, and the Eagle, the two former are described as the "symbols of St Matthew *and St Mark*," the two latter as those "of St Luke *and St John*." This is a warning not to accept, without examination, the statements of palæographers on such matters as those which are now before us. We may well suspect that a more careful scrutiny will bring to light in our libraries Irish Gospels, in which the order of either symbols or evangelists is different from that which is now received.

But some who have followed me thus far may now protest, You have caused us to wade through pages of argument, and at the end we are treated to an exhortation to caution and accuracy, which has no very close relation to the Book of Mulling. Benevolent reader, the charge is true. I crave pardon, and hasten to another subject whose relevance is indubitable. That the labour expended on the last few pages has not been altogether in vain may perhaps appear in the sequel.

[1] Compare also J. Romilly Allen. *Early Christian Symbolism in Great Britain and Ireland before the Thirteenth Century*, London, 1887, p. 383.

CHAPTER III.

THE SECTIONS.

M. BERGER has more than once [1] directed the attention of students of the Vulgate to the importance of certain accessories to the Biblical text found in many manuscripts. Among these are what he calls the "Summaries" (*sommaires*) of the Gospels, more usually known as *capitula* or *breves causæ*, which appear to have taken their origin in very early times from the lectionary system of the Western Church.

The Book of Mulling has no summaries. But in it the Synoptic Gospels, and to a certain extent St John also, are divided as originally written [2] into paragraphs or sections. It is the purpose of the present chapter to investigate the nature of these sections. The inquiry may be thought to be trivial; and to remove this impression it will be well to state at once the conclusion to which it leads us in the case of the Gospels of St Matthew and St Luke. The sections of these Gospels are not mere arbitrary divisions of the scribe : they will be found to have been, at least approximately, reproduced by him from his exemplar, and to correspond pretty closely to the divisions marked in the Book of Durrow and Ussher's manuscript, which in the main agree with the *capitulatio* of the Gospels preserved in the Books of Durrow and Kells, and elsewhere.

The easiest way to make good this assertion in the case of St Luke's Gospel is to place in parallel columns the beginnings of the sections in the Books of Mulling and Durrow and Ussher's Codex. The striking agreement between the three systems of division will thus immediately appear. Only those sections of the Book of Durrow which are numbered are represented in the table, and each is accompanied by the number which appears opposite it in the manuscript— similarly the numbers in Ussher's manuscript are added whenever they are legible. [3] In the left column are given the numbers of the

---

[1] *Revue Celtique*, vi. 356 ; *L'Histoire de la Vulgate*, pp. 307 *sqq.*, 343 *sqq.*

[2] The corrector of the manuscript has adopted a different system of division, as we shall see hereafter. With this we are not concerned in the present chapter.

[3] The numbers given are those of the first hand. They have been altered by a corrector as follows. The indication of the beginning of the section (iii. 1) which should have been numbered v. was omitted. Hence two consecutive sections were numbered respectively iv. and vi. This had the appearance of a blunder, which was remedied by depressing the sectional numbers above vi. (not apparently, however, vi. itself) by one. Similarly §§ 9, 10 were written together, the next section being numbered xi. Hence the numbers from xi. onwards were depressed by *two*. A

corresponding capitula as found in the summary in the Book of Durrow. The explanation of the asterisks and obeli I reserve for the present. The table, it is hoped, independently of its more immediate purpose, may prove useful to those who are engaged in studying the ancient sections of the Gospels.

CAPITULA.	BOOK OF MULLING.	BOOK OF DURROW.	CODEX USSERIANUS.
[I.]	* i. 1.		i. 1.
	* i. 5.		i. 5.
	i. 19.		
	† i. 20.		
	i. 23.		
	† i. 34.		
	i. 46.		
	i. 56.		
	i. 59.		
II.	† i. 68.		
	* ii. 1.		I[I.] (? ms.) ii. 1.
III.	* ii. 21.		ii. 21.
	ii. 25.		
	ii. 36.		
	ii. 38.		
IIII.		IIII. ii. 42.	IIII. (ms.) ii. 42.
			ii. 43. "Et dixit" (?)
V.	* iii. 1.	V. iii. 1.	
	iii. 3.		
	iii. 7.		
	iii. 10.		
	† iii. 16. " Ego."		
	† iii. 17.		
	iii. 19.		
VI.	* iii. 21.	VI. iii. 21.	VI. iii. 21.
	* iv. 1.		iv. 1.
	iv. 14.		
VII.	* iv. 16.	VII. iv. 16.	VII. iv. 16.
	iv. 22.		
			VIII. iv. 31.
VIII.	* iv. 33.	VIII. iv. 33.	
	iv. 38.		
	iv. 41.		
	iv. 42.		
VIIII.	* v. 1.	VIIII. v. 1.	VIIII. v. 1.
	v. 4.		
	v. 10. " Et dixit."		
X.	* v. 12.		
	v. 15.		
XI.	* v. 17.	XI. v. 17.	XI. v. 17.
	v. 18.		
XII.	* v. 27.	XII. v. 27.	v. 27.
	v. 36.		
XIII.	* vi. 1.	XIII. vi. 1.	XIII. vi. 1.
XIIII.	* vi. 6.		
XV.		XIII. vi. 13.	vi. 12.
	† vi. 20. " Beati."		
	† vi. 21.		
	† vi. 21. "Beati" sec.		
	† vi. 22.		
XVI.	vi. 39.	XV. vi. 41.	XV. vi. 41.
XVII.	* vii. 1.		XVI. vii. 1.
	† vii. 9. " Amen."		
XVIII.		XVII. vii. 11.	XVII. vii. 11.
XVIIII.		XVIII. vii. 18.	XVIII. vii. 19
	† vii. 28.		
	vii. 31.		
XX.	* vii. 36.	XVIIII. vii. 36.	XVIIII. vii. 36.

few numbers seem to have been overlooked by the corrector, and in at least two instances three instead of two has been subtracted (Abbott, pp. 603, 613). Dr Abbott's account of this, though substantially correct, is expressed in terms somewhat too general (p. iv).

CAPITULA.	BOOK OF MULLING.	BOOK OF DURROW.	CODEX USSERIANUS.
XXI. {	* viii. 1. viii. 4. viii. 11. viii. 16.	XX. viii. 1.	XX. viii. 1.
XXII.	* viii. 22.	XXI. viii. 22.	XXI. viii. 22.
XXIII.	viii. 32. viii. 37. "ipse."	XXII. viii. 26.	XXII. viii. 26.
XXIIII.	* viii. 40. viii. 42. "Et."	XXIII. viii. 40.	XXIII. viii. 40.
XXV.	ix. 6.	XXIIII. ix. 1.	X[XIIII.] ix. 1.
XXVI. {	ix. 12.	XXV. ix. 10.	XXV. ix. 10.
XXVII.	* ix. 18. ix. 21.[1]	XXVI. ix. 18.	
	ix. 33. * ix. 37.	XXVII. ix. 37.	XXVI. ix. 28. XX[VII]. ix. 37.
XXVIII.		XXVIII. ix. 51.	XXVIII. ix. 51.
XXVIIII.	* ix. 57.	XXVIIII. ix. 57.	XXVIIII. ix. 57.
XXX.	† x. 7. "Dignus." x. 10. x. 16.	XXX. x. 1.	x. 1.[2]
XXXI.	* x. 17.		XXXI. x. 17.
XXXII.	* x. 25. † x. 28. x. 31.	XXXI. x. 21. XXXII. x. 25.	XXXII. x. 25.
XXXIII.	* x. 38.	XXXIII. x. 38.	x. 38.
XXXIIII.	* xi. 2. "Pater." xi. 5. xi. 9.	XXXIIII. xi. 1.	XXXIIII. xi. 1.
XXXV. {	xi. 11.	XXXV. xi. 14.	XXXV. xi. 14.
XXXVI.	* xi. 27.		XXXVI. xi. 27.
XXXVII. {	xi. 35.	XXXVI. xi. 37.	XXXVII. xi. 37. xi. 48.
XXXVIII.	* xi. 44.		
XXXVIIII.	* xi. 53. xii. 4. xii. 8.[3] xii. 11.		XXXVIIII. xi. 53.
X[L]. {	xii. 15. xii. 16.	XL. xii. 13.	XL. xii. 13.
XLI.	* xii. 22. xii. 27.		
		XXXVIII. (sic ms.) [xii. 32.	XLI. xii. 32.
XLII. a.	xii. 40.[4] * xii. 49. xii. 54. † xii. 56.		XLII. xii. 49.
XLIII.			XLIII. xiii. 1.
XLII. b. (xiii. 6).	* xiii. 6. † xiii. 7. "Et ecce."		
XLIIII.	* xiii. 10. xiii. 18.[5]	XLIIII. xiii. 10.	XLIIII. xiii. 10.
XLV.		XLV. xiii. 22.	XLV. xiii. 22.
XLVI.	† xiii. 28. "uos." * xiii. 30.		XLVI. xiii. 31.
XLVII.	* xiv. 1. xiv. 12.[6]	XLVI. (ms.) xiv. 1.	XLVII. xiv. 1.
XLVIII.	* xiv. 25. xiv. 34 (?).	XLVIII. xiv. 25.	XLVIII. xiv. 25.
XLVIIII.	* xv. 1. xv. 4 (?). † xv. 6. "Congratu- lamini" (?).	XLVIIII. xv. 1.	XLVIIII. xv. 1.
L.	* xv. 11. xv. 20. "Cum au- xv. 29. [tem."	L. xv. 11.	xv. 11.

[1] Apparently a fresh capitulum begins here (or at v. 23) in the Book of Armagh.
[2] This division does not appear in Dr Abbott's edition. But above the word "hæc" in what he numbers l. 1 (p. 497) are distinctly visible the marks , , , indicating the termination of one and the commencement of another section.
[3] Apparently the beginning of a capitulum in the Codex Epternacensis.
[4] A capitulum begins here in the Codex Aureus.
[5] Begins a fresh section in the Codex Epternacensis.
[6] Beginning of a fresh capitulum in the Book of Armagh and the Codex Epternacensis.

CAPITULA.	BOOK OF MULLING.	BOOK OF DURROW.	CODEX USSERIANUS.
LI.	*xvi. 1.	LI. xvi. i.	LI. xvi. 1.
LII.	*xvi. 13.	LII. xvi. 13.	LII. xvi. 13.
LIII.	xvi. 14.		
	*xvi. 19.	LIII. xvi. 19.	LIII. xvi. 19.
	†xvii. 1 " Uæ."		
LIIII.	*xvii. 3.	LIIII. xvii. 3.	LIIII. xvii. 3. "Si autem peccauerit."
	†xvii. 8 "Et post."		
LV.	*xvii. 11.	LV. xvii. 11.	LV. xvii. 11.
LVI.	*xvii. 20.	LVI. xvii. 20.	LVI. xvii. 20.
	xvii. 28.¹		
	xvii. 34.		
LVII.	*xviii. 1.	LVII. xviii. 1.	LVII. xviii. 1.
LVIII.	*xviii. 9.	LVIII. xviii. 9.	LVII[I]. xviii. 9.
	xviii. 15.		
	†xviii. 17.		
LVIIII.	*xviii. 18.		LVIIII. xviii. 18. "Magister."
	xviii. 23.		
	*xviii. 31.	LX. xviii. 31.	LX. xviii. 31.
	xviii. 34.		
LX.	*xviii. 35.		
LXI.	*xix. 1.	LXI. xix. 1.	LXI. xix. 1.
LXII.	*xix. 11.	LXII. xix. 11.	LXII. xix. 11.
	xix. 12.		
	†xix. 26.		
LXIII.	*xix. 28.	LXIII. xix. 28.	LXIII. xix. 29.
	xix. 37.		
LXIIII.	*xx. 1.	LXIIII. xx. 1.	LXIIII. xx. 1.
LXV.	*xx. 9.	LXV. xx. 9.	LXV. xx. 9.
	†xx. 13.		
LXVI.		LXVI. xx. 20.	LXVI. xx. 20.
LXVII.	*xx. 27.	LXVII. xx. 27.	LXVII. xx. 27.
LXVIII.	*xx. 46.	LXVIII. xx. 45 (ms.).	LXVIII. xx. 45.
LXVIIII.		LXVIIII. xxi. 5.	LXVIIII. xxi. 5.
	xxi. 7.		
LXX.		LXX. xxi. 20.	LXX. xxi. 20.
	xxi. 23.		
LXXI.	xxi. 34.		
	*xxi. 37		LXXI. xxi. 37.
LXXII.	*xxii. 7.	LXXII. xxii. 7.	LXXII. xxii. 7.
	*xxii. 24.	LXXIII. xxii. 24.	LXXIII. xxii. 24.
LXXIII.	*xxii. 31.	LXXIIII. xxii. 31.	LXXIIII. xxii. 31.
[LXXIIII.]	*xxii. 39.	LXXV. xxii. 39.	LXX[V]. xxii. 39.
[LXXV.]	*xxii. 47.	LXXVI. xxii. 47.	xxii. 47 (?).
LXXVI.		LXXVII. xxii. 66.	LXXVII. xxii. 66.
	xxiii. 17.		
LXXVII.	*xxiii. 26.	LXXVIII. xxiii. 26.	LXXVIII. xxiii. 26.
	xxiii. 34.		
	xxiii. 38.		
	xxiii. 44.		
	xxiii. 47.		
LXXVIIII. (sic).	*xxiv. 1.		xxiv. 1 (?).
	xxiv. 10.		
	xxiv. 12.		
	xxiv. 13.		
	xxiv. 36.		
	xxiv. 50.		

In the above table an obelus (†) indicates that though the place thus signalised has indications which generally betoken the beginning of a section (*i.e.* in most cases a large letter, sometimes set out in the margin, and preceded by a mark of punctuation), it is yet not so to be regarded. The large letters, etc., in such places are obviously due to the fancy of our scribe, or of the writer of a manuscript from which his is derived. He shows, for example, his fondness for symmetrical

---

¹ Either this verse, or verse 34, seems to be the first of a fresh capitulum in the Book of Armagh and the Codex Epternacensis.

writing at vi. 20–22, he exhibits elsewhere a propensity to write such words as "dixit," "dicebat," etc., in the margin without any apparent purpose (xix. 26, etc.), and he is prone to give similar prominence to "Et ecce" (v. 18. xiii. 7). With more reason he detaches a remarkable saying (i. 68. iii. 16, etc.) or even a portion of a saying to which he wishes to give emphasis (xii. 56, etc.) from the context by writing the first letter in the margin. Omitting all such cases we have not more than 142 sections in St Luke's Gospel. Of these, 65 begin at the same places (or within a verse thereof) as sections of *durm* or r_1, or are distinctly supported in opposition to these manuscripts by the summary. These are marked with asterisks (*). In 6 other places *mull*, differing from *durm* and r_1, is consistent with the summary (vi. 39, ix. 12, xi. 11, 35, xii. 15, xxi. 7).[1] These 71 sections are all satisfactorily explained on the supposition that *mull* was copied from an exemplar having divisions similar to r_1 and *durm*. We come now to consider some cases which might be held to point in another direction.

There are in the first place divisions omitted in *mull* (vi. 12, vii. 11, ix. 51, x. 1, xiii. 22, xx. 20 [2]). These omissions, numerous though they be, need not surprise us, for similar omissions are frequent in *durm*, and occur also in r_1, as is proved by the numbers [3] or by comparison with the other authorities (iii. 1, v. 12, vi. 6, ix. 18, xviii. 35), and perhaps also in the summary (ix. 37, xviii. 31, xxii. 24). In other cases we cannot be sure whether a division has been omitted, or wrongly placed (ii. 38, vii. 31, ix. 6): but if we may trust the summary, misplacements are met with also in r_1 (ix. 28, xii. 32). On the whole we may say that the sectional divisions of *durm* and r_1, reappear in *mull* as accurately as could be expected on the supposition that the latter is copied, or descended from an exemplar in which these sections were preserved. There remain, however, about 50 or 60 divisions to which nothing corresponds in the other manuscripts. What is to be said of these? They will be found in almost all cases to be perfectly natural divisions of the text, a good many of them being in fact marked as paragraphs in printed editions. Some may correspond to sections the indication of which has been omitted in the other authorities, for all alike have been shown to be guilty of omissions.[4] Some again may be accounted for by the ambiguity of the summary, which now and then leaves it uncertain at which of two or more places a section is intended to begin. Our scribe in such cases may combine the testimony of

---

[1] A vinculum connecting two or more references indicates that the summary leaves it uncertain at which of these places the section was intended to begin.

[2] The capitulum (66) which begins at this verse is, however, part of the preceding in the summary in the Book of Armagh and the Codex Epternacensis, as in our manuscript.

[3] See above p. 30 note 3.

[4] Such may be the paragraphs beginning at ix. 21, xii. 8, 40, xiii. 18, xiv. 12, xvii. 28. See above.

several witnesses. See for example ii. 21, 25 ; xi. 11, 14 ; xii. 13,
15, 16 ; xix. 11, 12 ; xxi. 34, 37 ; xxiii. 17, 26, 34. But probably
the majority are to be regarded as sub-divisions of the sections,[1] due
either to our scribe or to the scribe of his archetype. It will be
observed, as might be expected, that these extra divisions are most
numerous where the older sections are longest, that is, at the beginning and end of the Gospel. At these places also, the indications
in the summary are unusually ambiguous and inadequate.

A good illustration of the way in which extra sections would have
appeared and some divisions been omitted in a manuscript written as
we suppose the Book of Mulling to have been, is found in the case
of the Codex Sangermanensis (g_1). The Gospel according to St
Matthew in this manuscript is divided into 74 numbered sections,[2]
which are further sub-divided. The first words of each section are
written in uncial rubric, and in the case of all but two (60, 61) the
beginnings of the sections are the beginnings of paragraphs. There
are in all about 163 paragraphs. Now if a transcript were made
from this manuscript, preserving with absolute fidelity its divisions,
but with the numbers omitted and the uncial writing copied in the
ordinary hand of the scribe, two of the sectional division marks
would be omitted, and there would be left no less than 91 indications
of division not corresponding to recognised capitula—quite as large a
proportion as we actually find in Mulling's St Luke. If the fancy
or the stupidity of the copyist were exercised, the proportion would
of course be still further increased. The Gospel of St Luke, in fact,
in our book would appear to have been copied by a careful scribe
from an archetype in which the sections were given less accurately
than in g_1, while the sub-divisions were less numerous.

The evidence in the case of St Matthew's Gospel for the connection
of the sections of the Book of Mulling with the ancient divisions is
exactly parallel to that just given for St Luke.

In the following table will be found marked the beginning of each
section of the first Gospel in our book. *Durm* and r_1 being almost
useless here for our purpose, I have had recourse to the Codex
Sangermanensis (g_1). This manuscript contains a "capitulatio" and
the corresponding sections are indicated in the text of the Gospels.
The numbers to the left are those found in the text and capitulatio
of the St Germain manuscript. In some cases our book agrees with
the text of this codex against the capitulatio: this is indicated by
the letters *marg.*, enclosed in brackets after the numeral. At other
times a section in the Book of Mulling is consistent with the summary, but at variance with the marginal number in g_1. When this
happens the letters (*cap.*) are added. In some instances of this kind
the summary and the text of g_1 contradict one another. Finally it

---

[1] Many of them are mentioned as separate headings in the *Capitula*. *E.g.*, ii.
36, v. 36, xi. 5, 9, xii. 27, xiv. 12, 34, xviii. 15, xxiii. 34, xxiv. 13, 50.
[2] The numeral has in one case (§ 60) been accidentally omitted.

happens pretty frequently that our manuscript has two marks of division either of which would accord with the commencement of the section as described in the summary. This is marked by the use of a vinculum. Thus, for example, a division is marked in our book at vii. 7, and again at vii. 13. Either of these may be the beginning of § 16 according to the capitulatio, though in the text of g_1 the corresponding numeral is found at the latter place.

Codex Sanger-manensis.	Book of Mulling.		Codex Sanger-manensis.	Book of Mulling.	
[I. (marg.)].	i.	1.	XXXIIII.	xi.	25.
I. (cap).	i.	18.	XXXV.	xii.	1.
II.	ii.	1.	XXXVI.	xii.	9.
III. (cap).	ii.	17.	XXXVII.	xii.	38.
IIII.	iii.	1.	XXXVIII.	xii.	46.
	iii.	5.	XXXVIIII.	xiii.	1.
	iii.	10 "Om-nis."	XL.	xiii.	24.
V.	iv.	1.		xiii.	31.
	iv.	5 (?).		xiii.	33 (?).
VII.	iv.	17.		xiii.	36.
	iv.	21.	XLII.	xiii.	53. }
	iv.	23. }	XLIII.	xiv.	1. }
VIII.	v	1.		xiv.	23 "Ues-pere."
	†v.	3–10.[1]		xv.	15.
	v.	13.		xv.	21 (?).
	v.	14.		xv.	28.
	v.	21. }		xv.	32.
X.	v.	26 (?). }	XLVI.	xvi.	13.
XI.		44.	XLVII.	xvii.	22 (?). }
XII.	vi.	2.	XLVIII.	xvii.	24. }
	†vi.	9 "Pater."	LI.	xviii.	1.
	†vi.	14.	LII.	xviii.	8.
XIII	vi.	16.		xviii.	15.
	vi.	23.		xviii.	19.
XIIII.	vi.	24.	LIII.	xviii.	23.
XV.	vii.	3.		xix.	1.
	vii.	7. }	LIIII.	xix.	13.
XVI.	vii.	13. }	LV.	xix.	16.[3]
XVII.	vii.	21.	LVI.	xix.	22.
XVIII.	vii.	28.		xix.	27.
	vii.	29 (?).)		xx.	1.
	vii.	29 "Non enim" (?). }	LVII.	xx.	17.
	viii.	1 (?).)	LVII. (marg.).	xx.	29.
XVIIII.	viii.	5.	LVIII.	xxi.	1 "Tunc."
	†viii.	11 (?).	LVIIII.	xxi.	17.
XX.	viii.	14.	LX.[4]	xxi.	23 (?).
XXI.	viii.	18.	LXI.	xxi.	33.
	viii.	23.[2]		xxii.	11.
XXII.	viii.	28 (?).	LXII.	xxii.	15.
XXIII.	ix.	2 "Et uidens."		xxii.	23.
XXIIII.	ix.	10.	LXIII.	xxiii.	1.
XXV.	ix.	14.	LXIIII.	xxiii.	13.
XXVII.	ix.	27.	LXV.	xxiv.	1.
XXVIII.	ix.	35.	XLVI.	xxiv.	14 (?).
	x.	5.	LXVIII.	xxv.	1.
	x.	16. }		xxv.	30 (?). }
XXX.	x.	23. }	LXVIIII.	xxv.	31. }
	x.	25 "Et si patrem" (?).		xxvi.	1.
XXXI. (cap).	x.	34.	LXX.	xxvi.	17.
XXXII.	xi.	1.	LXXI.	xxvi.	31.
	†xi.	10 "Ecce."	LXXII.	xxvii.	11.
XXXIII.	xi.	16.	LXXIII.[5]	xxvii.	45.
	xi.	20. }		xxvii.	62. }
			LXXIIII.	xxviii.	1. }
				xxviii.	16.

[1] First letter of "beatus" always written as if beginning a section.
[2] A capitulum begins here in the Codex Epternacensis.
[3] This, rather than xix. 13, is probably the true beginning of the section. See the authorities in Wordsworth's *Vulgate*, i. 33.
[4] The numeral is omitted in margin.
[5] Numbered lxxii. in margin by an error.

This table seems to need little comment. It does not appear to leave room for doubting that the divisions of our manuscript were ultimately founded on those represented in the summary and text of g_1. A good many of the ancient divisions are indeed omitted or misplaced (6, 9, 26, 29, 41, 44, 45, 49, 50, 67), but the coincidence of those which remain with the sections of g_1 is most marked.

It is worth while to remark that, whether the arguments just used are sound or not, it is quite certain that the divisions of St Matthew and St Luke in our manuscript have nothing to do with the Eusebian sections. These number 324 in St Luke, Mulling's paragraphs are about 160, and only about 100 of them begin at the same point as a Eusebian section. In St Matthew the number of paragraphs is less than 110, the Eusebian sections 355. The beginning of paragraph and section coincide in about 60 places.

When we turn to St Mark we discover that all is changed. This Gospel was most undoubtedly derived from an exemplar in which the principle of division was that of Eusebius. The proof is easy. The Eusebian sections marked in the first ten chapters of St Mark in Tischendorf's edition of the Codex Amiatinus are 116 in number. Of these at least 97 (more probably 102), coincide with Mulling's paragraphs, not more than 11 (probably 6) are omitted, and 6 are differently placed, while no sub-divisions are discernible. It is difficult to fix the numbers exactly, owing to the worn state of the manuscript, but those which I have given may be regarded as very nearly exact, and they tell their own tale.

It seems almost impossible to find order or system in the numerous divisions of St John. But punctuation marks (usually one or two points, . or . .) which elsewhere are used sparingly, are here so frequent, and capitals are used in such arbitrary fashion, that one is led to surmise that the text of this Gospel had as a not very remote ancestor a copy written *per cola et commata*. We may take as an example chap. xxi. vv. 19–23, which appear thus (the vertical lines indicating the ends of the lines of writing) :—

Hoc hautem dixit significans qua morte clari | ficaturus esset deum. et hoc cum dixis | set. dicit ei.sequere mé conuersus | petrus uidit.[1] illum discipulum quem dilegebat. ihs̄ | sequentem qui recubuit in coena | supra pectus eius. et dicit quis domine | qui tradit té . . Hunc ergo cum | uidisset petrus dicit ihū Domine | quid hic Dicit ei ihs̄ Sic eum uolo | manere donec ueniam quid ad té | tú mé sequeris exiuit ergo sermo iste | inter fratres quia discipulus ille | non moriretur Sed síc uolo ma | nere donec ueniam. quid ad té | Hic etc.

Better passages than this might have been chosen for exhibiting the punctuation of the manuscript. One reason for preferring this one will appear presently. We see at once that the scribe copied the marks mechanically from his exemplar, omitting some—and these not the least important from the point of view of the reader. Assuming

---

[1] The point here is doubtful.

that each of those which he preserves represents the close, and each capital letter the beginning, of a line, and guessing where such guidance is not forthcoming, we may write the passage "stichometrically" as follows :—

Hoc hautem dixit
significans qua morte clarificaturus esset deum
et hoc cum dixisset
dicit ei
sequere me
conuersus petrus uidit illum discipulum
quem dilegebat ihs
sequentem
qui recubuit in coena supra pectus eius
et dicit
quis domine qui tradit te
Hunc ergo cum uidisset petrus
dicit ihū
Domine quid hic
Dicit ei ihs
Sic eum uolc manere donec ueniam
quid ad te
tu me sequeris
exiuit ergo sermo iste inter fratres
quia discipulus ille non moriretur
Sed sic uolo manere donec veniam
quid ad te
Hic, etc.

We perceive that the marks have guided us correctly (except in one case) in the few places where they occur. We may now point out another fact. The scribe has omitted a few words before "sed sic uolo." We may suppose them to have run

et non dixit illud ihs quia non moriretur,

and to have been passed over through homœoteleuton. They would naturally form a single line (or perhaps two complete lines) of the exemplar, if it was written as I have supposed ; and so the error would be completely explained.

This is indeed only one of a number of similar cases. The fourth Gospel is written carelessly, and the scribe has been guilty of many omissions. The most notable are the following: iv. 23, 24 (qui adorent...deus et); v. 37 (et qui me misit); vi. 54 (amen amen dico uobis); vii. 8 (hunc...festum); 28 (docens...ihs et); 42 (de bethleem...dauid); viii. 13 (testimonium perhibes); 39 (dixit eis ihs); 46 ; ix. 20 (et quia...est); 21 (nos nescimus); 23 (ætatem habet); xi. 3 ; 25, 26 (etiamsi...credit in me); xii. 16 (tunc recordati...de eo); 34 (quis...hominis); xv. 16 (fructum afferatis et);

22-24 (nunc autem...haberent); xvi. 17, 18 (et non...modicum, apparently); xx. 6 ; xxi. 23 (see above).

Many, but not all, of the omissions are due to homœoteleuton. It is natural to suppose that the majority of them consist of one or more complete lines of the archetype. But if so it is quite certain that the lines must have varied very much in length. All, except perhaps those at vii. 28, viii. 13, would have formed lines or groups of lines in a manuscript correctly written *per cola et commata.* In one of them (viii. 46) our manuscript is in company with Codex Bezæ, where the omission is doubtless due to the cause which has been suggested.

One other reading may be mentioned in confirmation of our hypothesis. At v. 44 two clauses are inverted, namely "quomodo potestis uos credere qui gloriam ab inuicem accipitis," and " et gloriam quæ a solo est [deo] non quæritis." One or other had probably been omitted in the text of archetype, and had been restored in the margin. Does then either clause make a complete line or set of lines? The reading is at once explained if they do. Evidence is hardly needed, but the witness of *d* is here no doubt true, and it is on our side—

> quomodo potestis uos credere
> gloriam abinuicem accipientes
> et gloriam ab unico deo
> non queritis. nolite arbitrari

The point in the last line probably marks (see Harris, *Codex Bezae,* p. 241 *sq.*) a division of lines in the archetype.

We pause now to consider somewhat more carefully the sections into which the Book of Mulling is divided in St Matthew and St Luke, and to ascertain, if we may, what conclusion may be drawn from the presence of these sections as to the history of the manuscript.

First let us remark that in many copies we have not merely the sections, but also a summary or *capitulatio* at the beginning of the Gospels, indicating their contents. Now summaries of the type found in the Book of Durrow are almost confined to old Latin manuscripts of the European family, and Vulgate texts which have a considerable Old Latin mixture.[1] Their antiquity is thus assured. We are in fact warranted in the inference that in any manuscript in which the summary occurs it has been ultimately derived from an old Latin exemplar. The text, on the other hand, may bear unmistakable signs of derivation from a Vulgate archetype. But this does not make our conclusion as to the summary less certain. It only shows that at some step of the process by which the copy under consideration came into being, a scribe had two exemplars

---

[1] Berger, *op. cit.*, pp. 311, 353 *sqq.*

before him, from one of which he took his text, and from the other his *capitulatio*.

In some cases we may feel fairly confident that we have before us a manuscript, not merely ultimately derived, but actually copied in this fashion from two exemplars. Take for example the Book of Durrow. In this manuscript we have a summary. The text on the other hand is so slightly mixed that we may feel sure that it was transcribed or derived from a Vulgate. To increase our assurance we note the fact that in the body of the text the division into paragraphs does not agree with the *capitula*. But there is something more. The *numbers* of the *capitula* are in many cases entered in the margin, and copied in such a way that it is frequently difficult to discover the exact point at which the section indicated by a number was supposed to begin.[1] We may conclude that these numbers were taken, not from the copy which furnished the text, but from that which supplied the summary: and we are thus brought by another route to the opinion to which the consideration of the evangelical symbols has already led us, that the scribe of the Book of Durrow had before him two manuscripts, a Vulgate, from which he transcribed his text, and an Old Latin copy, from which he took the summary, the numbers just mentioned, and his conception of the symbols of the Evangelists.

This supposition is confirmed by another consideration. The summaries of St Matthew and St Mark in this codex precede the Gospels. Those of St Luke and St John are written (apparently in a different hand) after St John.[2] How did this come about? We can only guess, but our guess seems to have some likelihood of being correct. It is this. The summaries preceded the Gospels in the Old Latin exemplar from which they were copied, and came in the order : St Matthew, St John, St Luke, St Mark. The Durrow scribe wished to bring the order into conformity with that of his Vulgate " arguments " and Gospels. After transcribing the summary of St Matthew he therefore turned over to St Mark. This finished he had come to the end of the preliminary matter in his pre-hieronymian exemplar, and so, forgetting that he had omitted two of the summaries, he laid it aside and went on with his Vulgate copy. It may be said that this indicated great stupidity on his part, but we have many proofs that the scribe of the Book of Durrow was singularly wanting in intelligence.[3] His error was subsequently observed by another, who repaired it as best he could by writing the capitulatio of St Luke and St John at the end of the Gospels.

Turning now from the summary to the sections themselves we come to something which is of even more venerable antiquity. The sections are not only found in Old Latin texts: their origin can be traced to a Greek source. They are nearly identical with those of

---

[1] Abbott, *Evang. Vers.*, p. v.   [2] Abbott, *op. cit.*, p. xxvi.
[3] Abbott in *Hermathena*, viii. 200 ; *Evang. Vers. Anteh.*, p. xx, *sq.*

the Codex Vaticanus (B), the oldest copy of the original text of the Gospels in existence. Wherever then we find these divisions not merely marked in the margin of a Latin Gospel, but actually imbedded in its text, we may be assured that it is ultimately descended from a copy of an Old Latin version, however far removed its present text may be from the Old Latin type.

To apply all this to our book. The Gospels of St Matthew and St Luke are divided into the ancient sections, the marginal numbers having disappeared. These Gospels therefore have been derived from a manuscript of the Old Latin. The present text, indeed, as we shall see hereafter, is not for the most part pre-hieronymian. It must, therefore, in the course of time, have taken into itself many Vulgate readings. St Mark, on the other hand, is divided into Eusebian sections ; and the preliminary matter is, so far as it remains, such as properly belongs to Jerome's Version. The text therefore of the second Gospel and of the first volumen is derived in the long run from one or more[1] Vulgate manuscripts. While finally St John, with neither system of division, gives no indication of the ultimate source from which it was taken. But as one of its ancestors was written *per cola et commata*, and as the other Gospels bear no trace of this arrangement, it was probably ultimately derived from an exemplar different from that of the other parts of the book. Our conclusion is that the Book of Mulling, or one of its immediate ancestors, was compiled from at least two, probably from a greater number of separate exemplars.

[1] It appears more likely that St Mark and the preliminary matter were derived from different archetypes. For it will be argued hereafter (p. 71 *sqq.*) that the marginal numbers which appear in the former were copied from the same manuscript as the Eusebian Canons. But the divisions indicated by the numerals not seldom differ from those implied by the paragraphs of the text itself. Sections, for example, indicated by marginal signatures, begin without capitals at Mar. ii. 23, vi. 46, viii. 32 (Et adpræhendens), ix. 43, xiv. 36. At iii. 7 the number is placed opposite the beginning of the verse, while the second "Et" is written in the margin ; numbers are assigned to viii. 30, x. 28, xii. 28, xiv. 38, xiv. 64 (quid), while the corresponding capitals are found at viii. 29 (Respondens), x. 29, xii. 22, xiv. 37, xiv. 63 (Quid) respectively. Other instances might be added, but these may suffice.

CHAPTER IV.

THE BIBLICAL TEXT.

THE purpose of this chapter is to direct attention to two portions of the text of the Synoptic Gospels preserved in the Book of Mulling, which appear to be in themselves of considerable interest, and to have some bearing on the history of the manuscript, and on that of the Irish recension of the Latin Bible.

§ 1. *Corrections.*

It is necessary, however, by way of preface, to notice one of the palæographical features of the manuscript. It will be at once perceived by any one who inspects it, that the hand of a corrector has been busy on its pages. Corrections, it is true, are in some places much more frequent than in others ; but there is scarcely a page in the entire book which is altogether free from them.

The existence of a large number of these corrections is easily explained. The manuscript, as originally written, was not supplied with the numbers in the margin referring to the so-called Ammonian Sections and Eusebian Canons. The Gospels of St Matthew and St Luke, moreover, were divided into paragraphs, which, whatever may have been their origin, certainly had no relation to these sections. When, therefore, the numbers were subsequently added, an attempt was made to indicate the exact point at which each section began. This was effected in various ways. Usually the end of a section was denoted by a punctuation mark, resembling a colon followed by a comma (:,). The following word was sometimes marked with the sign ∕∙, and a similar sign was placed over the corresponding number in the margin (*e.g.* Mark viii. 30, f. 43 *v b*). More commonly, however, the first letter or two of the section were altered in such a way as to make them more prominent. Sometimes they were simply re-traced, as we may see, for example, in line 15 of the second column of f. 48 *r*.[1] At other times they were re-written in a larger character. Examples of this may be found in line 8, where the sign for 'et' (⁊) has been transformed into ⑄ , and line 23 of col. a, where, in the space occupied by *e*, the letter *ℓ* has been written, the original letter being left otherwise unaltered. Occasionally, when the first word of a section happened to be also the first word of a line, the scribe has placed one or more dots under it,

---

[1] A facsimile reproduction of this page will be found facing the title page.

re-writing the same word in the margin (f. 46 r b, ll. 3, 23). But not infrequently he has actually erased the original word and written it afresh, either in the margin (as in f. 48 r, col. a, l. 36), or in the space occupied by the erasure, or partly in one, partly in the other (f. 46 r a, ll. 15, 16). This is frequently done when it is desired that a section should begin with the first word of a line, where the original writing does not admit of its doing so. In this case the last word or two of the previous section are also erased, and transferred to the right margin opposite the preceding line. In such cases as those last mentioned, we can, of course, usually have no absolute certainty as to the original reading of the manuscript; but obviously we have no right to assume, in the absence of indications pointing in that direction, that it differed from that which the corrector has put in its room.

But besides the corrections made with the object of adapting the manuscript to the division into sections, there are very many others the purpose of which is undoubtedly to change the reading. Much the same methods are used in this as in the former case. A word has a dot placed under each of its letters, and that which is to be substituted for it is written above it (f. 48 r a, l. 20) or in the margin ; a word to be omitted is marked with a group of three dots above it, or with single dots above or below, or in both positions (f. 48 r a, ll. 25, 36) ; and in the case of a whole sentence so dealt with, a punctuation mark precedes and follows the omitted portion, and a wave line is drawn down the margin (f. 46 r a, ll. 29–31) ; a word to be supplied is written above the line or in the margin, with a mark indicating its place in the text (f. 46 r b, ll. 20, 35 ; f. 48 r b, l. 23) ; or, finally, a word is erased, and the resulting space is either left blank, or something else written in it (e.g. f. 48 r a, l. 30, where ů = nero is written over a partially erased h̊ = hautem, f. 48 r b, l. 20). Where we find a word written over an erasure not at the beginning or end of a section we are plainly warranted in the inference that the displaced word of the original text was different, and we can often conjecture with high probability what the original word actually was.

§ 2. *General Character of the Text.*

It is now our task to make an attempt to ascertain the general character of the text of the Gospels in the Book of Mulling *as originally written* (which we shall henceforth designate by the letter μ). This we shall most easily do by collating a few passages with the Codex Amiatinus (A). In parallel columns with the collation of these selected portions of μ, we shall place, for comparison, collations of the same passages as they are found in three other Irish manuscripts. We take first the Book of Durrow (*Durmach*), which may be regarded as the ancient Celtic manuscript of the Gospels which approaches most nearly to the ordinary Vulgate text. The Book of Kells (Q) is a good example of the usual type of Irish text,—having a Vulgate base, but with a large contingent of old Latin readings. While, as an example of pre-hieronymian Irish texts, we give in the fourth column the readings of Codex Usserianus (r_1). This manuscript is in a fragmentary state, and by this circumstance I have been mainly guided in selecting the passages to be collated. It is essential that all four texts should be approximately complete in the passages presented, and I have therefore chosen those places in which the Codex Usserianus is practically intact for at least two or three consecutive verses.

No complete collation or edition of the Book of Mulling has been published. The text of the Codex Usserianus has been printed by Professor Abbott, with collations of the Books of Kells and Durrow and another manuscript (r_2), which will be referred to lower down. I have re-collated all these texts, so far as it appeared necessary for my purpose, and where the reading of any of the manuscripts differs, in my judgment, from that given by Dr Abbott, I have indicated this fact by inserting the letters ' ms.' in brackets after the reading in question. Mere differences of spelling I have neglected, but a few readings which might perhaps have been included under this description I have retained, marking them, however, with an obelus (†), and building no argument upon them. Readings in which μ and r_1 agree are indicated by asterisks (*).

A 1.

LIBER MULLING.	CODEX DURMACHENSIS.	CODEX KENANENSIS.	CODEX USSERIANUS (r_1).
Matt. xxi.			
22.			
23.			*om.* docentem.
24.	aut *pro* et *tert.* (*ms.*).	eis *pro* illis.	
			uerbum *pro* sermonem.
* dicite′ mihi quem si dixeritis mihi *pro* quem si dixeritis mihi.			* q[uem dicit]e mihi *pro* quem si d. m.
25.			[fu]it *pro* erat. de cælo *pro* e caelo.
† intra *pro* inter.		† intra *pro* inter.	illi autem *pro* at illi.

A 2.

Marc. vii.			
29.		illi+iesus.	dix[it] *pro* ait. iesus *pro* illi (*vel* illi +iesus).
		sermonem hunc *pro* hunc ser.	uade propter hunc sermonem *pro* p. h. s. uade.
30. abisset+ad.	abisset+ad.	abisset+ad.	a *pro* de. uen[is]set *pro* abisset. *om.* suam.
† super *pro* supra.			
31.		Tyri+et. † medicos *pro* medios (*ms.*).	
32 deprecabantur *pro* deprecantur.			adferunt *pro* adducunt. depraecantes *pro* et deprecantur.
		inponant *pro* inponat.	inponeret *pro* inponat.
33.			ei *pro* illi. suscipi[e]ns *pro* adprehendens.
		deorsum *pro* seorsum.	
		auriculas+eius.	conspuens [mi]sit digitos suos in auriculas eius et *pro* misit d. s. in a. et expuens.
Marc. viii.			
2. hanc turbam *pro* turba.	† turbam *pro* turba.	turbam istam *pro* turba.	istam turbam *pro* turba.
			quoniam *pro* quia.
	† traditio *pro* triduo.		*om.* ecce. triduum iam *pro* iam triduo. est ex quo hic sunt *pro* sustinent me.

A 2—*continued.*

LIBER MULLING.	CODEX DURMACHENSIS.	CODEX KENANENSIS.	CODEX USSERIANUS (r₁).
Marc. viii.			
3.			dimittere *pro* si dimisero.
		domus suas *pro* domum suam.	*om.* suam.
			nollo ne fatigentur *pro* deficient.
		quia quidam *pro* quidam enim.	q[uo]niam quidem et aliqui *pro* quidam enim.
			his *pro* eis.
4. respondentes *pro* responderunt.			
			sui+dicentes.
			quis p[os]sit *pro* poterit quis.
			om. hic.
5. † interrogabit *pro* interrogauit			
	† quod (*ms.*) *pro* quot.		† quod *pro* quot.
		dixerunt+ei (*ms.*).	

A 3.

	LIBER MULLING.	CODEX DURMACHENSIS.	CODEX KENANENSIS.	CODEX USSERIANUS (r₁).
	Luc. iii.			
19.				faciebat *pro* fecit.
20.				et adiecit *pro* adiecit et.
	*† super *pro* supra. *om.* et *sec.*	*om.* et *sec.*	*om.* et *sec.*	*† super *pro* supra.
	† carcerem *pro* carcere.	† carcerem *pro* carcere (*ms.*).	† carcerem *pro* carcere.	
21.				baptizatus esset *pro* baptizaretur.
				populus+ab iohanne.
				cumque et iesus baptizatus esset *pro* et iesu baptizato.
				+ab eo *ante* et *sec.*
				orante+ipso.
				aperti sunt caeli *pro* apertum est caelum.
22.				quasi *pro* sicut.
			† columbam *pro* columba.	
				eum *pro* ipsum.
				filius meus es tu *pro* tu es f. m.
				om. dilectus.
	te+bene.	te+bene.	te+bene (*ms.*).	ego hodie genui te *pro* in te complacuit mihi.
23.	* putabatur *pro* putaretur.	putabatur *pro* putaretur.	putabatur *pro* putaretur.	qui* putabatur *pro* ut putaretur.

A 3—*continued.*

LIBER MULLING.	CODEX DURMACHENSIS.	CODEX KENANENSIS.	CODEX USSERIANUS (r_1).
Luc. xv.			
5. * eam *pro* illam.			* eam *pro* illam.
*† iuponet *pro* im-ponit.			*† inponet *pro* imponit.
			inp.+eam.
* super *pro* in.			* super *pro* in.
cum gaudio *pro* gaudens			
6. om. et.			amicos+suos.
domui *pro* domum.			
		uicinos+suos.	
	gratulamini *pro* congrat.		
			quod *pro* quia.
			inuenerim *pro* inueni.
7. dico+autem.		dico+autem.	in *pro* super.
	unum peccatorem *pro* uno pecca-tore.	unum peccatorem *pro* uno pecca-tore.	
(*hiat* μ.)	† habentem *pro* ha-bente.	† habentem *pro* ha-bente.	agente *pro* habente.
(*hiat* μ.)	istos *pro* iustis.	iustos *pro* iustis.	iustos *pro* iustis.
			egent *pro* indigent.
(*hiat* μ.)	† paenitentiam *pro* paenitentia.	† penitentiam *pro* paenitentia.	
8. (*hiat* μ.)			quae+est.
			decem+et.
			om. dragmam.
	uertit *pro* euertit.	uertit *pro* euertit.	scopis mundat *pro* euertit.
domum+suam.		domum+suam.	
			inueniat+eam.
9.		amicos et uicinos (*ms.*) *pro* amicas et uicinas.	
			quod *pro* quia.
			inuenerim *pro* inueni.

A 4.

Joh. i.			
16			quoniam *pro* et.
† accipimus.		† accipimus (*ms.*).	
	aco.+et (*ms.*).	aco.+et (*ms.*).	
17. (*hiat* μ.)			quoniam *pro* quia.
* gratia+autem.			* gratia+autem.
18. * umquam+nisi.		umquam + nisi (*ms.*).	* umquam+nisi.
19. * hoc+est.	hoc+est.	hoc+est.	* hoc+[es]t.
			cum nisisent *pro* quando miserunt.
miserunt+ei.			
om. ad eum.			illum *pro* eum *pri.*
			eum *sec.*+dicentes.
		qui *pro* quis (*ms.*).	

A 4—*continued.*

LIBER MULLING.	CODEX DURMACHENSIS.	CODEX KENANENSIS.	CODEX USSERIANUS (r₁).
Joh. i. 20. *om.* et confessus est *sec.*			*om.* et *tert.* [eg]o non sum *pro* non sum ego.
21. eum+*iterum′ tu. dixit *pro* dicit.			* eum+it[erum]. dicentes *pro* quid ergo. *om.* et *sec.* ait *pro* dicit. sum+numquid.
22.			*om.* et *tert.* +et *ad init.* (dixerunt [*ms.*]=*Am.*) *om.* ei.
es+dic nobis.			es+tu. nos miserunt *pro* miscrunt nos. +qu[i ei]s *ad init.*
23. *om.* ego.	essaias profeta dixit (*ms.*) *pro* dixit e. p.	ergo *pro* ego.	
24. añ *pro* erant.	*om.* erant.	*om.* erant.	*om.* erant. a *pro* ex. iudaeis *pro* pharisaeis. ut interrogarent *pro* et interrogauerunt. (*hiat* r₁.)
25. *om.* et (*sed spat. relict.*). illum *pro* eum. * +ei *ante* quid.	+ei (*ms.*) *ante* quid.	+ei *ante* quid.	* +ei *ante* quid.
Joh. xi. 30. * hautem *pro* enim. hic *pro* erat adhuc.	autem (*ms.*) *pro* enim.		* au[tem] *pro* enim. monumentum *pro* castellum. eo *pro* illo. quo *pro* ubi. obuiauerat (*ms.*) *pro* occurrerat.
31. * ea *pro* illa. ut consulentur *pro* et consolabantur.	ea (*ms.*) *pro* illa.	ea *pro* illa.	[a]utem *pro* igitur. * ea *pro* illa.
		om. quia *pri.*	ut uiderunt *pro* cum uidissent. quod *pro* quia *pri.* festina[ut]er *pro* cito. surrexisset *pro* surrexit.
† exit *pro* exiit.			*om.* et exiit. subsecuti *pro* secuti. quoniam *pro* quia.
32. * hautem *pro* ergo. uidisset *pro* uenisset. dicit *pro* et dixit.	uero *pro* ergo.	uero *pro* ergo.	* autem *pro* ergo. et uidisset *pro* uidens. procidit *pro* cecidit. dicens *pro* et dixit. *om.* ei.
*fuisset′ frater meus mortuus *pro* esset m. f. meus.			* fuisset *pro* esset.

A 4—*continued.*

LIBER MULLING.	CODEX DURMACHENSIS.	CODEX KENANENSIS.	CODEX USSERIANUS (r_1).
Joh. xi. 33. om. *ergo.* uidisset *pro* uidit.		uero *pro* ergo.	autem *pro* ergo.
fremit *pro* fremuit.		infremuit *pro* fremuit.	flentem *pro* plorantem. flentes qui uenerant cum ea *pro* qui u. cum e. plorantes. infremuit *pro* fremuit.
34. 35.	† turbabit (*ms.*) *pro* turbauit.	semet (*ms.*) *pro* se.	+in *ante* spiritu.
36. +et *ad init.*: dixerunt+ergo. 37.	dixerunt+ergo.	dixerunt+ergo. eis *pro* ipsis.	dixerunt+autem. illum *pro* eum. eis *pro* ipsis.
38. † rursus *pro* rursum. autem+quasi.	*om* et. † ¹apis *pro* lapis.		ne hic *pro* ut et hic non. autem *pro* ergo. *om.* rursum. intra semet ipsum *pro* in semet ipso

A mere glance over these four collations will enable us, so far as they go, to form a tolerably correct notion of the characters of the texts represented by them. *Durmach* approaches very closely to A, the best manuscript of the Vulgate : r_1 widely diverges therefrom. Midway between these two come μ and Q. And when we actually count the variants, this general impression is confirmed. The second column gives us 18 variants of *Durmach*; the fourth, 120 of r_1; while the first and third give respectively 43 (perhaps one or two more) of μ, and 37 of Q. The text of μ is therefore in these passages of the same general type as that of Q. It would, of course, be more than rash to make any inference as to the text of the entire manuscript from a few cases taken at random. But after working through a large part of the text I see no reason to alter the conclusion to which these passages appear to lead. In every chapter which I have tested—with certain exceptions to which I shall ask attention immediately—the result has been the same. The numbers of various readings in μ and Q are almost the same; the preponderance, when it exists, being for the most part on the side of μ. In St Mark the amount of variation from the Amiatine text in u is perhaps less than elsewhere, in St John greater.

§ 3. *The Old Latin Passages.*

I now come to deal with the exceptions just mentioned. They occur in the latter chapters of St Matthew and the earlier of St Luke. Following the same method as before, I append collations of a few passages.

B 1.

LIBER MULLING.	CODEX DURMACHENSIS.	CODEX KENANENSIS.	CODEX USSERIANUS (r_1).
Matt. xxiv.			
16. * in *pro* ad.			* [fugia]nt (*ms.*) in *pro* f. ad.
17. * tecto+sunt.			* tecto+sunt.
* discendent *pro* descendat.			* [desc]endant *pro* descendat.
† domu *pro* domo.		† domu *pro* domo.	
18. * agro+erit.			* agro+erit.
19.*† pregnantibus *pro* praegnatibus.	† praegnantibus *pro* praegnat.	† praegnantibus *pro* praegnat.	*† praegnan[tibus] *pro* praegnat.
20.	† fiet *pro* fiat (*ms.*).		[n]e *pro* ut non.
21. * sæculi *pro* mundi.			*om.* tunc.
			* sacculi *pro* mundi.
	(fiet = A.[*ms.*]).		
22. † brebiati *pro* brev.			
† fierit *pro* fieret.			*om.* illi.
† bræbiabunturtur *pro* breviabuntur.			
23.			hic+est.
			aut+ecce.
24. * exurgent *pro* surgent.			* exsurgent *pro* surgent.
			om. magna.
			† errore *pro* errorem.
		om. ut.	(f[ieri potest] = A[*ms.*].)
inducant *pro* inducantur.		† induantur *pro* inducantur.	
electos *pro* electi.			
26. † penitrabilibus *pro* penetralibus.	† penetrabilibus *pro* penetralibus (*ms.*).	† penitrabilibus *pro* penetralibus.	
credere *pro* exire.			
27.	ergo *pro* enim.	† exiit *pro* exit.	(*hiat* r_1.)
		apparet *pro* paret.	
* ad *pro* in.			* ad *pro* in.
om. et *sec.*		*om.* et *sec.*	
28. † illio *pro* illuc.			
aquilæ+et.		† +ali *ante* aquilæ (*ms.*).	(*hiat* r_1.)
29. +et *ad init.*			
eorum *pro* illorum.	obscurabuntur (*ms.*) *pro* obscurabitur.		
eorum *pro* caelorum.			

B 1—*continued.*

LIBER MULLING.	CODEX DURMACHENSIS.	CODEX KENANENSIS.	CODEX USSERIANUS (r_1).
Matt. xxiv.			
30. * apparebit *pro* par. † fili *pro* filii. plangent+se.	apparebit *pro* par.	apparebit *pro* par. p l a n g e n t (*ms.*) super se *pro* plangent. † nubus (*ms.*) *pro* nubibus.	* apparebit *pro* par. lamentabun[t] *pro* plangent.
31. † mittit *pro* mittet.			congrega[n]tur (?) *pro* congregabunt.
angulis uentorum *pro* uentis. summo *pro* summis		suos *pro* eius. uentis+et.	* angulis uent[o]rum *pro* uentis.
			summ[a] illorum *pro* terminos corum.
* *ad fin. vers.*+cum coepererent (*sic*) hæc fieri respicete et leuate caput quoniam adpropeat redemptio uestra.			* *ad fin. vers.*+cum coeperint autem haec fie[ri r]espicitae et leuate capud quia adpr[opinquet] redemptio uestra.
Matt. xxvi.			
24. *Ad init. vers* +et.	hominis quidem (*ms.*) *pro* quidem hominis.	*Ad init. vers.*+et.	(*hiat* r_1.)
tradetur *pro* uadit. *om.* de illo. *† tradetur *pro* traditur.	† tradetur *pro* traditur.	eo *pro* illo. † tradetur *pro* traditur.	† uadet *pro* uadit. eo *pro* illo. *† tradetur *pro* traditur.
* non nasci homini illi *pro* ei si natus non fuisset homo ille.	*om.* ei.	non natus *pro* natus non.	* non nasci hom[ini ill]i *pro* ei si natus non fuisset homo ille.
25.		respondit *pro* respondens.	iudas+scarioth.
* traditurus eum erat *pro* tradidit eum.		traditurus erat eum *pro* tradidit eum. eum+et. dixit+ei.	* tr[adi]turus eum erat *pro* tradidit eum.
* illi+iesus.		illi+iesus.	* illi+iesus.
26. * ipsis hautem manducantibus *pro* cenantibus autem eis.			* ipsis autem manducan[ti]bus *pro* cenantibus autem eis.
† accipit *pro* accepit.		† accipit *pro* accepit.	iesus accepit *pro* acc. iesus.
om. et *pri.* et *pro* ac. et dedit *pro* deditque.			(*hiat* r_1.)
* dicons *pro* et ait. * manducate *pro* comedite * est+enim.		dicens *pro* et ait. edite ex hoc omnes *pro* et comedite. est+enim: *ad fin. vers.*+quod confringitur pro sacculi vita.	* dicens *pro* et ait. * ma[nduc]ate *pro* comedite. * est+enim.

B 1—*continued.*

LIBER MULLING.	CODEX DURMACHENSIS.	CODEX KENANENSIS.	CODEX USSERIANUS (r₁).
Matt. xxvi.			
27. † bibete *pro* bibite.			
28.	† effundetur (*ms.*) *pro* effunditur.	effundetur pro uobis et pro multis *pro* pro multis effunditur.	† effundetur *pro* effunditur.
*† remisione *pro* remissionem.	† remisione(*ms.*)*pro* remissionem.		*† remisione (*ms.*) *pro* remissionem.
29. * uobis+quia.		uobis+quia.	* uobis+quia.
		† gemine (*ms.*) *pro* genimine.	ac creatura *pro* hoc genimine.
diem illum cum illud *pro* diem cum illum.	diem illum cum illum *pro* diem cum illum.	diem illum quo illud *pro* diem cum illum.	illud diem cum illud *pro* diem cum illum.
30.			
31.			*om.* illis. (ista=A[*ms.*].)
Matt. xxvii.			
20.	principes *pro* princeps.	principes *pro* princeps.	principes *pro* princeps.
* populo *pro* populis hautem *pro* ucro.			* populo *pro* populis. autem *pro* uero.
21. * de duobus dimittam uobis *pro* uobis de duobus dimitti.	*om.* uobis (*ms.*).	dimittam *pro* dimitti.	* [d]e duobus uobis dimittam *pro* uobis de duobus dimitti.
22. † qui *pro* quid. * ergo *pro* igitur.			* ergo *pro* igitur. fa[cia]mus *pro* faciam. *om.* de.
23. *om.* illis. pilatus *pro* praeses.	† praessit (*ms.*) *pro* praeses. *om.* magis (*ms.*).		
		clamauerunt *pro* clamabant.	*om.* dicentes. se nihil [pr]oficere *pro* quia n. proficeret. tumultum fieri *pro* tumultus fieret.
24. proficit *pro* proficeret. † fierit *pro* fieret.			[ac]cepit aquam *pro* accepta aqua.
fier.+in populo.			
† lauauit *pro* lauit. * manus+suas. dicens coram populo *pro* coram p. d.		coram+omni.	* manus+suas.
		ego innocens *pro* innoc. ego.	sum ego *pro* ego sum.
* *om.* iusti.		respondit *pro* respondens.	* *om.* iusti (*e spat.*).
25.			omnis turba *pro* uniuersus populus.
* huius *pro* eius.			* huius *pro* eius.
		uestros *pro* nostros. uero *pro* autem.	
26.			flagellis caesum *pro* flagellatum.
eum crucifigeret *pro* crucifigeretur.			* eum crucifigerent *pro* crucifigeretur.

B 1—*continued.*

LIBER MULLING.	CODEX DURMACHENSIS.	CODEX KENANENSIS.	CODEX USSERIANUS (r_1).
Matt. xxvii.			
27. * duxerunt *pro* suscipientes.			* duxerunt *pro* suscipientes.
prætorium *pro* praetorio.			* praet[orium] *pro* praetorio.
* præt. + et.			* præt. + [et].

B 2.

Luc. v.			
6. ut *pro* cum.			
multitudinem pisoium *pro* pis. m.			
* ita ut rumperentur *pro* rumpebatur autem.		ita ut rumpebatur hautem *pro* rump. autem.	* ita ut ru[m]perentur *pro* rump. autem.
* retia *pro* rete.			* retia *pro* rete.
7. tunc *pro* et *pri.*			
			innuerunt *pro* annu.
* socis + suis.			* sociis + suis.
qui cum *pro* et *tert. om.* et *quart.*			
* repleberunt *pro* impleuerunt.			* repleuerunt *pro* impl.
			ut *sec.* + paene.
8. hoc uiso *pro* quod cum uideret.		uidisset *pro* uideret.	uidisset *pro* uideret.
* *om.* Petrus.			* *om.* Petrus.
† procedit *pro* procidit.	† procedit *pro* procidit.	† procedit *pro* procidit.	
* dicens + rogo te.			* dicens + rogo te.
		me + domine.	
			quoniam *pro* quia.
		om. domine.	
9. * timor *pro* stupor.			* timor *pro* stupor.
* inuasserat *pro* circumdederat.			* inuaserat *pro* circumdederat.
* illum *pro* eum.			* illum *pro* eum.
10.			† capturam *pro* captura.
			autem + et.
* dixit *pro* ait.			* dixit *pro* ait.
			iesus ad simonem *pro* ad s. iesus.
* eris homines *pro* hom. eris.			* eris homines *pro* hom. eris.
			uiuificans *pro* capiens.
11. * nauiculis in terram *pro* ad t. nauibus.			* nauiculis in terram *pro* ad t. nauibus.
* eum *pro* illum.			* eum *pro* illum.
Luc. viii.			
10. ait *pro* dixit.			
scire *pro* nosse.			
autem + non est datum sed.			
similitudinibus *pro* parabolis.			

B 2—*continued.*

LIBER MULLING.	CODEX DURMACHENSIS.	CODEX KENANENSIS.	CODEX USSERIANUS (r₁).
Luc. viii. 11. hæc est hautem *pro* est autem haec. * similitudo *pro* parabola.	autem+uerbum.		haec autem *pro* est autem haec. * similitudo *pro* parabola. +qui seminat est filius hominis *ante* semen. semen+autem.
12. quod *pro* qui. autem+cecidit.			
* hii sunt *pro* sunt hi. * audiunt+uerbum.			uiam+seminati sunt. * hi sunt *pro* sunt hi. audiunt+* uerbum' in cordibus suis.
uenit hautem *pro* deinde uen. tulit *pro* tollit. * de corde corum uerbum *pro* u. de c. eorum.		tulit *pro* tollit.	* de corde illorum uerbum *pro* u. de c. eorum. uti ne credant et *pro* ne credentes.
13.			qui autem *pro* nam qui.
petrosam *pro* petram.			petram+seminati sunt.
* +hi sunt *ante* qui. audiunt *pro* audierint. * +uerbum *ante* cum sec. * accipiunt *pro* susc.	accipiunt (*ms.*) *pro* susc. .	accipiunt *pro* susc.	* + hi sunt *ante* qui. * + uerbum *ante* cum sec. * accipiunt *pro* susc.
* illud *pro* uerbum.			* illud *pro* uerbum. ipsi *pro* hi.
non habent * radices *pro* radicem non h. *† quia *pro* qui.	radices (*ms.*) *pro* radicem.	radices *pro* radicem. † quia *pro* qui.	* radices *pro* radicem. *† quia *pro* qui.
	om. et *sec.* (*ms.*). tribulationis *pro* temtationis.	tribulationis *pro* temtationis.	(et in tempore temtationis recedunt=A [*ms.*].)
14. audiunt *pro* audierunt.			cum audierint *pro* audierunt. aud.+uerbum. *om.* et *pri.*
per sollicitudinem *pro* sollicitudinibus. diuitiarum *pro* et diuitiis. dulcidinis *pro* uoluptatibus.	a sollicitudinibus (*ms.*) *pro* soll. uoluntatibus (*ms.*) *pro* uolupt.	a sollicitudinibus *pro* soll.	in sollicitudinibus *pro* soll. † uolumptatibus *pro* uoluptatibus. uitae+huius sacculi.
* *om.* euntes. * adferunt *pro* referunt.			* *om.* euntes. * adferent *pro* referunt.

A cursory inspection of these collations reveals immediately a remarkable difference between them and those with which we were previously occupied. Two facts at once strike us. The column which stands in closest relation to the first is no longer the third, but the fourth; and the number of asterisks in the first and fourth columns in proportion to the total number of readings has increased. Once more our first impression is borne out by a count. The number of various readings recorded for μ is 95, for r_1 99, for D*urm* 16, for Q 39. And of the 95 variants in μ and 99 in r_1, 51, or more than half, are marked with an asterisk. This suggests that the part of μ with which we are now concerned has a text substantially Old Latin with Vulgate mixture, rather than, as the remainder, a text substantially Vulgate with Old Latin readings. The relative number of variants in D*urm*, Q, and r_1 has not materially changed, while that in μ has been almost trebled. Again, the number of asterisks has advanced from 14 in 43, to 51 in 95. This is what we might expect to find if the text before us is really Old Latin. For the variations of any Irish Biblical codex from the Vulgate fall into two classes—errors of transcription and Old Latin readings. The number of the former would be about equal in two copies written under similar conditions; the latter will of course vary in proportion to the remoteness of the manuscript from the Old Latin type. Assuming, therefore, that there was one Old Latin recension in Ireland, the number of agreements in variation from the Vulgate between any two copies of that recension will be greater in proportion to the whole number of variations than between two manuscripts, one of which is mainly Vulgate and the other mainly Old Latin.

Now the passages of μ which have just been collated with A do not stand alone. The same test applied to the two passages, extending—to speak roughly—from the middle of St Matthew xxiv. to near the end of the Gospel, and in St Luke from the beginning of chap. iv. almost to the end of chap. ix., brings to light exactly similar phenomena. The text of these two passages is absolutely different in type from that which appears throughout the remainder of the Synoptic Gospels. It is essentially Old Latin.

It is naturally difficult to determine, within a verse or two, the exact points at which these Old Latin portions of our Book begin and end. It can be done, however, with more precision than might have been anticipated, as my third series of collations will demonstrate.

C 1.

LIBER MULLING.	CODEX DURMACHENSIS.	CODEX KENANENSIS.	CODEX USSERIANUS (r_1).
Matt. xxiv.			
1. accesserunt + ad eum.		accesserunt + ad eum.	
aedificationem *pro* aedificationes.		aedificationem *pro* aedificationes.	structuram *pro* aedificationes.
2. illis *pro* eis.	illis (*ms.*) *pro* eis.	illis *pro* eis.	[e]is dixit *pro* dixit eis.
			om. hic.
3.			*om.* co.
			in monte *pro* super 'montem.
		discipuli+eius.	discipuli+eius.
4.			(*hiat usque* -educat r_1.)
5.			(*hiat usque* meo *et a* christus *usque* -ent r_1.)
6. * audietis, hautem *pro* audituri enim estis. dicentes+quia.	autem (*ms.*) *pro* enim.	audietis enim *pro* audituri enim estis.	* audietis enim *pro* audituri enim estis.
			pugn[as] *pro* proelia. proeliorum+sed. exsurget *pro* consurget.
		contra (*ms.*) *pro* in *sec.*	contra *pro* in (*bis*).
8.	enim *pro* autem.		*om.* pestilentiae et. o[mnia] haec *pro* haec autem omnia.
9. † tribulationem *pro* tribulatione.	† tribulationem *pro* tribulatione.	† tribulationem *pro* tribulatione.	
10. * inuicem *pri*+se.		inuicem *pri*+se.	* inuicem *pri*+se. occid[ent . .] *pro* odio habebunt.
11. insurgent *pro* surgent.		insurgent (*ms.*) *pro* surgent.	exsur[gent] *pro* surgent.
12.			multos seducent *pro* sed. mult. quia *pro* quoniam.
iniquitas+et. *† refrigerescet (*sic*) *pro* refrigescet.	† refriget (*ms. p. m.*) *pro* refrigescet.		*† refrigerescit *pro* refrigescet.
13. permanserit *pro* perseuerauerit.	permanserit *pro* perseuerauerit.	permanserit *pro* perseuerauerit.	
14. * per totum orbem *pro* in uniuerso orbe.	† orbe regni in uniuerso (*ms.*) *pro* regni in uniuerso orbe.		* per totum (*ms.*) orbem *pro* in uniuerso orbe.
			(*hiat ab* hoc *usque* [reg]ni *et ab* in *sec. usque* -bus *et* ueniet consummatio r_1.)
15. hautem *pro* ergo.			(*hiat usque* -tum *et ab* -st *usque* intellegat r_1). [quod dic]tum e[st] *pro* quae dicta sunt.
per danielum profetam *pro* a danihelo propheta.			*aliqua uerba omissa sunt* (e *spat.*).

Taking first the early part of St Matt. xxiv., it will probably be agreed that there is no sign of an Old Latin base up to the end of v. 11. The variants in r_1 number *at least* (see vv. 4, 5) 17, in μ only 7, in Q 8, and in *Durm* 3 ; of the seven readings in the first column, no more than two have an asterisk. Here, then, we have the ordinary mixed text. From verse 16 onwards, on the other hand, the text is Old Latin, as we have already shown. About the intervening verses it is impossible to speak with confidence. In vv. 12–14, μ has three variants as against two in r_1 ; *Durm* and Q have one each. This gives us little to go upon. It must be observed, moreover, that only a portion of v. 14 remains in r_1 ; and that in the portion that is wanting the Codex Usserianus Alter (r_2) has an important reading—"finis" for "consummatio"— while, on the other hand, the reading "permanserit" in v. 13 (μ *Durm* Q) has every appearance of being an Old Latin survival, though unsupported by either r_1 or r_2. In v. 15 our difficulties increase : μ registers two variants, one of which is supported by r_2 ; *Durm* Q give none at all ; r_1, in the few letters that remain, two (one of which is an inference from the insufficiency of the space to contain the words of A). On the whole, I am inclined to think that the Old Latin text begins with v. 12 ; but if not, then certainly somewhere between the end of v. 11 and the beginning of v. 16.

What seems important to observe is, that the change in the type of text takes place suddenly. There is no gradual increase of Old Latin mixture, culminating in the almost total disappearance of the Vulgate element. We may fairly conclude from the facts that if r_1 were not so fragmentary just where we need its help most, in vv. 14, 15, we could fix, within a line or two of our manuscript, the place where the Vulgate and the Old Latin texts meet.

So much, then, for the starting-place of the Old Latin text in St Matthew. Where does it end? A collation of 25 verses of chapter xxvii. (vv. 40–64), which it would occupy too much space to print here, shows that the relation between the texts of r_1 and μ remains much the same as in the previous chapter. At the same time, however, we notice a considerable numerical increase in the variants of Q. The numbers are : readings in μ 43, in r_1 36 or more, in Q 33, in *Durm* 12, asterisks 23 or more. Our manuscript has therefore still an Old Latin text, while the Old Latin element in Q has become more marked. Let us now, therefore, collate the passage extending from xxvii. 65 to xxviii. 15, in order that we may determine, if possible, how far the Old Latin character of μ is maintained.

C 2.

	LIBER MULLING.	CODEX DURMACHENSIS.	CODEX KENANENSIS.	CODEX USSERIANUS (r₁).
	Matt. xxvii.			
65.	* milites *pro* custo-diam.		milites *pro* custo-diam.	* milites *pro* custodiam.
				ite+et.
66.	+ipsi *ante* scitis. *om.* abeuntes.		abeuntes + cum custodibus.	
	* et signauerunt *pro* signantes.			* et signauerunt *pro* signantes.
	lapidem + et dis-cesserunt.		lapidem + et dis-cesserunt.	
			om. cum custodibus.	
	Matt. xxviii.			
1.				
2.			de caelo discendit *pro* descend. de c.	
3.	hautem *pro* enim.	autem *pro* enim.	autem *pro* enim.	et erat *pro* erat enim.
	* uestimenta *pro* uestimentum.			* uestimenta *pro* uestimentum.
	* eius *sec.*+candida.		eius *sec.* + candidum.	* eius *sec.*+[ca]udida.
4			uel moltui (*ms.*) *pro* uelut mortui.	a *pro* prae. sicut *pro* velut.
5.				q[uaeritis q]ui crucifixus est *pro* qui c. est q.
6.			hic+sed.	dixerat *pro* dixit.
	* uenite+et.	uenite+et (*ms.*).	uenite+et.	* uenite+et. (*hiat ab* -ocum *usque ad fin. vers.* r₁.)
7.	surrexit + a mortuis.		surrexit + a mortuis.	
				ite [et] *pro* euntes.
	om. ecce *pri.* sicut praedixit *pro* ecce praedixi.	*om.* ecce praedixi uobis (*ms.*).	sicut dixit *pro* ecce praedixi.	(*hiat ab* [et] *usque ad* timore *v.* 8 r₁.)
8.	* gaudio magno *pro* magno gaudio.	gaudio magno *pro* mag. gaud.	gaudio magno *pro* mag. gaud.	* gaud[io magno] *pro* mag. gaud.
	* et current *pro* currentes.			* [et curren]t (*ms.*) *pro* currentes. (nuntiate [*ms.*]=A.)
			suis *pro* eius.	
		† aduerunt (*ms. p. m.*) *pro* ado-rauerunt.		
9.	† habete *pro* hauete.			† ille *pro* illac.
	om. autem. accesserunt + ad eum.			
				anplexerunt *pro* tenucrunt.
10.	timere+sed.		timere+sed (*ms.*).	quia praecedo uo[s] *pro* ut eant. galilaeam+et.
11.		† et+et (*ms.*).	aduntiauerunt (*ms.*) *pro* nunt.	
12.				sunt *pro* fuerant. consilium acceperun[t] *pro* consilio accepto. *om.* copiosam.
13.	uenerunt nocte *pro* nocte uen.			
14.				pers[uade]bimus *pro* suad. (*hiat* r₁).
15.	instructi *pro* docti.		edocti *pro* erant docti.	
		† deuulgatum (*ms.*) *pro* diu.	† deuulgatum (*ms.*) *pro* diu.	† deuulgatum *pro* diu.
				hoc *pro* istud.

It will be seen at once that there is a sudden change in the relation between μ and r_1 after xxviii. **3.** For xxvii. 65—xxviii. 3 the collation yields the following figures : μ **8,** r_1 **6,** Q **7,** Durm **1,** asterisks **4.** The ratio of these numbers agrees pretty closely with that of those already given for xxvii. **40–64.** But for xxviii. **4–15** the result is different. Here we get μ **11,** r_1 **16** or more, Q **10,** Durm **3,** asterisks **3** or more. The sudden decrease in the number of readings in μ and the almost more notable disappearance of asterisks are remarkable. Our conclusion is that the Old Latin text ends with xxviii. 3. This conclusion, however, could not, with the evidence now given, be held with absolute confidence, for the proportion of the variants of μ to those of r_1 is considerably larger than in the greater part of the manuscript. This might perhaps be accounted for by the specially imperfect state of r_1 just here, or by a greater amount than usual of Vulgate mixture in its text. But to place the matter beyond doubt, let us apply another test. The Clermont manuscript in the Vatican Library (h) agrees more closely than any other Old Latin manuscript of St Matthew with the Irish text. We may use it, then, in place of r_1 in these verses. Now let us examine the following collations of μ, Durm, Q, and h for St Matt. xxviii. **4–20.**

C 3.

Liber Mulling.	Codex Durmachensis.	Codex Kenanensis.	Codex Claromontanus (h).
Matt. xxviii.			
4.			a *pro* prae.
		uel moltui (*ms.*) *pro* uelut mortui.	
5.			
6.			quia *pro* quod. dixerat *pro* dixit.
7. * uenite+et.	uenite+et (*ms.*).	bic+scd. uenite+et.	* uenite+et. sed *pro* et *pri.* ite et *pro* euntes.
surrexit + a mortuis. * *om.* ecce *pri.*		surrexit + a mortuis.	* *om.* ecce *pri.* † praecedet *pro* praecedit. dixi *pro* praedixi.
sicut prædixit *pro* ecce prædixi.	*om.* ecce prædixi uobis (*ms.*).	sicut dixit *pro* ecce praedixi.	
8. * gaudio magno *pro* magno gaudio. et current *pro* curentes.	gaudio magno *pro* magno gaudio.	gaudio magno *pro* magno gaudio.	* gaudio magno *pro* magno gaudio. occurrentes *pro* currentes.
9.*† babete *pro* hauete *om.* autem. accesserunt + ad eum.		suis *pro* eius.	*† babete *pro* hauete.
10. timere+sed.		timere+sed (*ms.*).	amplexauerunt *pro* tenuerunt.
			ite+et. quia praecedo uos *pro* ut eant. galileam+et. uidebitis *pro* uidebunt.
11.	† et+et (*ms*).	adnuntiauerunt (*ms.*) *pro* nuntiauerunt.	† ciuitate *pro* ciuitatem.
12.			suut *pro* fuerant. consilium acceperunt et *pro* consilio accepto.
13.			magnam *pro* copiosam. et dixerunt *pro* dicentes. +illis *ante* dicite.
uenerunt nocte *pro* nocte uenerunt.			
14.			audierit praesis *pro* auditum fuerit a praeside. persuademus *pro* suadebimus.
15. * instructi *pro* docti.		edocti *pro* erant docti.	* instructi *pro* docti.
	† deuulgatum (*ms.*) *pro* diuulgatum.	† deuulgatum (*ms.*) *pro* diuulgatum. discipuli + eius (*ms.*).	hoc *pro* istud.
16.	† consituerat (*ms.*) *pro* constit.		
17.			
18.			cum uidissent *pro* uidentes.
19.		(iesus=*Am* [*ms.*].)	† est+est. *om.* ergo.
* +nunc *ante* docete.		+nunc *ante* docete.	* +nunc *ante* docete.
20. obseruare *pro* seruare.		obseruare *pro* seruare.	
	om. amen (*ms.*).		*om.* amen.

It is not too much to say that our inference is completely established by the foregoing table. The Codex Claromontanus yields 28
variants against 4 in *Durm*, 12 in μ and 13 in Q, while the asterisks
have dwindled to five. The Old Latin fragment of St Matthew
therefore begins at or a little after xxiv. 12 and ends at xxviii. 3.

Now let us turn to St Luke. That the portion upon which the
genealogy immediately follows (iii. 19–23) is mixed Vulgate will be
evident from the collation A 3. Omitting the genealogy, an examination of which would be valueless for our purpose, we next collate the
early verses of chapter iv.

D 1.

	LIBER MULLING.	CODEX DURMACHENSIS.	CODEX KENANENSIS.	CODEX USSERIANUS (r_1).
	Luc. iv.			repletus *pro* plenus.
1.				reuersus *pro* regressus.
	* deserto *pro* desertum.			* deserto *pro* desertum.
2.	+in *ad init. vers.*		+in *ad init vers.*	
				per dies *pro* diebus.
				(et tem.[*ms.*]=A.)
	* illis diebus *pro* diebus illis.			* illis diebus *pro* diebus illis.
			his *pro* illis *sec.*	his *pro* illis *sec.*
	† esurit *pro* esuriit.			+postea *ante* esuriit.
3				ut lapides [i]sti panes fiant *pro* lapidi huic ut panis fiat.
				om. et.
				illi *pro* ad illum.
	iesus+dicens.			om. quia.
	† uiuit *pro* uiuet.		† uiuit *pro* uiuet.	*vv.* 5–8 *post* vv. 9–12.
5.	* illum+iterum.			* illum+iterum.
	* diabolus+in montem excelsum ualde.		zabulus+in montem excelsum (*ms.*).	* diabolus+[in montem al]tissimum.
	ei *pro* illi.			
	mundi *pro* orbis terrae.			
6.				dixit *pro* ait.
				illi *pro* ei :
				+diabolus.
	ipsorum *pro* illorum.			
	* uoluero *pro* uolo.	uoluero *pro* uolo.	uoluero *pro* uolo.	* uo[l]uero *pro* uolo.
				dabo *pro* do.
		uero (*ms.*) *pro* ergo.	uero *pro* ergo.	† illam (*ms.*) *pro* illa.
	om. procidens.	om. procidens.	si cadens *pro* procidens si.	si procedens *pro* procidens si.
	* om. coram.			* om. coram.
	omnia tua *pro* tua omnia.			
8.				dixit illi iesus *pro* iesus d. i.
				iesus + uade post me satanas.
	est+enim.			diliges dominum deum tuum *pro* d. d. t. adorabis.
	om. soli.			
9.	eum *pro* illum.			illum+diabolus.
	ei *pro* illi.	† illis *pro* illi.		
10.	quoniam *pro* quod.			
	*† mandauit *pro* mandabit.	† mandauit *pro* mandabit.	† mandauit *pro* mandabit.	*† mandauit *pro* mandabit.
	custodiant *pro* conservent.			te conseruent *pro* cons. te.
11.	om. et.	om. et.	om. et.	om. quia.
	manibus+suis.	manibus + suis (*ms.*).	manibus+tuis.	
				† tollant *pro* tollent.

An analysis of this collation makes it clear, as I believe, that a sudden change in the character of the text takes place at the end of verse 4. For vv. 1–4 the numbers are, μ 4, D*urm* 0, Q 2, r_1 11, asterisks 2 ; while for vv. 5–11 we have μ 17, D*urm* 5, Q 6, r_1 15, asterisks 4. The beginning of the Lucan Old Latin fragment is therefore to be placed at verse 5. Its close may with no less confidence be assigned to ix. 54. Scarcely any part of the manuscript agrees so closely with r_1 as Luke ix. 45–54. As our collations of passages in this Gospel have not been numerous, we give a comparison of the four texts for these verses and a few which follow them in full, in order that the complete change which occurs in μ at v. 54 may the more easily appear. The number of variants are, for vv. 45–54, μ 27, D*urm* 6, Q 9, r_1 29 or more, asterisks 17 ; for vv. 55–62, μ 11, D*urm* 8, Q 7, r_1 23, asterisks 3. Our second Old Latin fragment therefore includes Luke iv. 5—ix. 54.

D 2

LIBER MULLING.	CODEX DURMACHENSIS.	CODEX KENANENSIS.	CODEX USSERIANUS (r_1).
Luc. ix.			
45. * hoc uerbum *pro* uerbum istud.			* hoc uerbum *pro* uerbum istud.
* erat hautem *pro* et erat.			* erat autem *pro* et erat.
* coopertum *pro* uelatum.			* coopertum *pro* uelatum.
illis *pro* ante eos.			illos *pro* eos.
* intellexerent (*sic*) *pro* sentirent.			* intellegerent *pro* sentirent.
			om. illud.
	om. et *sec.* tenebant *pro* timebant.	*om.* et *sec.*	
46. * in eis cogitatio *pro* cog. in eos.			* in eos cogitatio *pro* cog. in eos.
om. maior.			
47. * iesus hautem *pro* at iesus.			* iesus autem *pro* at iesus.
* corum *pro* illorum.		eorum (*ms.*) *pro* illorum.	* corum *pro* illorum.
adpræhendit *pro* adprehendens.			
puerum +et.			
* *om.* eum.			* *om.* eum.
48. * *om.* illis.			* *om.* illis.
* acciperit *pro* susceperit.			* acceperit *pro* suscepcrit.
† recipit *pro* recepit :	† recipit *pro* recepit.	† recipit *pro* recepit :	receperit *pro* recepit :
* +non me recipit sed.		+non me recipit sed.	* +no[n me recipit sed].
* *om.* omnes.			inter uos est *pro* est inter omnes uos.
			* (*om.* omnes).

D 2—continued.

LIBER MULLING.	CODEX DURMACHENSIS.	CODEX KENANENSIS.	CODEX USSERIANUS (r_1).
Luc. ix. 49. respondit *pro* respondens. dicens *pro* dixit.			(*hiat* r_1.) dixit+ad iesum.
* magister *pro* praeceptor.	† inmine (*ms.*) *pro* in nomine.		* magister *pro* praeceptor.
† qui *pro* quia. 50. eum *pro* illum. * iesus + sinite eum et.	*om.* qui enim.	iesus+sinite eum et. † aduersum *pro* aduersus.	*om.* ad illum. * iesus+sinite eum et.
			ad fin. vers.+nemo est autem qui faciat uirtutem in nomine meo et poterit male loqui de me.
51. coupleretur *pro* complerentur.	cum *pro* dum.	cum *pro* dum. † et ipse+et ipse (*ms.*).	
* iret+in. 52. illi+cœnam. 53. * euntis+in. 54.	iret+in.	iret+in. illi+cenam. † euntes *pro* euntis. cunt.+in.	* iret+in. euntes+nuntii. illum *pro* eum. * euntis+in. uidentes *pro* cum uidissent.
* uidissent+hautem. iohannes+et. † dicemus *pro* dicimus.	uidissent+autem.	uidissent+autem.	* uid.+autem. dixerunt+ad iesum. (*hiat* r_1 *a* vis *usque* et co-.)
	† igni (*ms.*) *pro* ignis.		eos *pro* illos. *ad fin. vers.* + sicut helias fecit.
55.			c[onue]rsus autem *pro* et conu. +iesus *ante* increpauit. quali spiritu *pro* cuius spiritus. animas+hominum.
om. cuius spiritus estis (*vide p.* 34). 56. *om.* filius . . . saluare (*vide p.* 34). 57.	*om.* et dixit *usque* estis. *om.* filius *usque* saluare.	*om.* et dixit *usque* estis. *om.* filius *usque* saluare.	† alium *pro* aliud. et factum est *pro* f. est autem. euntibus *pro* ambulantibus.
eum *pro* illum. 58.	† foueant (*ms.*) *pro* foucas.		† uiam *pro* uia. *om.* illi.
* nidos+ubi requiescant.	† capud+ûiû (*ms.*).	nidos+ubi requiescent.	* nidos+ubi requiescant. caput+suum.

D 2—*continued*.

LIBER MULLING.	CODEX DURMACHENSIS.	CODEX KENANENSIS.	CODEX USSERIANUS (r_1).
Luc. ix. 59.			et ait *pro* ait autem. † alterutrum *pro* alterum me *pro* mihi. et dixit *pro* dixitque : + * ei. *om.* ut.
60. * dixitque + ei. *om.* ut mortui se-peliant. uade + et.	iesus + ei. *om.* ut. † sepelient (*ms.*) *pro* sepeliant. adnuntiare (*ms.*) *pro* annuntia.	dixitque + ei. † sepelient *pro* se-peliant. adnuntiare *pro* an- - nuntia.	
61. alter *pro* illi. *om.* sed.	alter *pro* illi. mihi + ire.	alter *pro* illi.	ait autem *pro* et ait. alius *pro* illi. mihi + ire et.
* nuntiare *pro* re-nunt.	nuntiare *pro* re-nunt.	qui + in.	* nuntiare *pro* renunt. meis *pro* his. in domo *pro* domi.
62. *om.* suam.			dixit autem *pro* ait. illi *pro* ad illum. super *pro* in.

§ 4. *A Hypothesis.*

It may be well here to suggest a question which is not without interest. Granted that we have imbedded in Mulling's mixed text of the Gospels two fragments of genuine Old Latin,[1] how are we to account for this fact?

[1] The Book of Mulling is not unique in presenting the problem which we are attempting to solve. Readers of M. Berger's great work, *L'Histoire de la Vulgate pendant les premiers siècles du moyen age*, will have observed many parallels. Such are the text of the Epistle to the Hebrews (Vulgate, except chaps. x., xi.) in Brit. Mus. Harl. 1772 (Berger, p. 51); the Book of Job in St Gall 11, in which the text of Jerome's first revision of the Old Latin gives place to another in the middle of a word at xxxviii. 15, the handwriting changing at the same time (p. 122); the Chartres St John, Paris, B.N. 10,439 (Old Latin chaps. i.–vi., approaching to Vulgate chaps. vii.–xv., adhering still more closely to the Vulgate chaps. xvi.–xxi.: Berger, p. 89); the Sapiential Books in Metz 7 (Vulgate up to the middle of Wisdom, thenceforth "an exceedingly mixed text, abounding in passages taken from the ancient versions:" p. 101); the text of Acts in the Rosas Bible, Paris, B.N. Lat. 6 (Vulgate, except xi. 1–xii. 8, which is European: p. 25); and, most striking of all, the text of Acts in Paris B.N. 321. This is so closely analogous to our manuscript that M. Berger's words (p. 77) may be quoted: "Le livre des Actes des Apôtres est composé de deux parties fort différentes. Le premier tiers, jusqu'au verset 7 du chapitre xiii., représente un texte mêlé dans lequel les éléments anciens tiennent une si grande place, que l'on peut à peu près le considérer comme un texte ancien. Le texte antérieur à saint Jérôme reprend à xviii. 15 et occupe le fin du livre. Malheureusement les leçons anciennes ont été le plus souvent corrigées par grattage, de sorte qu'il est quelquefois difficile de les retrouver. Entre ces deux limites, le texte semble être un texte meridional," etc. The change of a few words would make this an accurate description of the text of St Matthew in our Book. Other parallels are mentioned in the text.

E

It will conduce to clearness if, before giving what we believe to be the most probable answer to this question, we state a theory which is obviously suggested by the facts, and which for some time appeared to the writer sufficient to account for them.

Let us suppose that the scribe—the writer, that is, either of the manuscript actually before us, or of one from which it was copied—had before him a codex from which a few pages were missing. The text of this was mainly Vulgate. When he reached the lacunæ, the deficiencies of the primary exemplar were supplied from another, the text of which was pre-hieronymian.

The truth of this hypothesis is, of course, incapable of proof. But it accounts for the facts by which it is suggested, and it is confirmed by various considerations.

It supposes, be it observed, that the main exemplar of the scribe was an imperfect copy of the Vulgate. This is proved to have been the case in another instance—the Stowe St John. In the Stowe manuscript the lacunæ of the exemplar are not supplied in the copy.[1]

It supposes, again, that our scribe used two exemplars, preferring the Vulgate, but having recourse to the other, an Old Latin manuscript, in case of need. That two different types of text should be current side by side in Ireland in early times, and that copies of both should be found in the library of a single monastery, will not surprise those who have studied Mr Haddan's account [2] of the gradual progress of the Vulgate in these Islands, or M. Berger's abridgment of the story.[3] And more direct proof in the shape of parallel cases is not wanting. The scribe of the Book of Durrow had in his hands, in like manner, two manuscripts—one of the Vulgate, another of the Old Latin.[4] So, again, had the scribe of Ussher's Codex. Its text is pre-hieronymian, and so lacked the *Pericope Adulterae*. This supposed deficiency is supplied from a Vulgate manuscript.[5] And, moreover, a similar hypothesis will be found to explain some of the phenomena of the Codex Usserianus Alter (r_2). This manuscript Professor Abbott regards as preserving an Old Latin text in St Matthew. In the latter chapters it certainly does so, but I venture to think the fact is not so clearly made out in the earlier portion of the Gospel. I must not encumber these pages with needless collations. It will suffice therefore to say that of the first half of St Matthew's Gospel only three fragments remain—i. 18–ii. 6, iv. 24–v. 29, and xiii.7–xiv. 1. In the two latter of these passages the variants of Q are almost identical in number with those of r_2; in the first there is a decided preponderance on the side of the latter manuscript. Now the existing portions of chapters iv., v., and xiii. are quite long enough to

---

[1] J. H. Bernard in the *Transactions of the Royal Irish Academy*, xxx. p. 316.

[2] Haddan and Stubbs, *Councils and Ecclesiastical Documents relating to Great Britain and Ireland*, vol. i. p. 180 *sqq.*

[3] Berger, *L'Histoire*, p. 30.

[4] See above pp. 21, 39.

[5] Abbott, *Evangeliorum Versio*, p. vii.

enable us to come to a satisfactory judgment as to the character of the text of which they are fragments, and the fact just mentioned leaves no room for doubt that it was Vulgate with Old Latin mixture. When we reach chap. xvi., and more especially when v. 19 is passed, we at once perceive a change. The variants of r_2 in xvi. 20–28 are nearly four times as numerous as those of Q.[1] May we not conclude that in r_2 part of St Matthew's Gospel was copied from a mixed text, the remainder from a manuscript of an Old Latin version?

The hypothesis, therefore, which we have provisionally assumed to account for the phenomena of μ, receives confirmation from the fact that a similar hypothesis serves to explain the textual features of the only other Irish Old Latin manuscripts of the Gospels known to exist.[2] And if we go a little further afield we shall find other parallels. Mr White[3] tells us, for example, that the Codex Palatinus (e) of the Old Latin, though mainly African, must have been copied from an ordinary European MS. in the last few chapters of St Luke; and he subjoins the remark that other similar instances of vacillation in the text of Old Latin manuscripts might be added. Dr Sanday, in like manner, suggests[4] that the last leaf of the archetype of a was lost or worn, and the text of this portion taken from some other copy. And a most interesting case of the same kind has recently been brought to light. The Earl of Crawford possesses a Syriac manuscript of the entire New Testament containing a version of the Apocalypse of which the only other known copy is a fragment in the British Museum. This version is akin to the Philoxenian rendering of the other New Testament books; but the exemplar from which the Crawford manuscript was copied had lost a leaf at the beginning, and the lacuna has been supplied from a manuscript of the later recension, akin to the Harkleian version, the *editio princeps* of which was published by De Dieu at Leyden in 1627, and which is now usually bound up with the Peshitto.[5]

[1] The numbers of the variants in the three MSS. *Durm*, Q, r_2 for the passages mentioned in the text may be exhibited in a table. Mere variations of spelling and unmistakable blunders are not reckoned. Several readings of r_2, however, are counted, which are almost certainly errors of the scribe.

	i. 19–ii. 6.	iv. 24–v. 29.	xiii. 8–58.	xvi. 13–19.	xvi. 20–28.
Durm	5	7	21	2	3
Q	6	14	57	10	10
r_2	15	18	61	15	36

[2] Excluding, of course, the St Gall fragment (p).
[3] Scrivener's *Introduction*, 4th ed., ii. p. 56.
[4] *Old Latin Biblical Texts*, ii. p. clxxv.
[5] Full proof of this fact is given by Professor Gwynn in his paper "On a Syriac MS. of the New Testament belonging to the Earl of Crawford and Balcarres, and on an in-edited version of the Apocalypse therein contained": *Trans. R.I.A.*, vol. xxx. part x., App. E, p. 414. See also *The Apocalypse of St John in a Syriac Version hitherto unknown*, edited by John Gwynn, Dublin, 1897, part ii. p. 37.

Our hypothesis is therefore well supported by parallel cases. We have next to remark that it seems to account sufficiently for two curious readings, one at the beginning, the other at the end of the Lucan fragment. To begin with the latter. It is found in St Luke ix. 55, 56. Our Lord's answer to the question of the two disciples is there cut down by our scribe to the single word "Nescitis." In many Greek MSS. the entire answer and the two preceding words "et dixit" are omitted, and this reading is followed by the Books of Armagh, Kells, and Durrow, Ussher's second Codex, and other Irish Vulgate manuscripts. The scribe of the Book of Mulling is conscious that there is something wrong in his (apparently unique) reading. For immediately after writing "Nescitis" he adds *in his text* the letter "d" (= "desunt") and places in the upper margin the remaining words of the sentence, reading the last five words, if not the whole clause, as they are found in r_1, which here differs from the Vulgate. It is not difficult to suggest an explanation. After copying v. 54 from his Old Latin exemplar, the scribe turns once more to the manuscript whose text he preferred, and which now again becomes available. But his memory of the other codex is still fresh, and so he writes "et dixit nescitis" before he observes that these words, with those that follow them, are absent from the text which he is transcribing. He allows the words which he has written to stand in his text, inserts after them the mark indicating omission, and relegates the remainder, which he takes from his Old Latin manuscript, to the margin.

We turn now to St. Luke iv. 5—the first verse, as we have already seen, of the fragment. It opens with the words "Et duxit illum *iterum* diabulus." What is the antecedent of "iterum"? Plainly neither "Agebatur in spiritu" (v. 1), nor "Dixit autem illi diabulus" (v. 3). "Iterum" is in fact meaningless as the text stands. But rearrange the narrative according to the order of r_1, in which the third temptation, according to the Vulgate, precedes the second, and all becomes clear. We now have "Et duxit eum in hierusalem" (v. 9) . . . "Et duxit illum *iterum*" (v. 5). What has happened is evident. The scribe was copying from an exemplar in which the temptations were given in the order in which they are found in all European Old Latin manuscripts.[1] He transposed the last two, but in other respects preserved the text unchanged. Now what prompted this clumsy dislocation of the text? The answer which the hypothesis under consideration suggests is this. The scribe has before him a Vulgate text. Suddenly at v. 5 it deserts him; but enough remains

---

[1] So *b, c, f, l, q, r₁*. The Vercelli manuscript (*a*) is no exception, for, in the first place, its text is not European in St Luke (Scrivener's *Introduction*, ii. 56); and moreover, though it here follows the African and Vulgate order, the marks of transposition in it are even clearer than in *μ*. The opening words of v. 5 in it are, "Et adduxit eum *hierusalem et statuit eum supra pinnam templi* et ostendit illi," etc. I know of no MS. except *μ* which reads "iterum" in v. 5 while following the Vulgate order; *e*, however, has "secundo."

to indicate that what immediately followed v. 4 in it was v. 5, and not, as in his secondary exemplar, to which he now turns, v. 9. It breaks off, let us suppose, with the words " Et duxit illum diabolus et ostendit illi omnia " . . This is sufficient as a cue. Following it as well as he can, he transcribes vv. 5–8 exactly as they stand in his second copy, before turning to v. 9, not perceiving that in so doing he deprives " iterum " of all meaning.

In spite of the many arguments by which our preliminary hypothesis may be supported, it lies open to one objection, not indeed absolutely fatal, but sufficiently serious. The Gospels of St Matthew and St Luke are in our Book divided into sections, according to a system found in many Old Latin texts.[1] These divisions embrace the Old Latin as well as the mixed portions of the text. This fact in itself makes it probable that these Gospels were ultimately derived not from two copies, but from a single exemplar of the Old Latin text, altered by the hands of successive copyists to its present state.

This is not, it is true, a necessary inference. The Old Latin exemplar would most probably have these sections. But experience shows us that quite possibly a mixed copy might have them also ; and so, on the supposition that our scribe used two exemplars, we are not absolutely prohibited from believing that both of them had sections such as we have mentioned. Probability, however, is against the supposition ; and so we come to suggest another hypothesis, or rather a hypothesis which is that already proposed, but in a slightly modified form. It is this : Our scribe copied from an Old Latin exemplar, which we may call x. This manuscript had, however, been previously corrected by means of an imperfect copy of the Vulgate, y. Where y failed, the pre-hieronymian text remained ; where it was available, the resulting text was mixed.

This hypothesis is supported by all the parallel instances which have been adduced above. It supposes, as before, in the hands of a scribe an imperfect Vulgate, y, evidently regarded as giving the better text, and an Old Latin, x. It explains, moreover, the reading "iterum" at iv. 5, just as readily as the other hypothesis. It accounts, too, though not so easily, for " et dixit nescitis " at ix. 56. The passage may have been expuncted in x by the corrector, though our scribe did not perceive the marks of deletion till he had written its first three words, or he may have mistaken the meaning of marks over the final words of the saying ascribed to Christ. It is, moreover, supported by the fact that in St Matthew and St Luke alone, the division into sections of the type referred to occurs. For these Gospels, therefore, and probably for these alone, we are obliged to suppose an ultimate Old Latin archetype. It will not, then, surprise us to find in them, and in them alone, a few pages passed over by the corrector, exhibiting an Old Latin text. And finally, it is supported by the fact that the Matthean Old Latin fragment is actually

[1] See above, p. 30 *sqq.*

corrected into conformity with the Vulgate, exactly in the way we
have supposed x to have been corrected by means of y. But this
will be seen more clearly in our next section.

§ 5. *The Corrector.*

We turn, then, to these corrections of the text with which our
fragments are so thickly studded. These corrections are, so far as
I can judge, all written by the same hand—the hand of him who
added the marginal numbers. They were certainly in some cases
made concurrently with or before the insertion of the numbers.
This may be seen, for example, by an inspection of f. 47 r a, l. 25
(St Matt. xxvi. 1). Here the words "omnia verba haec" have
been erased, and in their room "sermones hos omnes" has been
written. The correction extends, however, so far into the margin,
that the number referring to the Eusebian Canon, which had to
be inscribed opposite the corresponding line of the second column
(l. 24, Matt. xxvi. 26), is placed more to the right than is customary;
while, at the same time, the number of the section (cclxxiii.) is
begun too high and written in a slanting direction, so that the last
letter composing it is in its proper position.[1] Thus the correction
of the first column was completed before the numbers of the second
were written. And in the second column the first words of this
section, as originally written, were "et manducantibus." The word
"et" is erased, a punctuation mark set in its place, and "Et (in
prominent character) edentibus" written above the line. The text
is altered in the very act of marking the beginning of the section.
Thus it is quite clear that the corrector was identical with the
numerator,[2] and that he did both parts of his work concurrently.
It is important to note this fact, because it appears to lead us to a
further inference. The emendations and the numerals must have
been taken from the same exemplar. The large number of these
emendations shows us how thoroughly (too thoroughly) the corrector
accomplished his task in St Matthew's Gospel. His purpose seems
to have been to assimilate the text of μ to that of the copy which
he had in his hands. He was unsparing in the performance of this
work, and we may be pretty confident that, except by oversight,
he omitted to alter no word which differed from his codex. What,
then, was the character of the manuscript from which the corrections

---

[1] Similar phenomena are found at Matt. xxii. 46 (xxiii. 23), xxiv. 26 (40),
27 (42), Luke xix. 25 (39), etc. Specially interesting is Matt. xxvii. 3 (facsimile page, col. b, ll. 16, 17). Here the corrector wished to transpose "eum
tradidit." He therefore wrote a double stroke under "eum," and a single
stroke over "tradidit" in the usual way. The latter was found to interfere
with the signature, belonging to "Tunc." Hence it was replaced by a single
stroke *under* "tradidit." Obviously the signature was written after the first and
before the second of these single strokes.

[2] It may be remarked, in confirmation of this conclusion, that there is no
perceptible difference of hand between words introduced with the sole purpose of
emending the reading, and those by which the beginnings of sections are marked.

were drawn? Any copy of the Latin Gospels which is furnished
with the Eusebian Sections and Canons may be expected to contain
a substantially Vulgate text. That this was the character of the
text of the corrector's manuscript is proved by collating our first
fragment, as it left his hands, with the Codex Amiatinus. In a
very few instances an Amiatine reading is replaced by another:
now and then one reading gives way to another, neither of which is
Amiatine; but in the vast majority of cases, readings which differ
from those found in A are obliged to make way for rivals which it
supports. Let us take, for example, St Matt. xxiv. 21–31, which
has been collated above (B 1). It occupies lines 1–31 of the first
column of f. 46 r. In this passage μ varies from A 16 times.
In two cases the corrector introduces non-Amiatine readings, and in
nine he brings our text into agreement with the Amiatine. He
leaves therefore 7 variants. Q, in the same passage, has also 7.
Examining in the same way St Matthew xxvii. 20–26, we find the
13 variants of μ reduced by a similar process to 6, while again Q
has 7. If we extended our inquiry further, the result would be to
prove that the manuscript from which the Old Latin fragment was
corrected was of much the same character as Q or the greater part
of μ,—in fact, that it contained a mixed Vulgate text.

In the Lucan fragment the work of correction does not seem to
have been done in so thorough-going a spirit as in St Matthew.
Thus, in the two passages collated above (B 2), μ has 45 variants,
while there are only 6 corrections. Every one of these, however,
is an assimilation to the Amiatine text. The manuscript, therefore,
from which they were taken, if not the same, was at least probably
of the same character as that which the diorthotes used in St Matthew.

Who, then, was the corrector? I have already stated my belief
that the scribe who added the marginal numbers, and at the same
time divided the Gospels into sections, revised the text as he went
along. I must now express the further conviction that this reviser
was identical with the original scribe (or with one of them, if there
were several) of the manuscript. It is true some slight difference
may be detected in the writing of the text and of the corrections.
But the difference is not greater than that which is found to exist
in many cases between two pages of the text itself. And, independently of this fact, a difference in the script was to be expected,
owing to the difference of the conditions under which it was executed.
A man naturally writes better when his letters are penned upon
a blank sheet of well prepared vellum, than when he inserts them
where he can find space between closely written lines or over
erasures. And so the writing of the text in our fragments is *better*
than the writing of the emendations, but the difference extends, as
I believe, no further. It is quite consistent with identity of hand.

But, again, if we suppose that the corrections are not due to the
first hand, we are driven to one or other of two conclusions. The

Book of Mulling consists of five gatherings, forming what the colophon calls separate " volumina." The last four of these contain the evangelical text with some additions. The first is occupied with Jerome's letter to Damasus and other similar matter, including the Eusebian Canons. If we do not admit that our corrections and numerals are by the hand of the writer of the bulk of the manuscript, we are bound, therefore, to believe, either that the first gathering was penned by a different scribe from the last four,—in other words, that it is not really part of the Book of Mulling properly so called,—or that a manuscript, provided with a table of the Canons, was nevertheless unsupplied with the sections and marginal numbers, which were absolutely necessary if the table was to have either use or meaning.

It must be admitted indeed that the latter alternative is neither impossible nor without example. The Book of Armagh, for example, has the table of canons without the marginal numbers. Not only so. Its Gospel text is divided into regular sections, the beginnings of which are usually indicated, as in our Book, by capitals set out in the margin : and these sections are clearly quite independent of the Eusebio-Ammonian division. The Book of Armagh is therefore an exact parallel to our manuscript, supposing the latter to have been left by its original scribe without indication in the text, by numbers or otherwise, of the Eusebian sections. But even though the phenomena of the Book of Mulling may be illustrated by those of one or two other codices, we are still entitled to assert that the supposition which we are now discussing is *a priori* improbable. Nothing could be more natural than that a scribe who had added to his Gospel text the usual prefatory matter, should afterwards, when revising his work, bring the latter into agreement with the former in the way we have supposed.

On the other hand, the hypothesis that the scribe of the first " volumen " was different from that of the other four, does not seem to have occurred to such palæographers as Westwood and Gilbert. The writing of the first gathering does indeed present a different appearance from that of the Gospels to a superficial observer ; it is larger, and it is written all across the page, instead of in columns. But the form and character of the letters are similar ; the abbreviations used are, so far as I have observed, the same in both cases ; and I see, therefore, no reason to suppose a difference of hand.[1] It may, then, perhaps be granted that it is at least the more probable view that the entire manuscript (with the exception of the office for the Visitation of the Sick), including prefatory matter, numerals, and corrections, was the work of a single scribe. Assuming this to be true, and assuming also [2] that this scribe was not the Mulling of the colophon, but one who copied from him, we are now in a position to construct a tentative and hypothetical history of the writing of the

---

[1] See above, p. 8 *sq*. But compare also Appendix B.
[2] As has been already shown, p. 13 *sqq*.

Evangelium. St Molling of Ferns, in the latter half of the seventh century, wrote a copy of the four Gospels, in four gatherings of leaves, with a colophon in which this fact was stated. His exemplars were three in number,[1] including a mixed Vulgate text of St Mark, an Old Latin text of St Matthew and St Luke, and a copy of St John, written *per cola et commata*. The first and third Gospels were subsequently corrected from an imperfect Vulgate, or mixed copy. In the ninth century a transcript of Molling's Evangelium, thus corrected, and including the colophon, was made by a scribe of his monastery. This scribe possessed another mixed Vulgate Gospel manuscript, from which he took the numbers of sections and canons now found in the margin of the copy which he made. At the same time he adapted the text to them, made many corrections of the text, wrote an additional page which will be described hereafter,[2] and added a fifth " volumen " or gathering containing Jerome's prefaces and the Table of Canons, probably copied from the second manuscript just mentioned. The result was the Book of Mulling as we now have it.

Whether I have made it probable that this is a true history I must leave to others to decide. At least one thing is certain. We have succeeded in laying our hand on the adulteration of the text in its actual process. A copy made from the corrected text of our first fragment would have differed essentially from its archetype. The latter was Old Latin, the former would have been mainly Vulgate with Old Latin mixture. It is worth at least a sentence to remark, that such a text is formed, in this case at least, not by adulteration of the Vulgate with reminiscences of the older text, as we might have assumed to be the usual order of things,[3] but by the reverse process—by deliberately doctoring a pre-hieronymian text in order to bring it up to date. The text has in fact been constructed by exactly the same method as that which we have assumed to have given birth to that of the remainder of the Gospels of St Matthew and St Luke.

It may be well to add here a list of the readings of the corrector which differ from those of the Codex Amiatinus.

Matt. xxiv. 25. *om. vers.*	Matt. xxvi. 36. gezamani.
27. apparet *pro* paret.	39. procedit *pro* procidit.
46. dominus eius.	42. iterum hautem abiit *pro*
xxv. 2. his *pro* eis.	iterum secundo abiit.
14. *om.* peregre.	48. illum *pro* eum.
29. *om.* et *sec.*	eis *pro* illis.
34. *om.* eius.	56. adinplerentur *pro* im-
36. carcere eram.	plerentur.
37. *om.* ei (?).	58. finem rei *pro* finem.
39. [. .] *pro* et *pri.*	59. princeps *pro* principes.
xxvi. 14. dicitur *pro* dicebatur.	64. cum *pro* in.
26. *om.* et comedite.	67. *om.* in *pri.*
28. effundetur *pro* effun-	*om.* ei.
ditur.	

[1] See above, p. 41.   [2] Chapters vii. and viii.
[3] Compare Westcott and Hort's *New Testament*, ii. 81.

F

Matt. xxvi. 71. *om.* autem.
　　　　75. fleuit amarissime *pro* plorauit amare.
　xxvii. 1. aduersum *pro* aduersus.
　　　　3. tradidit eum *pro* eum trad.
　　　　　quia *pro* quod.
　　　　13. aduersus *pro* aduersum.
　　　　19. tibi sit *pro* tibi.
　　　　　illum *pro* eum.
　　　　20. princepes *pro* princeps.
　　　　22. faciemus *pro* faciam (?).
　　　　23. *om.* dicentes.
　　　　24. huius iusti *pro* iusti huius.
　　　　35. *om.* ut impleretur &c.
　　　　40. distruit . . reædificat *pro* destruebat . . reaedificabat.

Matt. xxvii. 41. inludebant eum *pro* inludentes.
　　　　43. confidit *pro* confidet.
　　　　　domino *pro* deo.
　　　　46. hel . i . hel . i .
　　　　49. liberare *pro* liberans.
Luke iv. 32. eius *pro* ipsius.
　　　　33. sinagoga + corum.
　　　　34. sis + tu es.
Luke v. 15. *om.* autem.
　　　　16. deserto *pro* desertum.
　　　　31. *om.* et.
　　　　37. ueteres uteres *pro* uteres uet.
　vi. 35. disperantes *pro* inde sperantes.
　viii. 2. e[x] *pro* de.
　ix. 20. ait *pro* dixit.

§ 6. *Value of the Text.*

We must now attempt to estimate the value of our fragments as witnesses to the text of the Gospels in Ireland before the influence of the Vulgate translation began to be felt. A rough and ready test at once suggests itself. For the greater part of the Matthew fragment we are able to compare our text with two others, r_1 and r_2. There are in fact about 540 places in which one or more of the three Old Latin manuscripts vary from the Codex Amiatinus, where the evidence of all three is available.[1] In about 140 of these μ r_1 r_2 agree in supporting a reading different from the Amiatine. In 17 all three vary from it, but without supporting each other. In 11, two vary independently, the third supporting the Amiatine reading. In about 50 cases μ alone differs from A, in 70 cases r_1, in 130 r_2. Again in 65 readings μ supports the Codex Amiatinus against the combined testimony of the other two, r_1 does the same 25 times, r_2 35 times. In all these latter cases we seem to have undoubted instances of Vulgate mixture in the several copies. Thus it will be seen that the Vulgate element in r_2 is more marked than in r_1, while in μ it is much greater than in either of these. On the other hand, r_2, as Mr Abbott remarks,[2] is full of blunders. The value of its singular readings is to a great extent discounted by this fact, and by it also their large number, as compared with those of r_1 and μ, is at least partially accounted for.

---

[1] The numbers given in this and the following paragraph are to be regarded as merely approximate, though I have taken pains to make them as accurate as possible. The general inference drawn from them is not likely, I believe, to be affected by any errors I may have made in the enumeration.

[2] *Evangeliorum Versio*, p. xvi.

On the whole, therefore, r_1 must be held to contain the purest Old Latin text, μ the most corrupted, while r_2—allowance being made for errors of the scribe—occupies a position midway between them.

In the Lucan fragment, the relation between μ and r_1 seems not to be quite the same as in St Matthew. In the former there are 1078 places in which one or other of the manuscripts varies from A. In 379 of these μ and r_1 agree, or, though not yielding exactly the same text, support one another in opposition to A; in 87 they vary from it independently. In 345 cases μ alone varies from A, in 267 cases r_1 alone. These figures point to the inference that μ has here an older type of text than r_1. That the variation in character has taken place rather in μ than in r_1 appears from the fact that while the number of variants in both manuscripts is greater than might have been expected, judging from the number found in St Matthew, the increase in variation is even more marked in μ than in r_1. The Lucan fragment is about half as long again as the Matthean, and the Codex Usserianus is here in a less fragmentary state. Now in St Matthew r_1 yields 336 variants; we might therefore expect rather more than 500 in St Luke. We have in fact 733, or about 50 per cent more. In μ, on the other hand, in St Matthew, there are nearly 275 variants, which warrants us in anticipating say 410 in St Luke. We actually find more than double the number—831. There is no evidence, so far as I have observed, to show that either r_1 or μ has suffered more from transcriptional errors in the third than in the first Gospel: we may thus pretty safely infer that the text of μ is in St Luke more ancient than in St Matthew,—more ancient indeed than that of r_1 in either Gospel, and less adulterated with Vulgate mixture.

CHAPTER V.

THE OLD LATIN PASSAGES.

The purpose of the following line for line copy of the Old Latin
portions of the Book of Mulling—St Matt. xxiv. 12–xxviii. 3 ; St
Luke iv. 5–ix. 54—is to reproduce these passages of the manuscript
as nearly as possible in the form in which they were originally
written.   Contractions are indeed expanded, but letters which had to
be supplied are printed in italics.   The manuscript has throughout
been corrected by a hand closely resembling, or, as I rather think,
identical with that of the original scribe.   All alterations of the text
made in the course of this correction are recorded in the lower margin.
In some cases the original writing has become, in consequence of erasure
or other causes, illegible : where this is so, the text is conjecturally
restored, and the letters by which the hiatus is filled are enclosed in
square brackets.   If the conjecture is not obvious, a note is added at
the end of the chapter stating the grounds on which it is based.   It has
been already remarked that the corrector divided the book into
Ammonian sections, and that in order to force the text into agreement with this division, he sometimes erased the opening letters of
the sections and re-wrote them in bolder character, sometimes contented himself with re-touching the first letter or two, so as to make
them more prominent.   In a few instances, in order to make room
for thé fresh writing, the scribe was obliged also to erase the closing
words of the preceding section and re-write them in the margin or
wherever space was available.   In such cases as these the *prima
facie* presumption clearly is that the original text was identical with
that which we now have.   I have therefore simply copied it without
comment, bracketing those letters which in the original script have
been so successfully erased as to be now illegible.   The end of a section is always indicated by an asterisk (∗) and those places in which
the sections of our manuscript do not coincide with those of *Codex
Amiatinus* are mentioned in the notes.

   I may add that the abbreviations ihs x̅p̅s̅ x̅p̅c̅ have not been
expanded.   Originally contractions of Greek words, they should be
represented by Greek expansions if at all, but no doubt by our scribe
they were regarded as merely conventional symbols.   How he would
have expanded the first it is impossible to say, for the word is not
once (if we except iessus, Luk. iii. 29) written in full in the manuscript.   The familiar symbol ħ I have ventured to expand *hautem*.
The word is frequently so spelt in Irish MSS. (*e.g.* Book of Kells at
St Luke, v. 6), and it seems not impossible that this spelling gave
rise to the customary abbreviation.

S. Matt. xxiv. 12–20.   f. 45 v. b.

25 tos *et* q*uoni*am habundabit i*n*iq*u*itas *et* refri
    gerescet caritas multor*um* q*u*i h*autem* per*m*an
    serit usq*ue* i*n* fine*m* hic saluus erit .—✱
Et pr*æ*dicabit*ur* h*oc* euangeliu*m* regni ¹pertotum¹
    ²orbe[*m*] i*n*testimonium oṁnibus gentibus
30 et t*unc* ueniet *con*summatio ✱ *cum* ³h*autem* uideritis
    abhominatione*m* desolationis q*uæ* dic
    ta*est* *per* danielum p*r*ofeta*m* stante*m* i*n*
    loco s*an*c*t*o qui legit intellegat ✱ t*unc* qui i*n* iudea
    s*unt* fugiant i*n* montes *et* qui i*n* tecto s*unt* no*n*
35 discendent tollere aliq*u*id de domu
    sua *et* q*u*i i*n* agro erit n*on* reuertat*ur* tollere
    tonica*m* sua*m* ✱ uæ h*autem* ⁴pregnantibus *et*
    nutrientibus i*n* illis diebus ✱ orate h*autem*
    utn*on*fiat fuga uestra hyeme u*el* sab

---

¹ ¹ *Expuncted : above the line, in un-*
    iuerso.
² *The line over* ꬱ (*representing* m) *erased.*

³ *Expuncted : in margin,* ergo.
⁴ *Above the line* (*over* e), i.

[bato * erit eni]m *tunc* tribulatio magna

qualis *non* fuit ab initio [1]sæculi us*que* mo

do ne*que* fiet * *et* n*i*si bre̦biati fuissent

dies illi *non* fierit salua omnis caro

5 *sed* prop*ter* electos [2] bræbiabunt*ur*[*tur*] dies

[illi * *tunc*] si *quis* uobis dixerit ecce hic x̄p̄s̄

aut illic nolite credere * [3][ex]urgent

enim seudox̄p̄i *et* seudoprofetæ et dab

unt signa magna *et* pr*o*digia ita ut i*n* er

10 rorem *in*ducant si fieri potest etia*m*

[4]elect[os] * [5] ecce *prædixi uobis [5] si *ergo* dixerint

uob*i*s ecce *in* deserto *est* nolite [6] credere

ecce *in* penitrabilibus nolite credere *

si*cut* *enim* fulgor ex*i*t ab oriente *et* [7] paret

15 us*que* [8] ad occidente*m* ita erit aduent*us*

f[ilii ho*minis* * ubi] *cumque* fuerit corpus ill*i*c *con*

gregabunt*ur* aquilæ * [9][et] statim h*autem* pos*t* tri

bulatione*m* dier*um* eorum sol obscurabit*ur*

et luna *non* dabit lumen suum *et* stelle

20 cadent d ecælo *et* uirtutes [10] eorum com

mouebunt*ur* * et *tunc* apparebit signu*m*

fili ho*minis* *in* cælo *et* *tunc* plangent [11] se om*ne*s

tribus terræ *et* uidebunt filiu*m* ho*minis* ue

nientem *in* nubibus cæli *cum* uirtute m

25 ulta *et* maiestate *et* mittit angelos

suos *cum*tuba et noce magna *et* *con*gre

gabunt electos *eius* a quattuor an

gul*i*s uentor*um* asummo cælor*um* us*que*

ad t*er*minos eor*um* [12] *cum* coepererent h*æc* fieri

30 respicete *et* leuate caput q*uoniam*

adpr*o*peat redemptio uestra [12] ab

arbore h*autem* fici discite para

bula*m* *cum* iam ram*us* *eius* tener fuerit

et folia nata cognoscetis

35   prope esse æstas s*i*c

et u*o*s *cum* uideritis h*æc*

omn*i*a scitote q*uoniam*

prope *est* ia   n*u*is amen dico

uob*i*s q*uia* *non* præteribit h*æc* generatio

---

[1] *Expuncted : above the line*, mundi.

[2] *The letters enclosed in brackets erased.*

[3] ex *erased : over the erasure* S.

[4] os *erased : over the erasure* i :,

[5]-[5] *Expuncted.*

[6] *Expuncted : in margin* exire.

[7] *Above the line (over* p) *is added* ap.

[8] *Expuncted : above the line* in.

[9] *Erased.*

[10] *Above the line* c l; e *changed into* ę : *the word being thus altered to* cęlorum.

[11] *Expuncted.*

[12]-[12] *Expuncted, and a line drawn down left margin.*

S. MATT. xxiv. 34–xxv. 3.

        g
donec omnia fiant cælum et terra [t]ran
sibunt uerba [1] hautem mea non [2] transibunt ✳
de die hautem illa et hora nemo scit neque
angeli cælorum nisi pater solus ✳ sicut [3] enim in diebus
5 noe ita erit et aduentus filii homi
nis sicut enim erant in   diebus ante diluium
manducabant et bibebant et nube
bant et uxores ducebant usque in diem
quo intrauit noe in arcam et non senserunt
10 donec uenit diluium et tulit omnes ita [3a] erit
aduentus filii hominis ✳ tunc [4] erunt [5] duo in agro
unus [6] adsumet[ur] [7] et [alte]r [7] relinquetur duæ [8]
in mola [9] unus adsumetur et [10] un[us] relinquetur ✳
[11] uigilate ergo quia nescitis qua die uel qua
15 hora dominus nester uenturus est ✳ illud hautem sci
tote quoniam si sciret pater familias qua
hora fúr uenisset uigilaret utique
et non sineret perfudiri domum suam ideo
et uos estote parati quia nescitis qua
20 hora filius hominis uenturus est ✳ [12] fidelis sernus
et prudens quem constituit dominus suus super
familiam suam ut det illís cibum in tempore ✳
beatus ille sernus quem cum uenerit dns [12a] in
uenerit síc facientem amen dico nobis
25 quoniam super omnia bona sua constituet eum ✳
sí hautem dixerit malus ille seruus in corde
suo moram facit dominus meus uenire et [12b] incip
conseruos suos percutere manducit
hautem et bibat cum ebriosís ueuiet dominus ser
30 ui illius in die qua non sperat et hora qua
ignorat et diuidit cum partem que eius ponet
cuminfidelibus illíc erit fletus et stridor denti[um] ✳
Tunc simile erit regnum cælorum x uirginibus
quæ[13] acciperunt lampades suas [14] et exierunt
35 [15] obiam sponso [16] quinque hautem ex [17] eis erant fa
tue et quinque prudentes [18] fatuæ hautem
acceptís lampadibus [19] suis

[1] *Expuncted: above the line,* uero.
[2] *Above the line,* præteribunt.
[3] *Above the line,* hautem.
[3a] *After this word is added* et.
[4] [5] *Marked for transposition.*
[6] *The mark indicating* [ur] *apparently erused and re-written.*
[7] [7] *Erased: over erasure,* et unus.
[8] *After* duæ *is added in margins* mo | lentes. [9] us erased: over erasure a.
[10] us erused: over erasure a.
[11] *Altered into* Uigelate.

[12] *Above the line,* quis putas est.
[12a] *In margin is added* eius.
[12b] *Some letters, apparently* iet, are added in margin.
[13] perunt expuncted: above the line, pi-entes.
[14] erased. [15] Above the line (over b), u.
[16] In lower margin is added, et sponsæ.
[17] e expuncted: over the line, h.
[18] In margin is added, sed quinq[ue].
[19] Expuncted.

S. Matt. xxv. 3–22.

[non sum]pserunt oleum secum prudentes nero acci
per[unt] oleum in uassís suís cum lampadibus suís
moram hautem faciente sponso dormita
uerunt omnes et dormierunt media hautem nocte
5 clamor factus est ecce sponsus uenit
exite obiam ei tunc surrexerunt omnes illæ
uirgines et accepierunt lampades suas
fatuæ hautem sapientibus dixerunt date nobis
deoleo uestro quia lampades nostræ exti
10 nguntur responderunt prudentes et
dixerunt non ne forte non sufficiat no
bís et uobís ite putius ad eos qui uendu
nt et emite nobis dum hautem irent emere
uenit sponsus et quœ parate erant
15 intrauerunt cum eo adnuptias et clusaest
ianna postea uenerunt reliquæ uir
gines dicentes domine domine aperi nobís
at ille respondens ait amen dico uobis quia
nescio uos uigilate itaque quia nescitis
20 diem neque horam ✳ sicut enim homo ¹ peregre pro
ficiscens uocauit seruos suos et tra
didit illis bona sua ✳ ² et uni ³ quidem dedit
quinque talenta alio hautem duo alio uero unum
unicuique secundum propriam uirtutem
25 et profectus est continuo hautem abít qui quinque
talenta acciperat et operatus est
in eis et lucratus est alia quinque simi
liter hautem et qui duo accipit lucratus est alia
duo qui hautem unum acciperat ⁴ habens fo
30 dit in terram et abscondit pecuniam domini
sui post multum tempus uenit dominus illorum
seruorum et possuit rationem cum eís
accessit qui quinque ⁵ talente acciperat et
obtulit alia quinque dicens domine quinque talen
35 ta tradidisti mihi ecce alia quinque superlu
cratus sum at illi dominus suus   euge ser
ue bonæ et fidelis quia super pauca fide
lis fuisti super multa té constituam
intra gaudium domini tui accessit et qui duo
40 talenta acciperat similiter dixit domine
duo talenta mihi tradidisti

---

¹ Expuncted.
² Above the line, Et.
³ Expuncted.
⁴ Above the line (over b), i.
⁵ The last letter expuncted: above the line, a.

S. MATT. xxv. 22–37.

ecce alio duo superlucratus sum [ait illi dominus]
suus euge serue bone et fidelis quia super
pauca fidelis fuisti super multa te con
stituam intra gaudium domini accedens hautem qui
5 unum talentum acciperat ait domine
scio quia homo durus es metis ubi non seminasti
et colligis ubi non sparsisti timui enim et
abí et abscondi talentum tuum in terra
ecce habes quod tuum est respondens hautem dominus
    eius
10 dixit ei serue mala piger sciebas quia
metuo ubi non semino et colligo ubi non sp
arsi oportuit ergo té dare pecuni
am meam nummularís et ego ueniens
recipissem utique quod meum est cum ussura
15 tollite itaque ab eo talentum et date
ei qui habet ·x· talenta * [o]mni enim ha
benti dabitur et habundabit ei hautem qui
non habet [1] etiam quod [2] [3] habet auferetur *
[4][ab eo et] sernum [5] nequam [6] proiecite [7] foras
20 intenebras exteriores illíc erit fle
tus et stridor dentium., * ff et omnes
Cum hautem uenerit filius hominis in maiestate sua
angeli cum eo tunc sedebit super sedem ma
iestatis suæ et congregabuntur ante
25 eum omnes gentes et seperabit [8] abinuicem
quem ad modum separat pastor ones
ab hedís et statuit quidem oues ad
extrís suís hædos hautem asinistrís
tunc dicet rex hís qui adextrís [9][eius]
30 [10] sunt uenite benedicti patris mei
percipite regnum quod uobís paratum
est ab initio mundi essuriui enim et
dedistis mihi manducare sitiui et
dedistis mihi bibere hospis
35 eram et colligistis me
nudus et operuistis mé
infirmus et uisitastis mé
in carcere [11] fui et uenistis ad me
tunc respondebunt [12] ei insti dicentes domine quando te

[1] *Expuncted.*
[2] *Added in margin, uidetur.*
[3] *The last letter expuncted and re sub-
    stituted (above the line).*
[4] *Erased : in margins and over erasure,
    ab eo :, | Et inutilem.*
[5] *Expuncted.*
[6] *pro erased.*
[7] *Expuncted.*
[8] *Above the line, eos.*
[9] *Erased : over the erasure and project-
    ing into margin* crunt.
[10] *Erased.*
[11] *Above the line, eram.*
[12] *Apparently expuncted.*

S. MATT. xxv. 37—xxvi. 8.

[uidim]*us* essurien*tem* *et* pauim*us* [1]té a*ut* siti
[ent*em*] *et* potauim*us* té *q*ua*ndo* té uidim*us*
hospit*em* *et* suscipim*us* té a*ut* nud*um* *et* co
operim*us* te [2]*uel* *q*ua*ndo* té uidim*us* i*n*firm
5 u*m* [3]*et* i*n* carcere *et* uenim*us* adte *et* res
pondit rex dicet illis amen dico uobis
quandiu fecistis uni ex fratribus
meis minimis m*i*hi fecistis t*un*c dicet hís
q*ui* asinistrís *eius* eru*n*t discidete ámé
10 maledicti i*n* ign*em* æter*n*um quem præpa
rauit pat*er* m*eus* diabulo *et* angelís *eius*
esuriui *enim* *et* n*on* dedistis m*i*hi manduca
re sitiui *et* n*on* dedistis m*i*hi potum
hospis era*m* *et* n*on* collegistis me
15 nudus era*m* *et*n*on* operuistis me
i*n*firm*us* *et* i*n* carcere fui *et* n*on* uisi
tastis me t*un*c respon*debunt* ei *et* ipsi dicen
tes dom*i*ne *q*ua*ndo* te uidim*us* esurien*tem*
a*ut* sitien*tem* a*ut* hospit*em* a*ut* nud*um* a*ut* i*n*fir
20 mu*m* *uel* i*n* carcere *et* n*on* ministraui
m*us* t*i*bi t*un*c respon*det* eis dicens amen
dico uobís quandiu n*on* fecistis uni
deminoribus hís nec m*i*hi fecistis t*un*c
ibunt isti i*n* ign*em* æter*n*um iusti h*autem* i*n* uita*m* eter*na*m
25 Et factu*m* *est* cu*m* *con*summasset ihs̄ [4][omn*i*a uerba
hæc] [4] d*i*xit discip*ul*ís suís ✻ scitis q*ui*a pos*t* biduum
pasca fiet *et*fili*us* hom*inis* tradet*ur* utcru
cifigat*ur* ✻ t*un*c *con*gregati su*n*t principes
sacerdot*um* *et* seniores populi i*n* atri
30 u*m* p*r*incipis sacerdot*um* q*ui* uocabat*ur*
caifas *et* *con*silium feceru*n*t ut ihm̄ dolo
tenerent *et* occiderent [5]dice[- -]bant
h*autem* n*on* i*n* die festo né forte tumul
tus fieret i*n* populo ✻ *cum* h*autem* [6]ihs̄ [7]esset
35 i*n* bethania i*n* domu simonis læpro
si accedens ad eu*m* mulier ha*bens* al
abastr*um* ungenti prætiosi *et* infudit
sup*er* caput *eius* recu*m*bente ipso
q*ui* *cum* uidissent h*autem* discip*uli* indignati su*n*t

S. MATT. xxvi. 8–27.   f. 47 r. b.

dicentes ut quid perditio hæc potuit
enim uenundari prætioso mu
lto *et* dari pauperibus sciens
h*autem* ihs ait illís quid molesti estis mulieri
5 bonum opus operata est in me nam semper pau
peres habebistis uobiscum mé h*autem* non semper
habe¹[bitis * ecce *enim* mittens]¹ unguentum hoc in
corpus meum ad sepeliendum me fecit amen
dico uobis ut ubicumque prædicatum fuerit hoc
10 euangelium intoto mundo dicetur et quod hæc fecit
in memoriam ipsius * tunc abít unus de duode
cim qui ² dic[e]batur indas scarioth ad princi
pes sacerdotum et ait illis quid uultis mihi
dare et ego uobís eum tradam at illi consti
15 tuerunt ei trigenta argenteos et exinde
querebat oportunitatem ut eum traderet
Pri ma h*autem* die ³ azimorum accesserunt discipuli ad
ihm dicentes ubi uís paremus tibi ⁴ manducare
pasca at ihs díxit ite in ciuitatem ad quen
20 dam et dicite ei magister dicit tempus meum propcest
apudté facio pascha cum discipulís meis et fe
cerunt discipuli sicut præcipit eís ihs et paruerunt
pascha uespere h*autem* facto discumbebat
cum duodecim discipulis * ⁵[et] ⁶ manducanti
25 bus illís díxit amen dico uobis quia unus uestrum
me ⁷ traditur * et contristati sunt ⁸ nimis cepe
runt siǵuli dicere numquid ego sum domine * [at]
ipse respondens ⁹ díxit qui intinguit mecum manum
in parabside hic mé ³ tradit ¹⁰ et filius
30 quidem hominis ¹¹ tradetur sicut scriptum est ¹² *
uæ h*autem* homini illi per quem filius hominis tra
detur bonum erat ¹³[non nasci homini illi * respondens]¹³
h*autem* indas qui ¹⁴ traditu[rus] eum ¹⁵[erat di]xit¹⁵ num
quid ego sum rabbi ait illi ¹⁰ ihs tú dixisti *
35 ¹⁶ i[psis h*autem* manducantibus]¹⁶ ³ accipit ihs
panem ¹⁷ benedixit ¹⁸ et fregit et dedit ¹⁹ disci
pulis suis ²⁰ dicens accipite ¹⁰ et ¹⁰ mandu
cate hoc est enim corpus meum * et accipiens
calicem gratias egit et dedit illís dicens

---

¹⁻¹ *Erased: over erasure,* tis :, Mittens
    enim hæc, *followed by space.*
² e *transformed by erasure into* i; ba
    expuncted. The word is thus chan-
    ged to dicitur.   ³ i *changed into* e.
⁴ *Expuncted: above the line,* comedere.
⁵ *Erased: above the line,* Et.
⁶ *Above the line,* edentibus.
⁷ *Above line, end of word* us (*see note*).
⁸ *Above the line,* ualde.
⁹ *Above the line,* ait.   ¹⁰ *Expuncted.*
¹¹ *Expuncted: above the line,* uadit.
¹² *Added in margin,* de illo.

¹³ *Erased: over erasure* ei si natus non
    fuisset homo ille, *and in left margin*
    opposite line 33, Respondens.
¹⁴ tu *changed into* di : rus *erased, and*
    over the erasure t, *the word being*
    thus altered to tradidit.
¹⁵⁻¹⁵ *Erased: over the erasure,* díxit.
¹⁶⁻¹⁶ *Erased: over the erasure,* Cænanti-
    bus hautem eis, *followed by space.*
¹⁷ *Above the line,* et.   ¹⁸ *Above line,* ac.
¹⁹ *Above the line is added,* que.
²⁰ *Expuncted: above the line,* et ait.

S. Matt. xxvi. 27–44.   f. 47 v. a.

bibete ex hoc omnes hic *est enim* san

guis meus noui testamen

ti qui pro multís [1] effunditur inre

misione peccatorum dico h*autem* uobis

5 [2] [quia] non bibam amodo de hoc genimine uitis us

que in diem illum cum illud bibam uobíscum nouum

in regno patris mei ⁕ [et] ymno dicto exi

erunt in montem oliueti., ⁕ ∬ ni in me inista

Tunc dicit illis ihs omnes uos scandalum patiemi

10 nocte ⁕ scribtum *est enim* percutiam pastorem

et dispergentur ones gregis [3] resurrexero

præcedam uos in [4] galieam ⁕ respondens h*autem* petrus

dixit sí omnes scandalizabuntur in té ego

enim numquam scandalizabor dicit illi ihs am

15 en dico tibi quoniam hác nocte antequam gallus

cantet ter mé negabis ⁕ [5] dicit illi petrus [6] si

oportuerit me mori técum non té ne

gabo similiter et omnes discipuli dixerunt ⁕ tunc ue

nit [7] cum illís [7] [8] ihs in [9] agrum qui [9] dicitur [10] gedzamani ⁕

20 [11] [et] dixit discipulis suís sedete híc donec uadam

illúe et [12] horem et adsumpto petro et du

obus filiis zebedei cepit contristari

et mestus esse ⁕ tunc [13] dicit illís [14] ihs tristis *est* ani

ma mea usque admortem sustinete híc

25 et uigilate mecum ⁕ et progresus pussillum [15]

[16] ce[ci]dit in faciem suam orans et dicens pater

sí possibile *est* transeat ámé calix

[17] [iste ⁕ sed] [17] tamen non [18] quod ego uolo sed [18] quod tu uis ⁕ [et]

uenit ad discipulos suos et inuenit eos dormi

30 entes et dixit petro síc non potuistis unam

horam uigelare mecum uigilate et orate

ut non íntretis intemptationem ⁕ spiritus quidem

prumtus *est* caro h*autem* in firma ⁕ [19] [abiit] h*autem*

[20] [iterum] et oranit dicens pater mí non potest

35 calix transire a mé nisi bibam illum

fiat uoluntas uenit iterrum et inuenit eos

dormientes erant *enim* oculi eorum graua

ti et relinquens eos iterrum abíit et oranit

---

[1] i *altered into* e.   [2] *erased* ?

[3] *In marg. is added,* postquam hautem.

[4] *Above the line (over* e), l.

[5] *Expuncted : above the line,* ait.

[6] *In margin is added,* etiam.

[7–7,8] *Marked for transposition.*

[9–9] *Above line* uillam quæ.

[10] d *expuncted.*

[11] *Erased : over erasure* Et.   [12] h *erased.*

[13] *Above the line,* ait.   [14] *Expuncted.*

[15] *In margin,* pro.   [16] ci *erased.*

[17–17] *Erased : over erasure,* Uerum, *followed by space* · iste *is re-written in margin after* calix.

[18] *Expuncted : above the line,* sicut (*bis*).

[19] *Erased : over erasure,* Iterum.

[20] *Erased : over erasure* abiit, *followed by space.*

S. Matt. xxvi. 44–58. f. 47 v. b.

tertio eundem sermonem * [tunc uenit ad discipulos]
suos et dicit [1] eis dormite iam et requiescite
ecce adpropinquauit hora et filius hominis
tradetur in manus peccatorum surgite
5 eamus ecce adpropinquauit qui mé tradet *
adhúc ipso loquente ecce indas unus
ex duodecim uenit et cumeo plurima mul
titudo cumgladiis et fustibus misi aprinci
pibus sacerdotum et senioribus populi *
10 qui hautem tradidit [2] eum dedit [3] illís signum dicens
quem [4] osculatus fuero ipse est tenete
eum et confestim accedens ad ihm dixit [5] [h]aué
rabbi et osculatus est eum [6] cui dixit [7] ihs am
ice ad quod uenisti fác tunc accesserunt
15 et manus iniecerunt inihm ettenuerunt eum *
et ecce unus ex hís qui erant cumihū exten
dit manum et exemit gladium suum et per
cussit sernum principis sacerdotum
et amputauit auriculam eius * tunc ait illi
20 ihs conuerte gladium tuum in locum suum omnes
enim qui [8] accipiunt gladium in gladio peri
bunt an̄ putas quia non possum modo
rogare patrem meum et exibet mihi modo
plusquam xii milia legiones angelorum
25 quomodo ergo inplebuntur scribturæ quia
síc oportet fieri * inilla hora dixit ihs
[9] ad [10] turbas quasi ad latronem uenistis cum
gladíis et fustibus conpræchendere mé
cotidie apud uós sedebam intemplo
30 docens et non mé tenuistis * hoc hautem totum fac
tum est ut [11] inpleretur scribturæ profetarum
tunc discipuli [12] [eius] omnes relicto eo fugierunt *
[13] illi [14] [hautem] tenentes ihm perduxerunt ad caifán
principem sacerdotum ubi scribae et
35 seniores [15] conuenerunt * petrus hautem sequebatur
eum alongue usque in atrium principis sa
cerdotum et ingresus [16] intus in [17] atrio

---

[1] *Above the line*, illis.
[2] *Above the line*, illum.
[3] *Above the line*, eis.
[4] *Above the line*, cumque.
[5] h *erased*.
[6] *Expuncted*.
[7] *Added in margin*, que illi.
[8] *Altered into* acciper int *by erasure*.
[9] *Expuncted*.
[10] *Above the line* (*over* a), i.
[11] *Above the line*, ad, *and* (*over* et)n., *the*

word *being thus changed to* adin-
plerentur.
[12] *Erased*.
[13] *In margin*, At.
[14] *Erased*.
[15] *Above the line* (*over last syllable*) a ;
*the word being apparently intended
to be read* conuenerant.
[16] us *expuncted : above the line*, tro.
[17] *Expuncted*.

S. Matt. xxvi. 58–71.   f. 48 r. a.

[sede]bat *cum* ministris utuideret [1] exitu*m*
[2] [rei * pri]ncip[e]s [2] [3] sacerdotu*m* *et* [4] uniuersu*m*
*con*cilium querebant falsum testi
moniu*m* [5] adu*er*sus ihm̄ ut eu*m* morti tra
5 derent *et* n*on* inuenerunt [6] in [6] [6]quicqua*m* cu*m*multi
falsi testes accessisent * nouissimæ
h*autem* uener*un*t duo falsi testes *et* dix*er*unt
audiuim*us* hune dixisse possu*m*
distruere templu*m* h*oc* d*ei* *et* p*ost* tridu
10 um ædificare illud *et* surgens
p*r*inceps sacerdotu*m* ait illi nihil
respondes ad ea qu*œ* isti testifican
t*ur* adu*er*sus té ihs̄ h*autem* tacebat *et* res
pondens p*r*inceps sacerdotu*m* d*i*x*i*t
15 illi adiuro té p*er* de*um* uiuu*m* utdi
cas nob*í*s s*í* tú es xp̄c̄ filius d*ei*
et d*i*c*i*t illi ihs̄ tú dixisti * uer*um*tame*n* dico
nob*í*s amodo uidebitis filium ho
minis sedente*m* [7] ad [8] dexteram uir
ი0 tutis *et* uenientem [9] in nubibus cæli *
tunc p*r*inceps sacerdotu*m* scidit uesti
menta sua d*i*cens [10] blasfemat quid [13] nu*n*c
adhúc [11] op*us* *est* testibus * ecce nu*n*c au
distis blasfemea*m* quid nob*í*s uidet*ur*
25 at illi [12] resp*on*derunt [6] omnes [6] *et* dixerunt reus *est*
mortis * tunc expuerunt [13] in faciem *eius et* co
laph*í*s eu*m* cæderunt [14] al*í* h*autem* palmas
in faciem [16] *eius* dederunt dicentes prophe
tiza nobis xp̄ē qu*i*s *est* qui té [15] percusset *
30 petr*us* [16] [h*autem*] sedebat foris i*n* atrio
et accessit ad eu*m* una [6] ex [17] ancellis
[18] d*i*x*i*t [6] illi *et* tú *cum* ihū galileo eras at
ille negauit cora*m* omnibus d*i*cens
nescio qu*i*d dicis [6] neq*ue* [6]intellego* [ex]
35 eunte [6] h*autem* illo ianua*m* uidit eu*m* alia
[6] anc ella *et* ait [19] ill*í*s qui erantibi

[1] *Above the line,* finem.
[2-2] *The letters enclosed in brackets erased:
in right margin, after l.* 1, rei ;
and over erasure, followed by space,
Pri : *the second* 1 *of* principes *is
transformed into* e *and* e *erased, the
word being thus changed to* princeps.
[3] *Above the line is inserted* hautem.
[4] *Above the line,* omne.
[5] *Above the line,* contra.   [6] *Expuncted.*
[7] d *erased.*
[8] am *erased : over erasure,* is.
[9] *Expuncted : above the line,* cum.

[10] *Above the line, before* t, ui.
[11] *Above the line,* egemus.
[12] *In margin (indicated as following* n),
tes : *the intention being that the
ambiguous* respon̄ *should be read as
a present participle* respondentes.
[13] *Erased.*   [14] i *added at end.*
[15] *The second* e *expuncted, and above it,* i.
[16] *Changed, partly by erasure, to* uero.
[17] is *changed, partly by erasure, to* a.
[18] x *transformed by partial erasure,
into* c ; s *added above the line ; the
word being thus altered to* dicens.
[19] *Expuncted : under the line,* his.

S. MATT. xxvi. 71–xxvii. 10.   f. 48 r. b.

et hic erat cum ihū nazareno [1]iterum nega
uit cum iuramento [2]dixit quia non noui hominem
et post pussillum accesserunt qui stabant et
dixerunt petro uere tú ex illís es nam
5 et loquella tua manifestum té facit
tunc cæpit detestare et iurare quia non nos
set hominem et [3]statim gallus cantauit *
[4]et recordatus est petrus uerbi ihū quod
dixerat prius quam gallus cantet ter
10 mé negabis egresus foras [5]ama
rissime [6]fleuit * mane hautem [7][cum] [8]factum [7][esse]t
consilium [9][fe]cerunt omnes principes sacer
dotum et seniores [10]plebis [11]aduersus ihm
ut eum morti traderent et uinctum [5]eum
15 [6]adduxerunt * et tradiderunt pontio py
lato præssidi * tunc [12]uedens indas qui [5]eum
[6]tradidit [13]quonia[m] damnatus est penctentia
ductus retulit trigenta argenteos
principibus sacerdotum et senioribus
20 dicens peccaui [7]quod [14]tradider[im] sangui
nem iustum at illi dixerunt quid ad nós
tú uideris et proiectís argenteís in
templo [15]processit et [16]laqueo [5]suspendit [6]se
[2]tunc principes [17]sacerdotum accepteís ar
25 genteis dixerunt non licet eos mittere in
curbán [2]hoc [2]est [2]in [2]oblationem quia prætium san
guinis est consilio hautem [18]facto [2]intersé emerunt
ex illís [2]hautem agrum figuli in sepulturam per
igrinorum propter hoc cognominatus est ager
30 ille acheldemath quod est ager sangui
nis usque in hodiernum diem tunc [19][ad]inpletum
est quod dictum est per heremiam profetam dicen
tem et acciperunt trigenta argenteos
prætium adprætiati [20]quod adprætiauerunt [21]filiis
35 israhel et dederunt eos in agrum figuli sicut constituit
mihi dominus . . , *

[1] Above the line, et.   [2] Expuncted.
[3] Expuncted : above the line, continuo.
[4] Altered into Et.
[5-6] Marked for inversion.   [7] Erased.
[8] The line representing m erased ; u altered into o.
[9] fec erased : over the erasure, ini.
[10] Above the line, populi.
[11] A line drawn over second u, and s expuncted : the word being thus changed to aduersum.
[12] The first e changed into i.

[13] m and the mark of abbreviation erased, and the remainder altered into quia.
[14] di erased, rī altered to ns, the word thus becoming tradens.
[15] pro expuncted : above the line, re.
[16] Above the line, abiens.
[17] Above the line, hautem.
[18] Expuncted : above the line, inito.
[19] ad erased.
[20] Expuncted, above the line, quem.
[21] Above the line, a.

[ih]s̄ hautem stetit ante pręsidem et interrogauit
  eum ¹ prœsis dicens tú es rex iudeorum dicit ei
  ihs̄ tú dicis * et cum accussaretur áprincipi
  bus sacerdotum et senioribus nihil resp
5 ondebat tunc dicit ² ei pylatus non audís
  quanta ³ aduersum té ⁴ testificantur et non
  ⁵respondit ei ⁶ ullum uerbum ita utmira
  retur ⁷ prœsis ⁸ multum * per diem ⁹sollemnem ¹⁰ consu
  etudo erat ¹⁰ ¹¹prœsis dimittere populo
10 unum uinctum quem uoluissent * habebant hautem
  tunc ¹² uintum insignem qui dicebatur barabas
  congregatis illís dixit pylatus quem uultis
  uobís dimittam barabán án ihm̄ qui
  dicitur xps̄ sciebat enim quod per inuidiam tra
15 diderunt eum * sedente hautem illo protribunali
  missit ad ¹³ eum uxor eius dicens nihil ¹⁴ sit ¹⁵ tibi
  et iusto illi multa ¹⁶ passa sum hodie
  per uisum propter ¹⁷ eum * ¹⁸ princeps hautem sacerdotum
  et seniores persuaserunt populo utpe
20 terent barabán ihm̄ hautem perdirent
  respondens hautem prœsis ait illís quem uultis de
  duobus dimittam uobís at illi dixerunt ba
  rabán * dicit illís pilatus ¹⁹qui ergo ¹⁹ ²⁰ faci[am de]²⁰
  ihū qui dicitur xps̄ dicunt omnes crucifigatur
25   ait ²¹ pilatus quid enim mali fecit at illi
  magis clamabant ²² dicentes cruci
  figatur * uidens hautem pylatus quia ²³ ni[c]hil ²⁴ pro
  ficit sed magis tumultus ²⁵ fierit in ²⁶ po
  pulo accepta aqua ²⁷ lauauit manus
30 ²⁸ suas dicens ²⁸ coram populo ²⁹ innocens ego
  sum ásanguine huius ³⁰ uós uideritis
  et respondens uniuersus populus dixit sa
  nguis ³¹ huius super nós et super filios nos
  tros * tunc dimisit illís barabán
35 ihm̄ hautem flagillatum tradidit eís

¹ i altered into e. ² Above the line, illi.
³ Above the line, over the final letter, s.
⁴ Above the line, dicant testimonia.
⁵ Above the line, at end of word, dit.
⁶ Below the line, ad. ⁷ i altered to e.
⁸ In margin, uel uehimenter.
⁹ Above the line, hautem.
¹⁰–¹⁰ Expuncted: above the line, consuerat.
¹¹ i changed into e.
¹² Above the line (over n), c.
¹³ Expuncted: above the line, illum.
¹⁴,¹⁵ Marked for transposition.
¹⁶ Above line, enim. ¹⁷ Above line, illum.
¹⁸ Above the line (after ep), e.
¹⁹–¹⁹ Altered into quid igitur (see note).
²⁰–²⁰ am de erased: over erasure and in margin at beginning of next line, emus | de (see note).
²¹ Above the line, illis prœses.
²² Expuncted. ²³ c erased (see note).
²⁴ Above the line (over final syllable), er.
²⁵ The second i altered into e.
²⁶ Expuncted. ²⁷ ua expuncted.
²⁸–²⁸ Expuncted. ²⁹ Above line, dicens.
³⁰ Above the line, iusti.
³¹ Expuncted: above the line, eius.

S. MATT. xxvii. 26–40.   f. 48 v. b.

ut [1] eum [2] crucifigeret * tunc milites præs[idis]
[3] duxerunt ihm̄ in prætorium [4] et congregauerunt
ad eum uniuersam cohortem [5] et uestier[unt]
eum tonicam porpoream [5] et [6] calamidem
5 cocciniam circumdederunt ei [7] plectentes
coronam despinís possuerunt super
capud eius et arundinem in dexteram eius
et genu flexu ante eum [8] adorabant
dicentes áué réx iudeorum * [9] [et] expuerunt
10 in faciem] eius [9] [10] [et] acciperunt arundinem
et percutiebant capud eius et postquam in
luserunt ei exuerunt eum calamidem coc
ciniam induerunt eum uestimentís eius
duxerunt eum ut crucifigerent [11] eum *
15 exeuntes hautem inuenerunt hominem [12] ciri
nensem [13] uenientem obiam illi [13] nomine
simonem hunc angarizauerunt [14]
[15] tollere crucem eius * et uenerunt in locum qui
dicitur golgotha quod est caluarie̦ locus *
20 [16] et dederunt ei uinum bibere cum felle
mixtum et cum gustasset noluit bibe
re * postquam [17] crucifixerunt eum di
uiserunt uestimenta eius sortem mit
tentes [18] utinpleretur quod dictum est per pro
25 fetam diuiserunt sibi uestimenta
mea et super uestem meam miserunt
sortem [18] et sedentes [19] [ob]seruaba
nt eum * et [20] possuerunt super capud eius
causam [21] illius [22] inscribtam hic est [23] rex
30 iudeorum * tunc [24] crucifix[e]runt cum eo [25] duos
latrones [26] unu[m] adextrís et [27] [alter]u[m]
asinistrís * [28] tunc euntes [28] blasphema
bant eum mouentes capita sua et
dicentes ua qui [29] distruebas templum
35 dei etintriduo illud [30] reædi ficabás

[1] Expuncted.   [2] Final lett. altered to tur.
[3] Expuncted : above the line, suscipientes.
[4] Expuncted.   [5.5] Expuncted.
[6] Above line, exuentes.   [7] Above line, et.
[8] Expuncted: above the line, inludebant.
[9-9] Erased : over erasure, and extending
    into right margin, Et exspuen | tes
    in eum, followed by space.
[10] Erased.   [11] Erased.
[12] nensem expuncted; the second i changed
    into e; in right margin, neum: the
    word being thus altered to cireneum.
[13-13] Expuncted.   [14] Added in marg., ut.
[15] Added at end, t.   [16] Changed into Et.
[17] Above the line, hautem.

[18-18] Expuncted, and a line drawn down
    left margin.
[19] ob erased.   [20] Above the line, in.
[21] Expuncted: above the line, ipsius.
[22] in erased.   [23] Above the line, ihs̄.
[24] Altered to crucifixi sunt.
[25] Last letter erased.
[26] Horizontal line (indicating m) erased,
    under the line, s.
[27] alter and line over u erased, nus
    added in margin.
[28-28] Expuncted : over the line, præter-
    euntes hautem.
[29] ebas expuncted : over the line, it.
[30] bas expuncted : over the line, it.

[saluu]*m* fac temet ipsum. sí filius d*e*i es
[di]scende decruce ＊ similit*er et* princi
[pe]s sacerdotu*m* [1] *in*ludentes cum scrib*í*s
et senioribus [2] *et* dicebant [2] alios saluos
5 fecit sé ipsum *n*on potest saluu*m* facere
sí réx isra*h*el [3] es [4] discend[e] *n*unc decruce
et cred emus ei [5] *con*fidat i*n* [6] domi*n*[um] [7] iam li
beret [8] eum sí uult [9] [eum ＊ d*í*xit] [9] *en*im qu*í*a [16] filius [17] dei
sum id ipsum h*au*te*m et* latrones qu*í* crucifixi
10 erant *cum* eo i*n*properabant ei., ＊
[10] A b ora h*au*te*m* [10] sexta [11] tenebr*ẹ* fact*æ* su*n*t
sup*er*uniuersam terram usque a*d* horam
[11a] [nonam] ＊ circa [7] [h*au*te*m*] horam [12] clamauit
ih͞s uoce magna d*í*cens [13] hel*í* hel*í* [13] [14] la
15 mazabathan.í. h*oc est* [7] [d*eu*s] deus meus [15]
ut quid [16] me [17] dereliqu*í*sti . quidam h*au*te*m* illíc
stantes *et* audientes dicebant he
liam uocat iste ＊ *et con*tinuo curr
ens unus ex eis acepta*m* [18] spungia*m*
20 i*n*plebit aceto *et* i*n*possuit [19] arun
dine*m et* dabat ei bibere ＊ [c]æteri u*er*o
dicebant [20] sine[te] [21] uidiam*us* [22] s*í* [23] uenit
helias [24] *et* saluet [24] eu*m* [25] alius h*au*te*m* accipit
lancia*m et* pupunguit latus e*í*us *et* ex*í*t
25 aqua *et* sanguis [25] ih͞s h*au*te*m* iterru*m* [26] excla
mauit uoce magna [7] [*et*]emissit sp*í*ritu*m* ＊
et ecce uelum templi scisum *est i*n duas
partes ásummo usq*ue* [27] ad deorsum ＊
[28] [et] [29] terr*æ* [30] mot[us] [27] factus [27] *est* [27] magnus *et* petr*ẹ*
30 scis*æ* su*n*t *et* monumenta aperta su*n*t
et [31] corpora sa*n*ctorum [32] domientiu*m* sur
rex*er*unt *et* exeuntes demonumentís
post resurrectione*m* [33] ipsius uener*un*t
i*n* sa*n*ctam ciuitatem *et* [16] mult*í*s [17] appa
35 rueru*n*t ＊ [34] [c]entorio h*au*te*m et* qu*í* cum eo erant

---

[1] ntes *expuncted : above line,* bant eum.

[2]-[2] *Expuncted : above the line,* dicentes.

[3] t *added at end of word.*

[4] *Final letter erased : over erasure,* at.

[5] a *expuncted,* i *above it.*

[6] *Final letter of* d͞u͞m *erased : over erasure,* o, *followed by slight space.*

[7] *Erased.*   [8] *Above the line,* nunc.

[9]-[9] *Erased : over the erasure,* DIXIT, *followed by space.*

[10]-[10] *Exp., save* A.

[11] *Above line,* h*au*te*m* hora.

[11a] nonam *erased : over eras.* Et, *followed by space ;* nonam *re-written in marg. opposite l.* 12.

[12] *Above the line,* nonam.

[13]-[13] *Points are inserted before and after* i *in each of these words, and in the margin is written* hel . i . hel . i .

[14] *Above the line (after* ba), c.

[15] *Added in margin,* deus meus.

[16], [17] *Marked for transposition.*

[18] u *altered to* o, i *to* e.   [19] em *altered to* i.

[20] te *erased.*   [21] *Second* i *altered to* e.

[22] *Expuncted : above the line,* an.

[23] *Above line (after* i), a.

[24]-[24] *Expuncted : above the line,* liberare.

[25]-[25] *Expuncted, and a line drawn down left margin.*

[26] ex *erased,* ui *altered to* ns, t *erased.*

[27] *Expuncted.*   [28] *Erased : over eras.* Et.

[29] *Altered by erasure to* terra.

[30] us *erased : over eras.* a ; *above line,* est.

[31] *Above the line,* multa.

[32] *Expuncted : above the line,* qui dormierant.

[33] *Expuncted : above the line,* eius.

[34] *Above the line (over first* o), u.

S. MATT. xxvii. 54–66.   f. 49 r. b.

    custodientes ihm̅ [1] cum uidissent terræ
    motum *et* ea [1] q*uæ* fiebant timuer*unt* ualde
    dicentes uere d*ei* filius erat iste * erant
    h*au*tem ibi mulieres multæ á longe uiden
5 tes q*uæ* s*ẹ*cut*ẹ* [2] fuerant ihm̅ agalilia
    ministrantes [3] illi *in*ter quás erat maria
    magdalenæ *et* maria iacobi *et* ioseph
    et m*a*ter filior*um* zebedei * [4] [cum sero h*au*tem esset]
    factum [5] uenit quidam homo diues ab ari
10 mathea nomine ioseph q*ui et* ipse
    discipulus erat ihū hic [6] accesset
    ad pilatu*m et* petit corpus ihū * [*tunc* py]
    latus iusit dari corpus [7] ihū *et* cum [7]
    [8] accipisset ioseph [9] corpus ihū [9] *in*uol
15 uit illud *in* sindone munda *et* possuit
    illud *in* monumento suo nouo qu*od* exci
    derat *in* petra *et* aduoluit saxum
    magnum ad [10] hostiu*m* monumenti *et* [11] dis
    cesset * erat h*au*tem ibi maria * magda
20 lena *et* altera maria sedentes *contra* sepulch*rum* *
A ltera h*au*tem die q*uæ est post* parasceuen con
    uener*unt* p*r*incipes sacerdotu*m et* pha
    risei ad pylatu*m* dicentes d*om*ine reme
    morati sum*us* quo*d* seductor ille d*ixit*
25 adhúc uiuens po*st* tres dies resurgam
    iubé ergo custodiri s*ẹ*pulchr*um* usq*ue in*
    diem tertium ne forte ueniant disci*puli*
    eius *et* furent*ur* eu*m et* dicant plebi sur
    rexit amortuís *et* crit nouissim*us*
30 error peior [12] p*r*iori ait illis pyla
    tus habetis [13] milites ite custodite
    sicu*t* [14] ipsi scitis illi h*au*tem [15] munierunt sæpul
    chrum [16] [et] [17] signa[uerunt] lapidem [18] et disces
    serunt [18] cum custodibus . .— *

[1-1] *Expuncted :* above *l.* 1, uiso terræ
    motu *et* his.
[2] fu *expuncted.*
[3] *Expuncted :* above *the line,*ei.
[4-4] *Erased :* over *erasure,* Cum sero hau-
    tem, *followed by space.*
[5] *Above the line,* esset.
[6] *Above the line* (over *second* e), i.
[7-7] *Expuncted.*
[8] et *before* accip. *in margin; first* i
    transformed into e; isset *expuncted;*
    above line, to corpore.

[9-9] *Expuncted.*
[10] h *expuncted.*
[11] *Expuncted :* above *the line,* abiit.
[12] *Final* i *changed to* e.
[13] *Above line,* custodiam.
[14] *Expuncted.*
[15] *Above the line,* abeuntes.
[16] *Erased.*
[17] ue *altered into* nt *; runt erased and
    replaced by* es *followed by space.*
[18-18] *Expuncted.*
  * *Altered to* magdalenæ.

S. Matt. xxviii. 1–4.   f. 49 v. a.

[Ues]pere hautem sabbati quæ lucescit in prima
[s]abbati uenit maria magdalenæ
[et] altera maria uidere sæpulch
rum et ecce terræ motus factus est magnus
5 angelus enim domini discendit decælo et
accedens reuoluit lapidem et sede
bat super eum erat hautem aspectus eius sicut fulgor
et uestimenta eius candida sicut nix præ timo

S. Luc. iv. 5.   f. 58 r. b.

25 in om*n*i ue*r*bo d*e*i et duxit illu*m* iter*um*
    zabulus inmonte*m* excelsum
    ualde *et* [1] ostendit ei omnia

[1] e *is written above* i

    regna mundi inmomento tem
    poris et ait ei *tibi* dabo potesta
    te*m* hanc uniuersa*m* *et* gloriam
    ipsor*um* qu*ia* m*ih*i tradita su*nt* *et* cui
5 uoluero do illa tu *ergo* si adora
    ueris me er*unt* om*n*ia tua *et* re
    spon*dens* ihs d*ixit* illi scriptu*mest* *eni*m
    dom*i*num d*e*um tuum adorabis *et* illi
    seruies *et* duxit eu*m* in hirusale*m*
10 *et* statuit eu*m* supra pinna*m* tem
    pli *et* d*ixit* ei s*í* f*ilí*us dei es mitte
    té hinc deorsum scriptum *est*
    *eni*m quo*niam* angel*ís* su*ís* mandauit
    deté ut custodiant té qu*ia* in
15 manibus su*ís* tollent té né for
    te offendas ad lapidem pedem
    tu*u*m *et* respon*dens* ihs ait illi scrip
    tu*mest* *non* temptabis dom*i*num d*eu*m tuu*m*
    et *con*summata om*n*i temptati
20 one zabulus recessit ab eo
    usq*ue* adtempus., ∗ ∫: ingalileam
Et egressus *est* ihs inuirtute sp*iritu*s
    et fama ex*í*t p*er* uniuersa*m* regi
    one*m* deillo, *et* ipse docebat
25 insinagog*ís* eor*um* *et* magnifica
    batu*r* ab omnibus., ∗ ∫: tritus
Et uenit nazareth ubi erat nu
    et intrauit *secundu*m consuetudine*m*

S. Luc. iv. 16–24.

suam die sabbati insinagogam
et surrexit legere *et* traditus *est*
illi liber esaiæ profetæ *et* utre
uoluit libr*um* inuenit locum ubi*est*
5 scriptum sp*iritu*s dom*i*ni sup*er* mé prop*ter*
quo*d* uncxit mé euangelizare
pauperibus misit me *præ*dicare
captiuis remisione*m* *et* cecís ui
su*m* dimittere *con*fractos inre
10 misione prædire annum d*o*m*i*ni
acceptu*m* *et* diem retributionis
et *con*plicuit libr*um* *et* reddidit
ministro *et* sedit *et* omnium insi
nagoga erant oculi intendentes
15 ineu*m* cæpit h*au*te*m* dicere ad illos ia*m*
hodie inpleta*est* scriptura
h*æc* in auribus uestrís.— *
Et omn*e*s [1] illi [2] testimonium dabant
et mirabant*ur* inuerbis gratiæ
20 q*uæ* procedebant deore ipsius
et dicebant no*n*ne hic *est* fili*us* io
[seph * et] ait illís utique dicitis mihi,
hanc similitudine*m* medice curá
té ipsum quanta audiuim*us* fac
25 ta incafarnauu*m* fác hic *et* in
patria tua, * [a]it h*au*te*m* [3] ih͞s amen
dico uobís qu*ia* nemo p*ro*feta acc
eptus *est* inpatria sua *

[1], [2] *Marked for transposition* | [3] *Expuncted.*

       ¹ [in] ueritate dico uobís multæ
       uiduę erant in diebus heliæ in
       israhel quando clusum est cælum
       annis tribus et mensibus séx cum
    5 facta est fames magna in omni
       terra et adnullam illarum misus est
       heleas nisi in sarepta sidoniæ ad
       mulierem uiduam et multi lepro
       si in israhel erant sub heleseo pro
  10 feta et nemo illorum mundatus est
       nisi neman syrus et repleti sunt
       omnes ira insinagoga hæc audien
       tes et surrexerunt et iecerunt illum
       extra ciuitatem et duxerunt illum usque
  15 ad supracilium montis supra
       quem ciuitas illorum erat ædifi
       cata utpræcipitarent eum ipse
       hautem transiens per medium illorum ibat ✱
       ² [et] discendit cafarnauum ciuita
  20 tem galileæ ibique docebat illos
       sabbatis ✱ et stupebant in doctri
       na eius quia in potestate erat ser
       mo ³ipsius ✱ ∫: nium inmundum
Et in sinagoga ⁴ erat homo habens dæmo
  25 et exclamauit uoce magna
       dicens quid nobis et tibi ihu naza
       rene uenisti perdere nós

¹ This word is apparently erased, and
   IN written in the margin.
² Erased : in margin, Et.

³ Above the line, eius.
⁴ Above the line, eorum

S. Luc. iv. 34–42.

scio ¹ qui sis ² sanctus dei et increpauit
illum ihs dicens obmutesce et exí
ab illo et cum proiecisset illum demo
nium inmedium exit abillo n[ihilque]
5 nocuit illum et factus est pauor
magnus in omnes et conloquebantur
ad inuicem dicentes quis est iste
sermo quod in potestate et uirtute
imperat inmundis spiritibus
10 et exeunt et deuulgabatur fama
deillo in omnem locum regionis . . — *
S urgens hautem ³ ihs desinagoga intra
uit indomum simonis socrus
hautem simonis tenebatur magnís
15 febribus et rogauerunt illum pro ea
et stans super illam imperauit
febri et dimissit eam et continuo
surrexit et ministrabat eis
occidente hautem sole omnes qui habe
20 bant infirmos uarís langori
bus adducebant illos ad eum at
ille singulís manum inponens
curabat eos.— * ƒ: mantia et di
Ex iebant hautem etiam demonia cla
25 centia qui tú es filius dei et increpans
eos non sinebat eis loqui quia sciebant
x̄p̄m̄ ipsum esse.— * ƒ: in desertum
F acta hautem die proficiscens ibat

---

¹ *Above the line*, te.
² *Above the line*, tu es.   ³ *Expuncted.*

locum *et* tur*b*a requirebant eu*m et* uene
ru*n*t usqu*e* ad ipsum *et* retinebant eu*m*
né discederet abe*í*s quibus ille ait
qu*ia et* aliis ciuitatibus oportet mé
5 euangelizare regnum dei ¹ ad hoc en*i*m ²
misus su*m et* erat *prœ*dicans insinago
gis galileæ.— * ∫: ut audirent
F actu*m est* ha*ut*em cum turbæ inruerent in eu*m*
uer*b*u*m* dei *et* ipse stáns secus stagnum
10 genezareth uidit duas naues
stantes secus stagnum piscatores
ha*ut*em exillis discenderant ut leuarent
retia sua ascendens ha*ut*em inunam
naue*m* qu*œ* erat simonis rogauit
15 eu*m* ut adduceret ate*r*ra aliqua
ntulum in altu*m et*sedens denaui
cula turbas.— * ∫: dúc in altum
Ut cessaunt ha*ut*em loqu*i* d*i*x*it* adsimone*m*
et laxate retia uestra i*n* captu*r*am
20 *et* respon*dens* simon d*i*x*it* ei *prœ*ceptor
*p*ertotam nocte*m* laborantes n*ihi*l
coepimu*s* se*d in* uer*b*o ³ tuo laxabo
⁴ retia *et* ⁵ ut h*oc* fecissent *con*cluse
ru*n*t multitudinem pisciu*m* copi
25 osam ita utru*m*peren*tur* retia coru*m*
tunc adnueru*n*t soc*í*s su*í*s qu*i* erant
in alia naui ut uenirent *et* ad
iuuarent eos qu*i* cum ueneru*n*t reple
beru*n*t ambas nauiculas ita
30 ⁶ utmer[e]geren*tur* * ⁷ [hoc uiso simon] ⁸

¹⁻² *Expuncted : above the line, uel quia*
ideo.
³ *Above the line, hautem.*
⁴ *Expuncted : above the line, rete.*
⁵ *Expuncted : above the line, cum.*

⁶ *The second* e *in* meregeren*tur* erased.
⁷⁻⁸ *Erased :* over *the erasure, Quod*
cum uidere, *and below the line,*
simon petrus.

S. Luc. v. 8–16. f. 59 v. b.

procedit ad genua ihū dicens rogo
té exí amé quia homo peccator sum
domine timor enim inuasserat illum
et omnes qui cum illo erant in captura
5 piscium quam coeperant similiter hautem ia
cobum et iohannem filios zebedei qui erant
socii simonis.— *∫: ex hoc iam eris
Et ¹ dixit ad simonem ihs nolitimere
homines capiens et subductis
10 nauiculis interram relictis om
nibus secuti sunt eum.— *∫: et ecce uir
Et factum est cum esset inuna ciuitatum
plenus lepra et ² ipse procedéns
infaciem ³ rogabat eum dicens ⁴ si
15 uís ⁴ ⁵ domine potes me mundare
et extendens manum ihs tetigit
eum dicens uolo mundare et confes
tim lepra eius discessit ab ⁶ eo et ⁷ præ
cipit illi ⁸ ihs utnemini diceret
20 ⁹ et dixit ⁹ ua de ¹⁰ et ostende té sacer
doti et offer pro emundatione
tua sicut præcipit moyses ut sit
intestimonium illis.— *∫: de eo ¹² et
Per ambulabat ¹¹ hautem magis sermo
25 conuenebant turbæ multæ ut
audirent et curarentur ab in
firmitatibus suís * ipse hautem ¹³ se
cessit in ¹⁴desertum et orabat *

---

¹ Expuncted : above the line, ait.
² Expuncted : above the line, uidens ihm̄.
³ ba expuncted : above the line, ui.
⁴·⁴, ⁵ Marked for transposition.
⁶ Expuncted : above the line, illo.
⁷ In margin, ipse.

⁸ Expuncted.
⁹·⁹ Expuncted above the line, sed.
¹⁰ Expuncted.
¹¹ Expuncted.
¹² Above the line, illo.
¹³ In margin, uel secedebat.
¹⁴ um expuncted : above the line, uel o.

Et factu*m*est inuna dier*um* *et* ipse [1] do
     cens *et* erant farisaei [2] *et* legis
     doctores q*ui* uenerant ex omni
     castello galileæ *et* iudæ *et* hi
   5 erusale*m* *et* uirtus erat d*om*ini
     ad sanandos eos.—   ✱ *ſ*: in lecto
Et ecce uiri portantes hominem
     q*ui* erat paralitic*us* [3] quærebant
     eu*m* [4] inducere *et* ponere ante eu*m*
  10 *et* no*n* inuenientes qua parte illu*m*
     ponerent p*ræ*tur̄ba ascenderunt
     sup*er*tectu*m* *et* p*er*tegulas sum̄miser*unt*
     eu*m* cu*m* lecto ante ihm̄ uidens hau*tem*
     ihs̄ fidem eor*um* d*ix*i*t* ho*m*ini remisa
  15 su*nt* t*i*bi peccata tua *et* coeper*unt*
     cogitare scribæ *et* farissei
     incordib*us* su*is* dicentes quis *est* hic
     q*ui* loquitu*r* blasfemiam quis pot*est*
     dimittere peccata n*i*si solus
  20 deus sciens hau*tem* ihs̄ cogitationes
     eor*um* d*ix*i*t* ad eos quid cogitatis
     mala in cordib*us* uestr*is* q*uod* *est*
     facilius dicere remisa su*nt*
     t*i*bi peccata tua aut dicere
  25 surge *et* ambula ut hau*tem* sciatis
     qu*ia* f*i*l*i*us hom*i*nis potestatem habet
     sup*er* ter*ram* dimittendi peccata
     d*ix*i*t* paralitico t*i*bi dico surge
     et tolle grabatum tuum *et* uade
  30 in domum tuam *et* confestim

---

[1] *Above the line,* sedebat.
[2] *Above the line,* sedentes.

[3] *Above the line,* et.
[4] *Above the line,* uel inferre.

S. Luc. v. 25–35. f. 60 r. b.

   surgens coram illís tulit in
   quo iacebat *et* abit in dom
   um suam magnificans dominum et
   stupor adpræhendit omnes
5 et magnificabant deum *et* re
   pleti sunt timore dicentes quia
   uidimus hodie mirabilia *
Et post hæc exiit *et* uidit puplicanum
   nomine leui sedentem adtylon
10 eum *et* ait illi sequere mé *et* relic
   tís omnibus ¹ secutus *est* eum * [et fecit]
   ² illi leui ³ cænam magnam in domu
   sua *et* erat turba multa pupli
   canorum *et* aliorum discumbentium
15 *et* murmurauerunt farisaei
   et scribæ dicentes ad discipulos eius qua
   re cum puplicanís *et* peccatori
   bus ⁴ manducat *et* ⁵ bibit ⁶ magister
   uester ⁶ * ⁷ [*et* ⁸ r]espondit ihs ⁹ *et* dixit eis non
20 egent qui sani sunt medico sed qui male
   habent non ueni uocare iustos sed
   peccatores in penitentia at
   illi dixerunt ei quare discipuli iohannis
   ieiunant frequenter similiter
25 et farisæorum *et* orationes
   faciunt tui hautem discipuli edunt
   et bibunt ait illis numquid
   possent filii sponsi ieiuna
   re quam diu cum illis *est* sponsus
30 uenient enim dies cum auferetur abeis

---

¹ *Above the line*, surgens.
² *Expuncted : over the line,* ei.
³ *In margin,* uel conuiuium mag.
⁴ *Above the line, at the end of the word,* uel is (*sic*).
⁵ *Above the line, over the final letter,* uel is.

⁶⁻⁶ *Expuncted.*
⁷ *et* r *erased : over erasure,* R.
⁸ *At the end of the word, above the line,* ens.
⁹ *Expuncted.*

   sponsus *et* tu*nc* ieiunabunt *i*nillis dieb*us*
D*ixit* h*aut*em parabula*m* ad eos qu*i*a nemo
   commissura*m* deuestimento no
   uo co*m*mittit in uestimentum
5 uetus alioqu*in* scinde*tur et* ueteri
   n*on con*ueniet commisura noua
   et nemo mittit uinu*m* nouum
   in ¹ utres ² ueteres alio quin ³ rum
   pet uinu*m* nouu*m* utres ⁴ ueteres
10 *et* ipsum effunde*tur et* utres p*er*i
   bunt se*d* uinu*m* nouu*m* in utres
   nouos ponunt *et* utraq*ue*
   *con*seruan*tur et* nemo bibens ue
   tus statim uult nouum *dicit* e*n*im
15 melius uetus *est.*, * *ſ*: primo
F actu*m* e*st* h*aut*em in sabbato secundo
   cum transiret ih̄s *per* segitem uel
   lebant disc*ipuli eius* spicas *et con*fri
   ngentes manibus manducab
20 ant q*ui*dam h*aut*em ex farisaeis di
   cebant eis quid facitis sab
   batis qu*od* n*on* licet *et* respon*dit* ih̄s
   ad eos nec h*oc* legistis qu*i*d fece
   rit d*aui*d cum essuriret ipse et
25 q*ui* cu*m*eo erant q*uo*modo intrauit
   in domu*m* dei *et* panes p*ro*possi
   tionis sumpsit *et* manduca
   uit *et* dedit eis q*ui* cum eo erant

¹, ² *Marked for transposition.*   ⁴ *Expuncted.*
³ *Above the line (over e), i*

S. Luc. vi. 4–14.   f. 60 v. b.

quos n*on* licebat manducare
n*i*si solis sacerdotibus *et* d*i*x*it* eis qu*i*a
dom*i*nus *est* fil*i*us hom*i*nis etiam sabbati ⁕
F actu*m* *est* h*au*t*em* in alio sabbato ut
5 intraret in sinagoga *et* doce
ret *et* erat homo ibi h*a*b*en*s manum
arida*m* dextera*m* obseruabant
h*au*t*em* scribæ *et* farisaei si in sa
bbato curaret ut inuenirent
10 accussare eu*m* ipse u*e*ro sciebat
cogitationes eor*um* *et* ait hom*i*ni q*ui*
habebat manum arida*m* surge
et stá in medium *et* surrexit *et*
stetit ait h*au*t*em* ad eos ih͞s inter͞rogo
15 uos s ilicet sabbatis bene
facere a*ut* male a*ut* animam
saluam facere a*ut* p*er*dere *et* cir
cu*m*spect*í*s illis omnibu*s* d*i*x*it* hom*i*ni
extende manum tuam *et* extendens
20 manum restituta *est* man*us* e*i*us sic*ut*
et alter*a* ipsi h*au*t*em* repleti su*nt* insipientia
et co*n*loquebant*ur* ad inuice*m* q*ui*dna*m*
facerent de ¹hom*i*ne ⁕ factum *est* h*au*t*em* in
ill*í*s dieb*us* exiit in montem oilare
25 *et* erat p*er*noctans in oratione dei ⁕
[et] c*um* dies factus *es*set uocauit ad
sé disc*i*p*ulos* suos *et* elegit duodecim
ex ips*ís* quos *et* apostolos nomi
nauit simone*m* quem cognominauit

¹ *Expuncted: above the line,* ih͞u.

[petrum et andream] fratre*m* e*ius* *et* iaco
[bum et ioh] annem *et* philippu*m* *et* bar
[th]alomeu*m* *et* thoma*m* *et* matheum
et iacobu*m* alfei *et* simonem q*ui* uocat*ur*
5 zelotis *et* iudam iacobi *et* iudam
scarioth q*ui* fuit ¹ traditor ✻ [et dis]
cendiens cum eis in loco campestri
stetit *et* t*ur*ba disci*pulorum* e*ius* *et* multitudo
copiosa plebis abom*n*i iudea *et*
10 hierusale*m* *et*transfretu*m* *et* ma
ritimatiri *et* sidonis q*ui* uenerant
ut audirent eu*m* *et* sanarentur alan
goribus suis *et* q*ui* uexabant*ur* aspiri
tibus inmundís curabant*ur* *et* om*n*es
15 t*ur*bæ querebant eu*m* tangere qu*ia*
uirtus deillo ² exi[e]bat *et* sanabat
omnes ✻ *et* ipse ³ adleuans ⁴ oculos
⁵ ad discipulos suos dixit.——
B eati pauperes ⁶ sp*iritu* qu*ia* uestr*um*est reg
20 num dei.—— ✻ ∫: turabemini.—— ✻
B eati q*ui* nunc esuritis quia sa
B eati q*ui* nun*c* ⁷ lugitis ⁸ quo*n*ia*m* ridebitis.—— ✻
B eati eritis cum uos oderint homines
et cum uos sep*er*auerint *et* exprob
25 raberint *et* iecerint nomen uestr*um*
tamquam malum prop*ter* filiu*m* hom*in*is gau
dete in illa die *et* exultate ecce
*eni*m mercis uestra magna *est* in cæ
lís sec*un*d*um* hæc *eni*m faciebant p*ro*fetis pa
30 tres eor*um* ✻ ueru*m* tame*n* uæ uobis di
uitibus qui habetis consulatione*m*

---

¹ *Above the line,* uel p*ro*.
² *The second* ө *erased.*
³ *Expuncted: above the line,* eleuatis.
⁴ *Above the line* (over *the second* o), i.
⁵ *Expuncted: above the line,* in.

⁶ *Expuncted.*
⁷ *Above the line,* fletis.
⁸ *The last lett*er *expuncted, and the* remainde*r altered into* qu*i*a.

S. Luc. vi. 25-34.   f. 61 r. b.

    uestram uæ uobis qui saturati estis
    quia essurietis uæ uobis qui riditis nunc
    quia flebitis et lugebitis * uæ uobís cum
    benedixerint homines secundum hæc facie
5 bant psedoprofetis patres eorum *
    sed uobis dico qui auditis dilegite
    inimicos uestros et benefacite
    hís qui uos odierunt benedicite ma
    ledicentibus uobís orate pro calum
10 niantibus uobís * et qui te [1] percusserit
    in maxillam præbe illi et alteram et ei
    qui aufert tibi tonicam etiam pallium
    noli prohibere omni petenti té
    tribue et qui aufert quæ tua sunt ne
15 repetas * et prout uultis uobis fa
    ciant homines sic facite illis. simi
    [liter * et] si dilegitis eos qui uos dilegunt
    quæ uobis est gratia. nam et peccatores
    diligentes sé dilegunt. etsi benefi
20 ceritis eis qui uobis benefaciunt
    quæ uobis gratia est. cum et peccatores
    hautem ipsud faciunt. et si motuum de
    deritis eís a quibus speratis uos
    recipere quæ gratia est uobis. nam
25 et peccatores peccatoribus fe
    nerant ut recipiant æqualia :
    uerum tamen amate inimicos uestros
    et benefacite eís et motuum date [2]
    [3] [nec] [4] desperantes et crit merces uestra
30 in cælis multa. et eritis filii alti
    ssimi quia ipse benignus est super

[1] sser *expuncted : above the line,* t.
[2] nihil *is added in the margin.*
[3] *erased.*
[4] *Above the line* (over *first* e)*,* i.

S. Luc. vi. 35–44.　　　　　　　　　　　　　　　f. 61 v. a.

　　ingratos *et* malos estote miseri
　　cordes si*cut* et pate*r* ueste*r* misericors *est* *
　　[n]olite iudicare né iudicet*ur* de
　　uobis nolite co*n*dempnare ne
5　co*n*dempnemini dimitite *et* dimi
　　ttet*ur* uobís. ¹ *et* dabit*ur* uobis mensu
　　ra*m* bonam co*n*uersa*m* *et* coagitata*m*
　　et supereffluente*m* dabunt insinu*m*
　　uestr*um*. eadem quippe mensura qua
10　mensi fueritis remetiet*ur* uobis., *
²D*ixit* ha*u*te*m* illis *et* similitudine*m* nu*m* quid
　　pote*st* cæcus cæcum ducere n*on*
　　né utriq*ue* infouea*m* cadent * [n*on est*]
　　disci*pulus* supe*r* magistru*m*. pe*r*fectus ha*u*te*m*
15　om*n*is erit si sit si*cut* magister e*i*us * [quid]
　　ha*u*te*m* uides fistuca*m* in oculo fratris
　　tui *et* trabe*m* qu*œ* in oculo tuo *est* n*on*
　　co*n*sideras. a*ut* quomodo potes di
　　cere fratri tuo sine frater
20　iecia*m* fistuca*m* de oculo tuo. *et* in
　　oculo tuo trabis *est* ipse in ocu
　　lo tuo ³ trabre*m* n*on* uides. hippo
　　chrita eice p*r*imum trabe*m* deocu
　　lo tuo *ettunc* pe*r*spicies iecire fis
25　tuca*m* deoculo fratris tui * [n*on est* e*ni*m*]
　　arbor bona qu*œ* faciat fructus
　　malos. neq*ue* arbor mala qu*œ* fa
　　ciat fructus bonos unaqu*œ* q*ue*
　　arbor ⁴ exfructu suo cognosc
30　[*itur* * neq*ue*] e*ni*m* collegunt despinís

---

¹ *Above the line*, date.
² *Under this word, in the margin, is*
　written u*e*l dicebat.
³ *The second* r *expuncted.*
⁴ *Above the line*, de.

ficus neque de ro[bo uindemiant]
[uuam * b]onus homo de bono [thesauro]
cordis sui profert bona malus
homo demalo profert malum ex abun
5 dantia enim cordis ós eius loquitur * [quid]
hautem uocatis mé domine domine et non fa
citis quæ dico * [1][omnis] qui uenit ad me
et audit uerba mea et facit ea
ostendam uobis cui sit similis
10 similis est homini ædificanti domum
suam et fodit in altum et posuit
fundamenta super petram inun
datione hautem facta inlisum est flu
men domui illi et non potuit eam
15 mouere fundata enim erat su
pra petram Nam qui audit uerba
mea et non facit ea similis factus
homini ædificanti domum suam sine
fundamento super terram inlisum est
20 flumen domui illi et continuo con
cidit et factaest ruina magna
domus illius., * ſ: in aures plebis
Et factum est cum conplesset omnia uerba
intrauit in cafarnauum centori
25 onis hautem cuiusdam seruus male
habens erat moriturus qui illi
prætiosus erat qui cum audisset deihu
misit seniores iudeorum rogans
eum ut ueniret etsanaret ser
30 uum suum at illi uenerunt et rogābant

1 *Erased : over erasure, Omnis.*

eum sollicete dicentes quia dignus
est ut hoc ei præstes dilegit enim gentem
nostram et sinagogam ipse ædi
ficauit nobís ibat hautem cum illís
5 ihs et cum iam non longue esset ado
mu missit adeum centorio ami
cos dicens domine noli uexari non enim dig
nus sum ut intres . sub tec
tum meum propter quod et me ipsum non
10 sum dignum arbitratus ut
uenirem adte sed dic uerbo tuo et
sanabitur puer meus. nam et ego ho
mo sum subpotestate constitus
et habeo subme milites. et dico
15 uni uade et uadit et alio. ueni et
uenit. et seruo meo dico fac hoc
et facit. et hoc audito ihs mira
tusest et conuersus sequentibus sé dixit
A men dico uobís innullo talem
20 fidem inueni inisrahel * et reuersi
sunt in domum qui misi erant
et inuenerunt seruum qui langue
bat sanum * [et] factum est de
inceps ibat in ciuitatem quæ uo
25 catur nauim et ibant cum illo disci
puli eius et turba copiosa cum ad
propinquaret portam ciuitatis
et ecce ferebatur mortuus
filius unicus matris suae
30 et hæc uidua erat etturba multa
ciuitatis sequebatur cum ea
quam cum uidisset dominus mise
ricordia motus dixit illís
nolite flere et accessit et
35 titigit loculum et qui porta
b ant steterunt. et ait ihs adu

S. Luc. vii. 14–27.

liscens tibi dico surge et rese*dit* p*ro*
tinus q*ui* mortuus erat et coepit
loq*ui* *et* dedit matri suae. accepit
h*au*t*em* timor omnes *et* magnificabant
5 dom*in*um dicentes qu*ia* p*ro*feta magnus sur
rexit i*n* nobis *et* qu*ia* uisitauit deus ple
bem suam ¹ in bono ¹ * [et] exiit hic ser
mo inuniu*er*sam iudeam *et* in omnem
regionem de eo * [et nuntiauer*un*t io]
10 hanni discipuli e*ius* de omnibu*s* his
et c*on*uocauit duos de discipul*is* su*is*
iohannes *et* misit ad ih*m* d*icens*
tú es q*ui* uenturus es añ alium ex
spectamus illa h*au*t*em* hora cura
15 uit multos á langorib*us* et pla
g*is* *et* spiritib*us* inmund*is* *et* cae
cis mult*is* dedit uisum et res
pondens ih*s* dix*it* ite nuntiate
iohanni qu*æ* uidistis *et* audistis
20 caeci uident clodi ambulant
leprosi mundant*ur* sordi au
diunt mortui resurgunt et
pauperes euanguelizant*ur*
et beatus q*ui* inme n*on* fueritn*on*
25 scandalizatus. Et cum disces
sissent nuntii iohannis coepit
ih*s* dicere deiohanne babtis
ta adt*ur*bas. quo*d* existis indeser
to uidere harundinem áuen
30 to moueri se*d* q*uod* existis uidere
hominem mollib*us* uestitum
ecce q*ui* inueste s*unt* pr*æ*tiosa et
in diliciis in domibus
regum s*unt* : se*d* ² quo*d* existis uidere
35 p*ro*fetam dico uobis etiam
plus qu*am* p*ro*fetam * hic *est* de quo

¹·¹ *Expuncted.* | ² *Altered into* quid.

S. Luc. vii. 27–38.

scriptum*est* ecce mitto anguelu*m*
me*u*m an*te* faciem tuam q*u*i pr*œ*parabit
uiam tuam ¹ * dico ² uob*í*s qu*ia* nemo *m*ai
or *est* exnat*í*s mulier*um et* amplior in p*ro*
5 fet*í*s quam iohannis *h*abtista *
D ico h*autem* uob*í*s minor q*u*i *est* in regno *dei*
*m*aior illo *est* * et om*ni*s populus audi
ens [*et*] puplicani iusti magnifica
bant deum babtizari babtismo iohan
10 nis. farissei h*autem et* legis doctores co*n*si
lium d*ei* co*n*tempserunt i*n* semet ips*í*s
ab iohanne no*n* *h*abtizati. * ⫾ genera
CUi ergo similes dicam homines h*uius*
tionis. similes su*n*t puer*í*s sedenti
15 b*us* inforo loquentib*us* a*d* inuicem di
centes cantauimus uob*í*s et no*n* sal
tastis lamentauimus uob*í*s et no*n*
planxistis uenit *enim* iohannis neque
*m*anducans nequ*e* bibens *et* d*ic*u*n*t da*e*
20 monium habet uenit f*il*ius hominis.
*m*anducans *et* bibens *et* d*ic*u*n*t ecce ho
mo deuorator *et* bibens uinum
amicus puplicanor*um et* peccator*um*
et iustificata*est* sapientia ab om
25 nib*us* filiis su*í*s * ‖ utmanduca
Ro gauit h*autem* eum q*u*i dam fariseus
ret cum eo *et* ingresus in do
mum farissei recubuit. et ecce
mulier in ciuitate q*ua*e erat pecca
30 trix utcognouit quo*d* recubuit
in domu farissei retulit alabas
tr*um* ungenti plenu*m* et stans retro
secus pedes e*i*us *et* lacrim*í*s riga
bat pedes e*i*us *et* capill*í*s sui ca

¹ *Above the line*, ante te.   ⎮   ² *In margin, enim.*

S. Luc. vii. 38—viii. 2.   f. 62 v. b.

pitis tersit eos et osculabat[ur pedes eius]
et ungebat ungento. quod cum uidisset fa
riseus qui eum rogauerat ait intra se
dicens hic si esset profeta sciret utique qua
5 lis est mulier quæ tanguit eum quia peccatrix
est et respondens ihs dixit adeum. symon habeo
tibi dicere aliquod at ille ait magister
dic cui ihs dixit duo debitores erant
cuidam feneratori unus debebat
10 denarios quincentos et alius denarios
·l· non habentibus illis unde redderent
donauit utrisque quis ergo illum plús
amauit respondit hautem simon existimo quod is
cui plus donatum est atihs dixit ei
15 recte iudicasti et conuersus ad mulie
rem dixit simoni uides hanc mulie
rem intraui in domum tuam aquam
pedibus meis non dedisti hæc lacrimis suis
rigauit pedes meos et capillis suis
20 tersit osculum mihi non dedisti hæc hautem ex quo
intraui osculari pedes meos non ces
sat . oleo caput meum non unxisti hæc ¹ ungen
to ² pedes meos propter quod tibi dico remitten
tur illi peccata multa quoniam dilexit mul
25 tum. cui hautem paruum dimittitur paruum
diligit . et ait mulieri remisasunt
tibi peccata tua et coeperunt qui simul
recubuerunt cum eo dicere intra
sé quis est hic qui etiam peccata re
30 mittit et ait ad mulierem fides
tua té saluam fecit uade in pace *
Et   factum est deinceps
et ipse iter faciebat per ciui
tates et uicos prædicans et euan
35 guelizans regnum dei . et exierunt
· xii · discipuli cum eo et mulieres

___

¹ *Above the line,* hautem. | ² *Above the line,* unxit.

[aliqu*æ* qu*æ* era]nt curat*ę* aspiritib*us*
inmund*ís* *et* ab infirmitatibus
et maria qu*æ* uocat*ur* magdalenæ
¹ de qua demonia uii exierant
5 *et* iohanna uxor chuzæ *procu*
ratoris herodis *et* sussanna
et aliæ multæ qu*æ* ministrabant
adeum exeis quæ habebant.,
C um ² ergo tur*bæ* *conuenissent* et qui
10 deciuitati*bus* ad ueniebant d*ixit*
similitudin*em* talem ad eos ecce ex
it q*ui* seminat seminare semen
suu*m* *et* du*m* seminat aliud cecidit
secus uiam *et conculcatum est et* uolue
15 res illud comeder*unt et* aliud ce
cidit sup*er* petrosa*m et* cum natu*m est*
exaruit q*uia non* habebat umore
aliud cecidit inter*spinas et* exor
te s*unt*spin*ę* suffocauer*unt* illud
20 aliud h*aut*em cecidit sup*er* terra*m* bona*m*
et obtima*m et* exortu*m est* et fecit fr
uctu*m* centuplu*m* et h*œc* dicens cla
mabat q*ui* h*ab*et aures audiendi
audeat inter*rogauerunt* eu*m* disc*ipuli eius*
25 qu*æ* esset h*œc* similitudo quibus ipse
ait uobis datum *est* scire mist*erium*
regni d*ei* * cæteris h*aut*em ³ *non est* datum
se*d* ³ insimilitudinib*us* ut uiden
tes n*on* uideant *et* audientes
30 non intellegant..,*

¹ *Above the line is written* e[x].   ^{3 3} *Expuncted.*
² *Above the line,* hautem.

S. Luc. viii. 11–20.   f. 63 r. b.

Hæc est hautem ¹ similitudo . semen est uerbum dei
    quod hautem cecidit secus uiam hii sunt
    qui audiunt uerbum uenit hautem zabo
    lus et tulit decorde eorum uer
5   bum né credentes salui fiant
    Nam qui supra petrosam hí sunt
    qui cum audiunt uerbum cum gaudio
    accipiunt illud et hí non ha
    bent radices quia ad tempus
10 credunt et intempore temp
    tationis recedunt quod hautem inspi
    nis cecidit hí sunt qui audiunt et
    per sollicitudinem diuitiarum et
    dulcidinis uitæ soffocantur
15 et non adferunt fructúm quod hautem ceci
    dit interram bonam hii sunt qui in cor
    de bono et obtimo audiunt uer
    bum et tenent et fructificant per
    patientiam .. , * ∫: uasso aut subtus
20 N emo ² enim accensam lucernam cooperit
    lectum ponit sed supra cande
    labrum ut omnibus luceat * ³ [non] est
    enim absconsum quod non manifestatur
    neque ocultum quod non cognoscatur
25 et in palam ueniat * ⁴ [uidete ergo] ⁴ quomodo
    ⁵ audietis qui enim habet dabitur ei et qui
    cumque non habet et quod habet auferetur
    ⁶ [ab eo] * uenerunt hautem mater eius et fratres
    et non poterant uidere eum
30 præ turba et nuntiatum est illi

---

¹ *Above the line, uel* parabula.
² *Above the line,* hautem.
³ *Erased : over erasure,* Non.
⁴⁻⁴ *Erased : over erasure,* Uidete ; *above line,* ergo.

⁵ *e expuncted.*
⁶ ab eo u *erased : in margins,* ab illo :, | U, *followed by space containing the erasure.*

quia mater tua et fratres tui stant
foris uolentes té uidere atille
respondit mater et fratres mei hí sunt
qui uerbum dei audiunt et faciunt ✳
5 Et factum est in una dierum et ipse as
cendit innauem cum discipulis suís et ait
adeos transcamus transfre
tum et ascenderunt nauigantibus hautem
illís obdormiuit et discendit
10 tempestas magna in stagnum
et conplebatur nauis fluctibus et peri
clitabantur accedunt hautem discipuli
suscitauerunt eum dicentes præcep
tor perimus at ille surgens
15 imperauit uento et tempestati
aquæ et cessauit et facta est tr
anquellitas magna dixit hautem eís ubi
est fides uestra et timentes mira
ti sunt dicentes ad inuicem quis est hic
20 quia uentís imperat et mari et obę
diunt ei pernauigauerunt hautem inre
gionem gerasinorum quæ est contra
fretum et contra galileam exit ad
terram et occurrit illi uir quidam
25 qui habebat demonium iam temp
oribus multís et uestimentum nonin
duit neque in domu manebat
sed in monumentis uidens hautem ihm
exclamauit uoce magna

dicens *et* procedit ad pedes [eius]
qu*id* m*ih*i ett*ib*i e*st* ih*ū* fili d*e*i altissi
mi obsecro té né métorqu
eas pr*æ*cipit h*aut*em sp*irit*ui inmundo
5 ut exiret ab homine multis e*n*im
temporibus arripiebat eum
et alligabat*ur* caten*is et c*onpe
dib*us et* custodiebat*ur et* disru
pt*is* uincul*is* agebat*ur* ade
10 mone in deserta loca *et* int*er*
rogabat eu*m* ih*s* ~~respon~~ dic
ens q*uod* t*ib*i nomen e*st* at ille resp
ondit legio multa e*n*im demoniā
erant *et* rogabant eu*m* né im
15 p*er*aret e*is* ut in abisu*m* irent.—
E rat h*aut*em ibi grex porcorum mu
ltor*um* pascentiu*m* in monte et
rogauer*unt* eu*m* demonia dicentia
si iceis nós mitte nós in grege*m*
20 porcorum at ille d*ix*it ite *et* illi
euntes introier*unt* inporcos
et impetu abiit grex porcor*um*
p*er* pr*æ*ceps in mare *et* suffocati
s*unt* uidentes h*aut*em q*u*i eos pascebant
25 pastores quo*d* factum e*st* fuger*unt*
et nuntiauer*unt* in ciuitatem
et in agros exier*unt* h*aut*em uidere
quo*d* factum fuerat *et* uener*unt*
ad ih*m* et inuener*unt* hominem

S. Luc. viii. 35–43.

    s[edent]e[m] aq*uo* demonia exierant
    uestitu*m et* sana mente nuntia
    uer*unt* hau*tem* illís q*ui* uiderant q*uo*mo*do* fac
    tus *es*set san*us* alegione roga
 5 uer*unt* hau*tem* illu*m* om*n*is multitudo re
    gionis gerasinor*um* ut discede
    ret ab eís q*uia* timore magno
    tenebant*ur* . .— * *ſ*: *et* reuersus *est*
I pse hau*tem* ascendit innauiculu*m*
 10 rogabat hau*tem* illum uir aq*uo* demo
    nia exierant ut *cum* ipso *es*set di
    missit hau*tem* illum d*ice*ns redí in dom
    um tuam *et* na　　rrá quanta
    t*ib*i fecerit dom*i*nus et habiit p*er*
 15 uniuersa*m* ciuitate*m* pr*œ*dicans
    quanta ihs̄ fecit illi . .— *
F actu*m* *est* hau*tem* *cum* ihs̄ redisset exco
    epit eu*m* *tur*ba erant hau*tem* om*n*es
    exspectantes eu*m* *et* ecce uenit
 20 uir cui nomen erat zari*us*
    et hic erat pr*i*nceps sinagog*ę*
    et p*ro*cedit adpedes ihū rogans
    eu*m* ut intraret in domu*m* sua*m*
    q*uia* filia sua unica q*uœ* erat illi
 25 fere annor*um* xii *et* h*œc* moriebat*ur*
Et factum *est* dum iret ihs̄ a*tur*bís síc
    *con*primebat*ur* ut soffocarent eu*m*
    mulier quædam q*uœ* fluxum

S. Luc. viii. 43–50.   f. 64 r. b.

    sanguinis patiebat*ur* ab annís
    xii q*uæ* medicís erogauerat om
    ne*m* sub stantia*m* suam nec ob ullo
    potuit curari accessit retro
 5 et tetigit fimbrias uestimen
    ti *eius et con*festi*m* stetit fluxus san
    guinis ihs̄ h*aut*em uidens quo*d* exierat
    ab eo uirtus in*ter*rogabat
    quis *est* q*ui* mé tetigit negabant
10 h*aut*em om*n*es d*ixit* pétrus *et* q*ui cum* illo
    erant *turbæ* té *con*primunt et
    dicis quis mé tetigit atille d*ixit*
    tetigit mé aliq*uis* ego *enim* scio ´á
    mé exisse uirtute*m* uidens h*aut*em
15 mulier quo*d* no*n* lateret uenit
    tremens *et* p*r*ocedit ante pedes
    ihū et ob q*uam* causam tetigit eum
    indicauit cora*m* om*n*i populo
    et quem ad modum sanata*est* at
20 ille d*ixit* filia fides tua té sal
    ua*m* fecit uade inpace ad
    húc eo loquente uenit adp*r*in
    cipe*m* sinagogæ nuntius
    d*icens* qu*ia* filia tua mortua *est*
25 nolí uexare magist*rum* ihs̄
    ue*r*o audito uerb*um* hoc ait pa
    tri puellæ· nolí timere
    crede *tantum et* saluá erit

et cum uenisset ad domum non per
missit intrare quemquam secum
nisi petrum et iacobum et iohannem
et patrem puellæ et matrem
5 flebant omnes et plangebant
eam at ille dixit nolite flere
non est enim mortua puella sed
dormit et diridebant eum sci
entes quod mortua esset ipse
10 hautem tenens manum eius clamauit
dicens puella surge et reuer
sus est spiritus eius et surrexit continuo
et iusit ei dari manducare
et stupuerunt parentes eius et ex
15 pauerunt quibus præcipit né ali
cui dicerent quod factum est *
conuocatís ¹ xii discipulis dedit
eís uirtutem et potestatem super
omnia demonia ut curarent
20 omnem languorem et missit
eos prædicare regnum dei et sana
re infirmos * [et] ait ad ² eos nihil
tuleritis in uiam non uirgam non pe
ram non panem non pecuniam neque
25 duas tonicas habueritis
in quamcumque domum intraueritis
ibi manete et inde ne exea
[tis * et] quicumque non ³ reciperit uós

Above the line, hautem. | ³ *Above the line (above* t), n.
² *Above the line,* illos.

S. Luc. ix. 5–12.

    exeuntes deciuitate ex[cuti]
    te puluerem depedibus uestris
    intestimonium illís.— *ʃ: ella
E gressi hautem circum ibant per cast
  5 et ciuitates euangelizantes et cu
    rantes ubique * audiuit hautem he
    rodis tetracha omnia quœ era
    nt facta ab eo et hesitabat
    eo quod diceretur aquibus dam quia iohannis
 10 surrexit amortuis ¹ aquibus
    uero quia helias apa
    ruit ab aliis hautem profetaunus
    deantiquís su   rrexisset
    et ait herodis ² iohannem hautem ego de
 15 collaui quis hautem est iste de quo
    audio ³ talia et quesiuit eum uidere *
    [et] reuersi apostoli dixerunt ei quœ
    cumque fecerunt * et adsumptís illís
    secessit seorsum in locum deser
 20 tum qui uocatur bethzaida quod
    cum cognouissent turbæ secutæ
    sunt eum et excoepit eos et loque
    batur eis deregno dei et eos qui
    curari indigebant sanabat *
25 D ies ⁴ uero coeperat declinare et
    accesserunt xii discipuli eius dixerunt
    ei dimitte turbas ut eant cir
    ca castella et uicos et refici
           ant sć

¹ *At end, in margin,* dam.   ³ *Above the line,* ego.
² *In margin,* nem.   ⁴ *Expuncted : above the line,* hautem.

[et inue]nient escas qu*ia* hic i*n* loco
deserto sumus ait h*au*t*em* ad eos
date illís u*ó*s manducare
at illi dixer*unt* n*on* s*unt* nob*í*s plus
5 q*uam* quinq*ue* panes *et* duo pisces n*i*si
n*ó*s camus *et* emamus in omne*m*
hanc tu*r*bam escas erant *enim* fere
quinq*ue* milia uiror*um* ait h*au*t*em* ad
disci*pulos* suos facite eos discum
10 bere p*er con*uiuia quinquagenos
et ita fecer*unt et* discu*m*ber*unt* om*n*es
accept*í*s h*au*t*em* quinque panib*us et* duobus
piscib*us* respexit in cælum *et* be
nedixit sup*er* illos *et* fregit de
15 dit disci*pulis* su*í*s ut ponerent
ante tu*r*bas *et* manducauer*unt*
om*n*es *et* saturati s*unt et* sublatu*m est*
qu*od* sup*er*fuit ill*í*s fragmento
ru*m* cophini xii.— * ƒ: disci*pulis* su*í*s.
20 Et factum *est* cum[1] solis *es*set orans c*um*
int*er*rogauit eos dicens que*m* m*é*
*es*se dicunt turbæ at illi dix
er*unt* iohanne*m* babtistam alii
h*au*t*em* heliam aut unum ex p*ro*fet*í*s
25 prioribus[2] at h*au*t*em* e*í*s u*ó*s h*au*t*em* que*m* m*é*
dicitis *es*se respon*dens* sim*ó*n
petrus d*í*x*it* xp*m̄* dei . — *
At ille increpans illos præcipit

---

[1] i *expuncted : above the line,* u. | [2] *Above the line (after* a), i.

S. Luc. ix. 21–28.

né cui dicerent hóc dicens
quia oportet filium hominis multa
pati et reprobrari aprincipibus
et senioribus et scribís et occidi
5 et post tertium diem resurgere *
[d]icebat hautem ad omnes sí quis uult
post mé uenire abnegat sé
ipsum sibi ettollat crucem suam
etsequatur mé qui enim uoluerit ani
10 mam suam saluam facere per
d[e]t eam Nam qui perdiderit ani
mam suam propter mé hic saluam
faciet eam quod enim proficiet homini
sí ¹ lueretur uniuersum mundum
15 sé ipsum hautem perdat et detrimen
tum sui faciat * nam qui mé eru
buerit et meos sermones hunc
et filius hominis erubescet cum ue
nerit in maiestate sua et pa
20 tris sui et sanctorum angelorum *
[d]ico hautem uobís uere sunt híc ali
qui stantes qui non gustabunt
mortem donec uideant filium
hominis in gloria sua factum
25 est hautem post hæc uerba fere post dies
octo adsumpsit petrum
et iohannem et iacobum et ascen
dit inmontem ut oraret

¹ First e changed into c.

S. Luc. ix. 29–36.

 et dum oraret facta*est* spe
 cies aspectus e*i*us altera et
 uestitus e*i*us albus *et* refulgens
 et ecce duo uiri loquentes
5 *cum* eo erant hau*t*em moyses *et* helias
 apparentes inmaiestate
 et dicebant excessu*m* e*i*us quem
 *con*pleturus erat in hirusa
 lem petrus hau*t*em *et* q*u*i c*u*meo erant
10 grauati s*unt* somno *et* euige
 lantes uider*unt* maiestatem
 *ei*us *et* duos uiros q*u*i adstabant c*u*millo
Et factum e*st* cum discederent ab eo
 ait petrus ad ihm magiste*r*
15 bonu*m* e*st* h*í*c e*ss*e nob*í*s *et* faci
 amus tria tabernacula
 unum t*i*bi *et* unum moysi *et* unum
 heliæ nesciens quo*d* diceret
 h*ec* [1] eo loquente facta*est* n*ub*s
20 *et* inumbrauit e*ó*s *et*timue
 r*unt* intrantib*us* hau*t*em ill*í*s innu
 bem uox facta *est* innube
 d*i*cens hic *est* filius meus dilec
 tissimus hunc audite *et* c*um*
25 uox facta e*ss*et inuentus e*st*
 ih*s* solus *et* ipsi tacuer*unt*
 et [2] nemi dixerunt inill*í*s di
 eb*us* q*u*icq*uam* ex ill*í*s q*uæ* uiderant *

[1] *In margin,* hautem. | [2] *Above the line, at the end of the word,* ni.

S. Luc. ix. 37–44.

F actum *est* ha*ut*em in sequent[i die]
   discendentib*us* illís demonte
   occurrit illís t*ur*ba mul
   ta *et* ecce uir deturba
5 exclamauit *dicens* magist*er*
   obsecro té respice infi
   lium meum qu*ia* unicus *est* m*i*hi *et* ecce
   sp*iritu*s inmundus adp*ræ*hendit
   eum *et* subito clamat eledit
10 et disipat eu*m* *cum* spuma *et* de
   laniens eu*m* uix discedit ab eo
   et rogaui disci*pulos* tuos ut cicere
   nt illu*m* *et* n*on* potuer*unt* ipse ha*ut*em
   respon*dens* d*ixit* ógeneratio incre
15 dula quo usqu*e* patiar uós quo
   usqu*e* s[um] apud uos addúc
   filiu*m* tuum huc dum accidisset
   elidit eum demoniu*m* *et* dissipa
   uit eum *et* increpauit   ihs̄
20 sp*iritu*m inmundu*m* *et* sanauit
   puer*um* *et* reddidit [2] patri
   [3] [eius * *et*] stupebant om*n*es in
   magnitudine*m* dei * *et* mira
   bant*ur* omnes sup*er* om*n*ia qu*æ*
25 faciebat ihs̄ d*ixit* ha*ut*em ad dis
   cipulos suos ponite uos in cor
   dib*us* uestrís sermones istos
   filius ha*ut*em hom*i*nis tradetur

---

[1] *Erased : over the erasure,* ero.
[2] *Above the line,* illum.
[3] *Erased : in right margin* (l. 21) *eius ;*

and partly in margin, partly over erasure, Et, *followed by space.*

S. Luc. ix. 44–52.

   [inma]nus hominum at illi igno
   rabant hóc uerbum erat hautem co
   opertum illís utnon intellexerent
   illud et timebant interrogare
5 eum de hoc uerbo * intrauit hautem in eís
   cogitatio quis eorum esset ihs hautem
   uidens cogitationes cordis
   eorum adprœhendit puerum et sta
   tuit secus sé et ait quicumque ac
10 ciperit puerum istum innomine
   meo me recipit et quicumque mé
   recipit non mé recipit sed re
   cipit eum qui mé missit Nam
   qui minor est interuós hic maior
15 [est] * respondit hautem iohannis dicens magis
   ter uidimus quendam innomine
   tuo eicientem demonia et prohi
   buimus eum qui non sequitur nobiscum et
   ait ad eum ihs sinite eum et noli
20 te prohibere qui enim non est aduersus
   uos pro uobis est * factum est hautem dum
   conpleretur dies adsumptionis
   eius et ipse faciem suam firma
   uit ut iret in hierusalem
25 et missit nuntios ante conspec
   tum suum et euntes intrauerunt
   in ciuitatem samaritanorum
   ut pararent illi cænam

S. Luc. ix. 53–56.   f. 66 r. b.

    et non receperunt eum quia facies eius erat
    euntis in˙hierusalem cum uidissent
    hautem discipuli eius iacobus et iohannis et
    dixerunt domine uís dicemus ut
5 ignis discendat decælo et con
    sumat illos et conuersus increpa
    uit illos et dixit nescitis đ/· ¹ et abi

¹ *The words* [cuius spiritus esti]s fi*lius*   um perdere sed sanare *are supplied in*
  hominis non uenit animas homin-   upper *margin.*

NOTES TO CHAPTER V.

  p. 77. l. 15. The section in the Amiatine manuscript ends with traderent (l. 14).

  p. 77. ll. 27, 28. The punctuation mark, and Et in margin, are probably due to the corrector.

  p. 78. l. 5. The second tur is not quite certain.

  p. 78. l. 7. The erased x appears to be legible. Exurgent is read by r_2, exsurgent by r_1 h, insurgent by Q (*ms.*) R.

  p. 78. l. 11. Traces of the final letter of electos remain. The section should have ended with uobis. But ecce præd. u. being rejected by the corrector, the mark indicating the close of a section is placed after electos. This appears to confirm the supposition that the corrector and the numerator were the same person.

p. 78. l. 21. The section ends with in cælo (l. 22) in Cod. Am.

p. 78. l. 34 *sqq.* A hole in the vellum extends from l. 34 *to* l. 37, and is the cause of the space in the middle of ianuis. l, 38.

p. 79. l. 3. Possibly et is a correction from *uel.*

p. 79. l. 6. The space after *in* is not large enough to have contained illis : nor is there any appearance of erasure.

p. 79. l. 12. Apparently *tur et* unus is written over an erasure. Traces of et . r remain.

p. 79. l. 23. Some traces of cum remain.

p. 80. l. 36. The space after suus is due *to* a hole in the vellum.

p. 81. l. 18. The words ab eo are followed by the mark (:,) indicating the end of the section.   Here is a further proof that whoever divided the Gospels into sections revised the text as he went along.

p. 81. l. 19. Et is possibly due *to* the corrector. If so, ab eo (l. 18) may be written in part over the same word erased.

p. 81. l. 20. There is a mark before *in*, which may possibly be a partially erased letter.

p. 81. l. 29. eius is read by $r_1 \, r_2 \, h$ A etc., and suits the space.

p. 81. ll. 34–37. A hole in the vellum extends down these lines.

p. 82. l. 1. tê may be read as above, regarding the point above it as a mark of omission ; or possibly the line as well as the point is due *to* the corrector.   In this case it should be printed te, the symbol /. being an indication of a marginal note now illegible.

p. 82. ll. 25, 26. The conjecturally restored reading of the erased words (which exactly fits the space) is that of $r_1 \, r_2$ E *.

p. 82. l. 26. In A the section begins with the words (l. 25) Et factum *est.*

p. 82. l. 33. There is a mark before the first letter of forte.   Possibly something was written here and afterwards erased.

p. 83. l. 1 *sqq.* A hole in the vellum extends down ll. 1–3.

p. 83. l. 7. The letters tis are plainly a correction. We therefore infer that habetis was not the original reading.   In the absence of all trace of the original letters I substitute for those of the corrector bitis with r_2 (not r_1) DELQR *Durm,* etc.   Again, it seems clear that the word before unguentum cannot have been hac.   Otherwise this word must have been erased, for no assignable reason, merely to be re-written. This sufficiently disposes of the claim of the reading of the corrector to represent the text as originally written. No trace of the original writing remains. What I have substituted for it suits the space, and is supported by $r_1 \, r_2$ h (haec enim mittens).

p. 83. l. 26. Possibly the original reading was tradit, the final *t* being changed into *tur* by the corrector.

p. 83. l. 32. No trace of the erased words remains. The restored text is supported by r_1 (L) (R*) etc. r_2 is wanting.

p. 83. l. 33. I have followed the reading of r_1 L (DQR).

p. 83. l. 35. The reading as restored is required by the space and supported by r_1 L.

p. 84. ll. 1 *sqq.* A hole extends from the top of the column to l. 4.

p. 84. l. 5. No traces of quia remain : but there is a space which may have contained it.   It is read here in r_1 h (r_2 is wanting) DE꜔ⁱⁿᵍLQR.

p. 84. l. 20. dixit is uncertain. The word may have been dicit ($= r_1$ L), perhaps corrected into dixit.

p. 84. l. 28. The space appears to be too small for iste uerum : sed is the reading of r_1.

p. 84. ll. 33, 34. I know of no other authority for the reading abiit *hautem* iterum.   But both r_1 and r_2 are unfortunately wanting at this place.   The original reading was certainly not iterum hautem abiit ; for in that case abiit would not have been erased, merely to be re-written, and moreover the abiit of the corrector, though the letters are spread out, does not nearly occupy the space left by the erasure, iterum, if written in full would about fill it. Accordingly I have restored the reading on the analogy of v. 44 as read in r_1 f (abiit iterum). The original reading, however, may have been abiit hautem secundo.   In any case hautem seems to belong to the original writing.

p. 86. ll. 1, 2. exitum rei, which is the reading of $r_1 r_2$ (ms.) h etc. suits the space. I have sometimes persuaded myself that I could read the erased e of rei, and pri of principes. Be that as it may the original reading of the manuscript can scarcely be regarded as doubtful.

p. 86. l. 17. The section ends in Cod. Am. at filius dei (l. 15).

p. 86. l. 23. In Cod. Am. the section ends with blasphemauit (see l. 22).

p. 86. l. 26. in, which suits the space, is supported apparently by all other MS.

p. 86. l. 30. uero may possibly be original.

p. 86. l. 36. The space in the middle of ancella is due to a rent in the vellum.

p. 87. l. 11. mane cum factum esset, is the reading of h ; r_1 being here wanting.

p. 87. l. 12. fecerunt is the reading of Q r_2. Traces of the first letter remain.

p. 87. l. 28. Is hautem a scribe's blunder for hoc?

p. 87. l. 31. ad supplied on the authority of r_1 h. These letters suit the marks which have survived, which, however, would rather have suggested ex.

p. 87. l. 34. For filiis the correct reading may possibly be fili, the final is being added as a correction.

p. 88. l. 1. traces of the letters hs seem to be legible.

p. 88. l. 23. quid igitur may be original. A portion of the second a in faciam remains, transformed into e. Possibly us | de are original.

p. 88. l. 27. It is quite possible that the original reading may have been nullum, the second stroke of the first u being erased, ll being changed into h, and ū into il. But as nullum seems otherwise unsupported I have put nichil into the text.

p. 89. ll. 9, 10. There can be little doubt that the words enclosed in brackets are correct. They exactly suit the space, and are supported by $r_1 r_2$: eius, though erased, is distinctly legible, as is also the lower part of the first letter of faciam, which has escaped erasure. Thus in faciem eius is certain. The space remaining in l. 9 is too small for et expuentes (A etc.), et expuebant (h etc.) or et conspuentes (d), unless the writing projected considerably into the margin, but is quite sufficient for expuerunt.

p. 89. l. 10. et is most uncertain, but there appears to be room for it after eius, and it is required by the sense, and supported by h r_1.

p. 89. l. 27. Some traces of ob remain.

p. 89. l. 30. In very good light the e in crucifixerunt seems legible.

p. 89. l. 31. alterum is the reading of h ; alium would suit the space equally well ; unum ($=r_1 r_2$) and unus are both excluded. There are some traces of the erased letters, but I have found it impossible to read them.

p. 89. l. 35. A rent in the vellum causes the space in reædificabás.

p. 90. l. 1. The horizontal line over the final letter of the first word is legible. There is some writing above this line, of which only the two letters su (above temet) are legible.

p. 90. l. 6. That es has been altered to est is quite evident ; es would require descende, and the t in descendat has all the appearance of being inserted ; but a shows little trace of being due to the corrector. It exhibits, however, signs of compression as if to make room for the following t.

p. 90. l. 7. ei looks as if it had been written by the corrector. Perhaps it replaced si. h reads cred. ei si confidet.

p. 90. l. 8. eum dixit: so $h_1 r_2$. The section begins with id (l. 9) in A.

p. 90. l. 9. The two last letters of crucifixi are perhaps due to the corrector.

p. 90. l. 13. autem is read by h.

p. 90. l. 21. The section ends with eum (l. 23) in A.

p. 90. l. 22. sinete : so d (hiat r_1). Parts of the letters et remain.

p. 90. l. 25. ihs is made prominent by the corrector, as if to mark the beginning of a section, but there is no numeral in the margin.

p. 91. l. 8. The reading may|have been hautem sero (h $r_1 r_2$).

p. 91. l. 12. The section begins in the next line (et) in Am.

p. 91. l. 33. et signauerunt suits the space, and is supported by h r_2 (hiat r_1).

p. 98. l. 30. hoc uiso simon suits the space, which is not sufficient for the reading of the corrector. It is taken from a. In r_1 we find quod cum uidisset simon, which may have been written in our manuscript. But if so it must have projected into the margin.

p. 100. l. 1. Slight traces of Et remain in the MS. The word is distinctly legible in a photograph of the page.

p. 100. l. 10. Opposite this line in left margin is the letter s.

p. 101. l. 19. The space of the erasure is too great to have contained only r. *et* is therefore inserted with A r_1 etc.

p. 103. l. 3. In A the section ends with sacerdotibus (l. 2). Our numerator makes its close coincide with that of the paragraph in his manuscript.

p. 103. l. 4. The section begins a verse earlier (l. 2 et dixit) in A.

p. 103. l. 24. oilare (*sic*) : a slip of the pen, not very difficult to explain, for orare.

p. 104. ll. 1–3. The letters enclosed in brackets are for the most part torn away.

p. 104. l. 6. et dis is erased and re-written in large character as if for the beginning of a section, but there is no number in the margin.

p. 104. l. 30. uerum is retouched as if for beginning of section, but no number appears in the margin.

p. 105. l. 3. In A the section begins two lines further back (uæ nobis *qu*i saturati).

p. 105. l. 19. Probably dilegentes is correct : but it may be diligentes (the second i perhaps altered into e).

p. 105. l. 29. The word (of two or three letters) erased at the beginning of the line cannot have been n*ihil*, though this would suit the space ; for there is no reason why this word should have been erased and re-written by the corrector. On the other hand a very slight mark remaining before d looks like the upper part of c. Hence the conjectural restoration, nec. Perhaps, however, we may read non or ne ; or again in, *i.e.* inde sperantes, though the space is more than sufficient for this. Whatever may have been the erased word there appears to be no other authority for the reading as originally written.

p. 106. l. 7. Possibly the mark over coagitata*m* may indicate omission, or at least doubt. The word is not found in r_1.

p. 106. l. 10. The second e of remetiet*ur* may have been corrected from i.

p. 106. l. 14. Possibly a word is erased in left margin before discipulus.

p. 106. l. 15. Apparently traces of q in q*u*id remain.

p. 106. l. 17. The u in oculo has been corrected from some other letter.

p. 107. ll. 1, 2. The greater number of the letters enclosed in brackets are torn away.

p. 109. On the extreme edge of this page above the second column there is some writing partly torn away, of which a few letters appear to be legible—incipit nim . r m . . .

p. 109. l. 13. There appear to be marks over the two last words, thus : álium eẍ.

p. 109. l. 25. Perhaps scandulizatus.

p. 109. l. 33. A space is left after domibus sufficient to have contained regum.

p. 110. l. 8. The space between ens and puplic. is sufficient for *et*. A crease in the vellum makes the word illegible.

p. 113. ll. 27, 28. The words ab illo, written in the right margin opposite l. 27, are regarded above as having been penned by the corrector. It would be natural to conclude that these words were originally written at the beginning of l. 28. The space of the erasure there seems however too small to have contained ab illo u. Hence the conjectural reading ab eo, which is supported by r_1. Some traces of the erased letters remain, which appear to be of the e of eo, and the first letter of uenerunt, the latter being indeed quite certain.

p. 115. l. 11. *sic* : respō̄n (*i.e.* respon*dens* or respon*dit*) deleted.

p. 116. l. 1. Traces of s remain.

p. 116. l. 13. The space in the middle of narrá is caused by a hole in the vellum.

p. 117. l. 3. ob *sic*.

p. 117. l. 26. uerb*um* = uerƀ, the horizontal stroke being perhaps not original.

p. 119. l. 13. Space after su due to hole in vellum.

p. 122. l. 16. tria is badly written. It might be read trai.

p. 125. l. 1. no*n* might be read hæc the form of the n approaching very closely here, as occasionally elsewhere, to that of h.

p. 125. l. 7. đ = desunt (cf. Abbott's *Evangeliorum Vers. Anteh.* pp. 645, 699). It refers to the words written in the upper margin. The position of this symbol as part of the original writing proves that the omission of the words which follow nescitis in the Vulgate text is not solely due to the carelessness of our scribe. See above p. 68 *sq.* In restoring the illegible words of the marginal reading I have followed the Codex Amiatinus. The first three words may have been (as in r_1) quali sp*iritu* es*t*is.

CHAPTER VI.

AFFINITIES OF THE IRISH OLD LATIN TEXT.

IF the reasoning of our fourth chapter has conducted us to a correct conclusion, we have in our hands three copies[1] more or less complete of the Irish Old Latin recension of the last five chapters of St Matthew, and two for six chapters of St Luke. With their help we may now enter upon a further stage of our inquiry. Our object is to discover the affinities of the Irish Old Latin text. It is generally agreed that it belongs in the main to the European family, of which the Codex Veronensis (b) is the typical representative. We shall make the attempt to discover whether there are any variations from that type, and to what extent these are derived from the Italian or African recensions.

§ 1. *Binary Combinations* (*St Matthew*).

For the Matthean fragment we have three witnesses—$\mu\ r_1\ r_2$—and our task will here perhaps be most thoroughly and easily performed by giving in the first place a list of the readings in which at least two of these mss. are in agreement against the Vulgate, omitting those which are found in b.[2] With these we have noted the principal mss. of the pre-hieronymian text in which they are found. We confine ourselves to the Codex Brixianus (f) for the Italian family, to the Codex Palatinus (e) and Cyprian's quotations for the African (Codex Bobiensis (k) not being available), and to the Vercelli manuscript (a) and Codex Bezae (d) as representing other ancient types of text. The references for the Cyprianic readings are to the pages of Hartel's edition in the Vienna *Corpus*.

I. *Readings in which at least two of the three MSS.* $\mu\ r_1\ r_2$ *agree.*

Matt. xxiv. 12. $r_1\ r_2$ (*ms.*) quia *pro* quoniam=*d*.
*$\mu\ r_2$ iniquitas et ref.
14.[3] $\mu\ r_1\ r_2$ per totum orbem=*e* (+terrarum) Cyp. i. 335 (+terrae).

[1] One of these, an extract from "the Garland of Howth" (r₂), is printed in the Appendix to this volume.
[2] The number of variants recorded in the following list is over 200 : it would have been about 350 had those been included which are supported by b.
[3] The text of this verse is of peculiar interest. St Patrick, in his Confession (Whitley Stokes, *Tripartite Life*, ii. p. 369), quotes St Matt. xxiv. 14 as follows : "Predicabitur hoc euangelium regni *in uniuerso mundo* in testimonium omnibus gentibus ; et tunc ueniet *finis*." And elsewhere (p. 367) he says that our Lord had foretold that His Gospel would be preached "in testimonium omnibus genti-

Matt. xxiv. 15. μ r_2 ($hiat$ r_1) per danielum profetam (-tum r_2)=d (e) Cyp. i. 335.
16. *μ r_1 in montes ; r_2 in montibus=a b d e . f ad montes.
17. μ r_1 r_2 in tecto sunt.
      μ r_1 r_2 discendant (-dent μ).
18. μ r_1 in agro erit ; r_2 in agro sunt . $e f$ Cyp. i. 335 in agro est.
23. r_1 aut ecce illio ; r_2 ecce illio : r_1=a Cyp. i. 336, r_2=b e.
24. μ r_1 ($hiat$ r_2) exsurgent=a $d f$.
27. μ r_1 usque ad=$e f$ Cyp. i. 336.
      μ r_2 ($hiat$ r_1) erit aduentus=a d.
30. μ r_1 r_2 apparebit=$e f$ Cyp. i. 336.
      r_1 lamentabun[t . .] ; r_2 lamentabunt se . e lamentabuntur ;
      e vel r_2=Cyp. i. 336.
31. μ r_1 r_2 (ms.) quattuor angulis uentorum . b quat. angulos caeli.
      μ r_1 r_2 ad fin + cum coeperint autem ($om.$ autem μ) haec fieri
      respicite et leuate caput quoniam (quia r_1) adpropiat re-
      demptio uestra=b (capita uestra) d (incipientibus   . his
      . . . capita uestra quia).
32. μ r_2 ($hiat$ r_1) cognoscitis (-cetis μ) pro scitis=d e (-cite).
      μ r_2 ($hiat$ r_1) prope esse aestatem (aestas μ).
33. μ r_2 ($hiat$ r_1) sic pro ita.
      μ r_2 ($hiat$ r_1) quoniam pro quia=d e.
      *μ r_1 (? ms.) r_2 prope est ianuis.
35. μ r_1 r_2 (ms.) autem pro uero=a d $e f$.
37. μ r_1 r_2 (ms.) enim pro autem=d e.
38. μ r_2 manducabant ; r_1 manducantes : μ r_2=a ; r_1=b d $e f$.
      μ r_2 bibebant=a.
      μ r_1 r_2 et ($om.$ r_1) nubebant.
      μ r_1 r_2 uxores ducebant=a.
      μ r_1 (? ms.) r_2 usque in=a $d f$.
      μ r_2 $om.$ eum=f.
      μ r_1 r_2 noe in arcam=$d f$.
39. μ r_1 r_2 non senserunt.
40. μ r_1 r_2 erunt duo.
      μ r_1 alter relinquetur ; r_2 alius rel.
42. *μ r_1 r_2 qua die uel (+qua μ) hora . e qua hora aut qua die.
45. r_1 r_2 $om.$ suus=a d e.
      μ r_2 super=a d e.
49. *μ r_2 conseruos suos percutere.
      μ r_1 r_2 ebriosis=$d f$.
51. μ r_1 cum infidelibus.
xxv. 1. r_1 r_2 similabitur=d.
      *r_1 r_2 prodierunt
2. r_1 (? ms.) r_2 sapientes=d.
3. μ r_2 ($hiat$ r_1) fatuae autem . d stultae ergo.
4. r_1 r_2 sapientes=d.
      r_1 r_2 (ms.) autem pro nero=d.
      r_1 r_2 $om.$ suis.
9. μ r_2 et ($om.$ r_2) dixerunt.
      μ r_1 r_2 ad eos qui uendunt.
      *r_1 r_2 emite nobis oleum.
11. μ r_1 (c $spat.$) r_2 postea pro nouissime=f.
      μ r_2 ($hiat$ r_1 [ms.]) uenerunt (-iarunt r_2)=$d f$.
12. μ r_2 (ms.) ($hiat$ r_1) uobis+quia=f.
14. r_1 r_2 substantiam suam=$d f$.
15. μ r_1 r_2 +quidem $ante$ dedit=d.

bus ante *finem* mundi." These two passages suffice to show that St Patrick read
the last word of the verse as it is found in r_2 d f q δ Cyp. i. 335, though μ r_1
agree in this case with the Vulgate. In the earlier part of the verse, on the other
hand, his reading agrees with the Vulgate against the unanimous testimony of our
three manuscripts, which have there adopted the African " per totum orbem " of
Cyp. i. 335. This is the only passage within the limits of our fragments quoted
by St Patrick.

Matt. xxv. 16. μ r_1 r_2 autem abiit (abhiis r_2)$=f$.

17. μ r_1 similiter autem.

    μ r_1 r_2 et qui$=a$ d f.

19.   *μ r_2 om. nero.

    μ r_1 r_2 tempus$=d$ f.

    *μ $_{r1}$ illorum seruorum.

20.   *μ r_2 om. et pri.

    μ r_1 r_2 accessit . . et.

    μ r_1 r_2 (ms.) om. talenta sec.

    r_1 r_2 lucratus.

21. μ r_1 r_2 serue bone$=$d f.

    μ r_1 r_2 fidelis fuisti.

23. μ r_1 dominus suus$=d$.   [r_2 om. vv. 22, 23.]

    μ r_1 fidelis fuisti.

24. μ r_1 colligis.

25.   *μ r_1 r_2 timui ergo (enim μ) et.

26. r_1 r_2 serue nequam$=a$ (nequa) . d nequa serue.

    μ r_1 r_2 colligo$=f$.

27. μ r_1 te dare pecuniam ; r_2 uenundari pecuniam.

    μ r_1 r_2 ego ueniens.

29.   *r_1 r_2 om. autem.

    μ r_1 etiam quod ; r_2 quod . . . etiam.

34. μ r_2 regnum quod nobis paratum est$=$Cyp. i. 391, 430[1] . Cyp. i. 100, 112, quod uobis paratum est regnum.

35. r_1 r_2 suscepistis pro collexistis.

36. μ r_1 r_2 carcere (-rem r_2) fui$=d$ f Cyp. i. 100, 112, 181, 391, 700.

    a b carcerem eram.

37. μ r_1 r_2 aut sitientem$=d$ f.

    *μ r_1 potauimus te ; r_2 pauimus te . d f Cyp. i. 100, 112, 391, potauimus.

38.   *r_1 r_2 + aut ad init.

    μ r_1 r_2 suscepimus (suscip. μ r_2)$=a$.

39. μ r_1 r_2 uel pro aut.

40. μ r_1 r_2 ex pro de$=$Cyp. i. 100, 112, 392.

    μ r_1 r_2 om. his.

41. μ r_1 r_2 quem praeparauit (par. r_1) pater meus$=d$ (quod) Cyp. i. 100 (L) : $r_1=a$ (quod) b Cyp. i. 100 (Hartel), 112, 392.

42. r_1 r_2 bibere ([. . . .]e r_1).[2]

43. r_1 r_2 suscepistis$=f$.

    r_1 r_2 cooperuistis$=f$.

44. μ r_1 (ms.) r_2 respond. + ei $=f$.

45.   *r_1 r_2 respondet (respōn μ).

    μ r_1 r_2 eis$=d$.

    r_1 r_2 minimis$=a$ Cyp. i. 101, 112, 392   d minimorum.

46. μ r_1 r_2 et tunc ibunt (om. et μ).

    μ isti pro hi ; r_1 [. .]s[t]i (? ms.) ; r_2 iniusti : $\mu=$Cyp. i. 101, 112, 392.

xxvi. 1. μ r_1 r_2 omnia nerba haec.

3.   *μ r_1 r_2 (ms.) uocabatur.

8. μ r_2 quod (qui μ) cum uidissent.

9. r_1 hoc pro istud ; r_2 haec (ms.) : $r_1=d$.

    μ prætioso multo ; $_{r1}$ praetio ; r_2 praetio magna : $r_1=a$ b . f multo praetio.

10.   *μ r_1 r_2 bonum opus.

12.   *μ r_1 r_2 ecce enim mittens.

    *μ r_1 r_2 om. haec.

19. μ r_1 eis$=a$ d.   [hiat r_2 usque v. 45.]

21. μ r_1 manducantibus$=a$ d.

23. μ r_1 dixit$=a$ d.

---

[1] So also Lebar Brecc, p. 450. See Bernard in Trans. of R.I.A., xxx. p. 323.
[2] So Lebar Brecc, p. 418, Trans. R.I.A., xxx. 323.

Matt. xxvi. 24. $*\mu\ r_1$ non nasci homini illi . b homini illi non nasci.

        25. $\mu\ r_1$ traditurus eum erat . $a\ b\ f$ traditurus erat eum.

        26. $\mu\ r_1$ ipsis autem manducantibus$=d$. $a\ b$ ipsis autem cenanti-bus.

               $\mu\ r_1$ dioons *pro* et ait$=f$.

        29. $\mu\ r_1$ uobis$+$quia$=f$.

        34. $*\mu\ r_1$ quoniam.

        35. $\mu\ r_1$ dicit$=d$.

        36. $\mu\ r_1$ cum illis iesus . f cum eis iesus.

               $\mu\ r_1$ agrum qui$=d$.

        38. $\mu\ r_1$ dicit$=d$.

        45. $r_1\ r_2$ (*ms.*) ait$=f$.

        47. μ plurima multitudo ; r_1 plurima turba.

        50. $\mu\ r_1\ r_2$ cui dixit.

               $\mu\ r_2$ uenisti fac.

        51. $r_1\ r_2$ abscidit.

        53. $r_1\ r_2$ putatis$=f$.

               r_1 non posse me ; r_2 non . . possum me . $a\ b$ non   posse me.

               $*r_1\ r_2$ exiberet ; μ exibet.

        55. $\mu\ r_1\ r_2$ ad turbas . a ad turbam.

               $r_1\ r_2$ eram *pro* sedebam.

               $r_1\ r_2$ tenuistis me$=a$ d.

        56. $*\mu\ r_2$ inpleretur.

               $\mu\ r_1\ r_2$ discipuli eius$=a$.

        57. $\mu\ r_1\ r_2$ illi autem$=d$.

               $*\mu\ r_1\ r_2$ perduxerunt.

        58. $\mu\ r_1\ r_2$ intus$=d$.

               $\mu\ r_1\ r_2$ (*ms.*) exitum rei *pro* finem$=a$ $b\ d\ f$ finem rei.

        59. $\mu\ r_1\ r_2$ aduersus$=a$ df.

        60. $\mu\ r_1\ r_2$ inuenerunt in eum (eo μ) quicquam (quiquam r_2) . d in-uenerunt sequentia.

               $*r_1\ r_2$ *om.* cum . . . accessissent.

        61. $*r_1$ (?) r_2 dei hoc ; μ hoc dei : $\mu=b$ d.

        63. $\mu\ r_1$ dixit *pro* ait$=a$ d.

        64. $\mu\ r_1\ r_2+$et *ad init.*

               $r_1\ r_2$ dixit.

        65. $*\mu$ (*hiat* r_1) opus est *pro* egemus ; r_2 opus uobis d opus habemus.

        69. $\mu\ r_1\ r_2$ petrus autem.

               $\mu\ r_1$ ex (de r_1) ancillis$=f$.

               $\mu\ r_1\ r_2$ dixit ([. . . .]t r_1).

        71. μ illis *pro* his ; $r_1\ r_2$ eis : $\mu=a$ (illi).

        72. μ dixit quia ; r_1 dicens quia ; r_2 diciens : $r_1=f$; $r_2=b$.

        74. $\mu\ r_1$ statim.

        75. $\mu\ r_2$ (*hiat* r_1) amarissime flenit . f flenit amare ; b amarissime plorauit.

xxvii. 1. $\mu\ r_2$ (*hiat* r_1) fecerunt *pro* inierunt$=a\ f$.

       2. $\mu\ r_1$ eum adduxerunt . a d eum duxerunt.

       3. μ r_1 quoniam *pro* quod ; r_2 quia : $\mu\ r_1=d$; $r_2=a\ b\ f$.

       5. $\mu\ r_1$ (*e spat. ms.*) *om.* abiens.

       6. $\mu\ r_1$ eos mittere$=f$.

             $*\mu\ r_2$ corb. hoc est in oblationem (locum r_2) . b loculum.

       7. μ r_1 autem facto.

       8. μ r_1 cognominatus est.

       9. $\mu\ r_1$ adimpletum$=f$.

             $\mu\ r_2$ (*hiat* r_1) *om.* a$=f$.

      13. μ r_1 ei.

             $\mu\ r_1$ testificantur$=f$. d testantur.

      14. $*\mu\ r_1$ multum *pro* uehementer.

      15. $*\mu\ r_2$ *om.* autem.

             $*\mu\ r_1$ consuetudo erat.

      17. $\mu\ r_1$ nobis dimittam$=d$.

             $r_1\ r_2$ (*ms.*) aut *pro* an$=d$.

      18. μ r_1 r_2 (*ms.*) tradiderunt$=f$. $a\ b\ d$ tradiderant.

Matt. xxvii. 19. μ r_2 eum *pro* illum $= a$ d.

20. μ r_1 r_2 (*ms.*) autem *pro* uero $= d$.

21. μ r_1 r_2 de duobis dimittam nobis (u. dim. r_1) $= d$. f ex d. dim. nobis ; b ¦de duobus nobis dimittam ; a nobis de du. mittam.

24. μ r_1 r_2 (*ms.*) manus suas $= d$.

25. μ r_1 huius *pro* eius $= d$ f.

26. μ r_1 eum crucifigerent . a b cruci eum figerent ; d crucifigerent eum.

27. *μ r_1 r_2 duxerunt . . . et *pro* suscipientes.
μ r_2 (*hiat* r_1) praetorium $= d$.

28. *μ r_1 (*e spat.*) r_2 uestiarunt eum (*om.* eum r_2 tonicam purpuream et. a b f induerunt eum (*om.* eum b) tunicam purpuream et ; d vestientes eum tunicam purpuream.

30. *μ r_1 r_2 expuerunt . . . et (*om.* et r_2). a expuebant . . et.

31. *μ r_2 *om.* et *sec.*

32. μ r_1 cirinensem ([c]yr. r_1).
*μ r_1 r_2 uenientem obuiam illi (sibi r_2) . $r_2 = a$; b d obiuam sibi uenientem.

35. *μ r_2 *om.* autem.

38. μ r_1 r_2 crucifixerunt . f crucifixissent.
μ r_1 r_2 duos $= f$.
μ r_2 (*hiat* r_1) unum *pro* unus *pri.* $= f$.
r_1 r_2 unum *pro* unus *sec.* $= f$.

40. μ r_1 saluum fac.

41. r_1 [eu]m cum ; r_2 eum : $r_1 = f$.

43. μ r_2 filius dei.

44. *r_1 r_2 crucifixerant (-runt r_2).

45. μ r_1 ab ora autem sexta $= d$. a ab hora sexta.
r_1 usque in ; r_2 in : $r_1 = a$ Cyp. i. 91.

46. μ r_1 (? *ms.*) *om.* meus *pri.*

49. μ r_1 si uenit $= a$ d f : r_2 si ueniat ; b si ueniet.
μ et saluet ; r_1 et saluabit.
*μ r_2 + *ad fin. vers.* alius hautem accipit lanciam et (accepta lancia r_2) pupungit latus eius et exiit (exit μ) aqua et sanguis.

50. *μ r_1 exclamauit . . . et ; r_2 exclamans.

54. *μ r_1 r_2 cum uidissent terrae motum . d uidentes t. m.
μ r_1 r_2 ea *pro* his $= a$ (*sic*).

55. μ r_1 r_2 fuerant *pro* erant *sec* $= a$.
μ r_1 r_2 illi *pro* ei.

57. r_1 r_2 autem sero $= f$.

58. μ r_1 r_2 dari *pro* reddi $= f$.

59. μ r_1 cum accepisset ioseph corpus $= a$. [*hiat* r_2 *usque fin. ev.*]

60. μ r_1 discessit (-et μ) *pro* abiit.

65. μ r_1 milites *pro* custodiam.

66. μ r_1 et signauerunt.

Most of these readings may fairly claim to have found place in the Irish recension of the Old Latin, and about one-fifth of them have no other pre-hieronymian attestation so far as I have been able to discover. These I have marked with asterisks. Some few of them may seem to suggest that the Irish Old Latin recension was based to some extent on a study of the original Greek. Such are the omission (supported by the Greek cursives 24*, 39, 180, 198, etc.) of a part of xxvi. 60, and the narrative of the piercing of the Saviour's side, found in the uncials ℵ B C L Γ U and some cursives and versions at xxvii. 49. But M. Berger's caution (*L'Histoire* p. 34) on this subject must not be forgotten.

Among the remainder, Dr Sanday's remarks on the St Gall frag-

ment (p) [1] lead us to expect to find some of Italian origin. In the
search for these we are indeed confined to a somewhat restricted area.
The Italian origin of a reading cannot be proved, though it may be
sometimes very probable, in the absence of opposing African testimony.
Now, for the entire extent of our Matthew fragment the Codex Bobiensis (k) is wanting, the Codex Palatinus (e) is available only for xxiv.
12–49, xxviii. 2 *sqq.*, Cyprian's citations for xxiv. 12–31, xxv. 31–
46, xxvi. 28, 29, 39, xxvii. 3, 4, 45. Or, in other words, African
evidence is forthcoming only for about one-quarter of the fragment.
Keeping within the limits of these passages, a few readings, supported
by f alone among the group a b e f Cyp., may be classed under this
head. Upon several of them, indeed, no stress can be laid : but the
more significant are xxiv. 38 *usque in diem . . . noe in arcam*, xxv. 43
suscepistis . . . cooperuistis.

Far more important is the African element, of which no instances
were brought to light by Dr Sanday's comparison of p with r_1.
African readings are found in our passages from St Matthew at the
following places : xxiv. 14, *per totum orbem* ; xxiv. 15, per danielum
profetam ; xxiv. 30, *lamentabuntur*, or *lamentabunt se* ; xxiv. 32, *cognoscitis*; xxiv. 42, *qua die uel* (*qua*) *hora* ; xxv. 34, *regnum quod
uobis paratum est*; xxv. 46, *isti*; and perhaps also at xxv. 40, *ex.*
We may be allowed also to add xxiv. 31, *a quattuor angulis uentorum*,
and xxiv. 51, *cum infidelibus*, supported by m alone among old Latin
authorities, and xxiv. 39, *senserunt*, found elsewhere in h m only.
We shall perhaps not be wrong in concluding that African influences
played a larger part in shaping the Irish text of St Matthew's Gospel
than Italian.

When, still keeping within the same limits, we come to look for
coincidences with d, which appear so strikingly in p, disappointment
awaits us. Three only, and those of little importance, are found
xxiv. 12, *quia*; xxv. 45, *eis*; xxvii. 45, *ab ora autem sexta.*

What, now, is the significance of these coincidences of reading ?
Are we to infer direct literary contact with the African and Italian
texts and the text represented by d ? By no means. M. Berger
has remarked the resemblance of the text of the Codex Claromontanus (h) to that of r_1. Of the 350 variants in our passage of St
Matthew in which two of the three MSS. μ r_1 r_2 are together, it
supports them in about 230, or in two-thirds of the entire number.
Among the readings attested by it are both those which we have
classed as Italian (one however only partially), the three in which it
coincides with d, and seven of the eleven which we regard as African.
The thought is thus suggested that the Irish recension may not be in
the strictest sense indigenous. The version upon which it was founded,
and from which its African, Italian, and d elements were derived, may
have been imported from the region which gave birth to the text
represented by h. If the provenance of h can be fixed, we shall

___

[1] *Old Latin Biblical Texts*, ii. p. ccvi *sqq.*

perhaps have advanced one step towards ascertaining the local origin of the Irish Old Latin text.

§ 2. *Individual readings of μ, r_1, r_2 in St Matthew.*

I now proceed to give a list of the individualisms of μ—variants, that is, in which it stands apart from both r_1 and r_2. For the sake of completeness, I include those which appear to be mere scribe's errors, marking them, however, with an obelus. Opposite each reading is given a list of its supporters among the Old Latin MSS. *a b c d e f ff₁ g₁ h n q δ*. Where r_1 or r_2 gives a rival variant, I have recorded it with its Old Latin supporters. In all cases where this is not done, r_1 and r_2 agree with, or at least support, the Amiatine text.

II. *Readings in which μ stands alone.*

Matt. xxiv. 13. permanserit $= b\ c\ q$. *a* remanserit.
    15. hautem *pro* ergo (*hiat* r_1).
    24. inducant $= c\ f\ h$.
        electos $= c$ d $f\ ff_1\ h$.
    26. credere *pro* exire (*hiat* r_1) $= c\ ff_1$ (*sed et* exire *pro* credere) $r_2\ om.$
        exire *usque* nolite . *b om.* nolite exire.
    29. [et] statim hautem.
        eorum *pro* illorum.
        eorum *pro* caelorum.
    30. plangent se $= a\ c\ m\ q$. r_1 lamentabun[t . .] ; r_2 lamentabunt se
        —*vide sup.*
    31. a summo.
    35. transibunt *pro* praeteribunt $= d$ (transient) *e* (transient).
    41. *om.* molentes . r_1 *om.* in mola $= a$.
        †unus (*bis*) $= q$.
    43. fur uenisset (*hiat* r_1) . r_2 fur ueniet . *a b c f h* q fur uenit . *d e δ*
        fur ueniret.
    45. *om.* quis putas est . $r_1\ r_2$ quisnam est $= a\ b\ c\ f\ ff_1\ h\ m$. d *q* quis
        enim est.
  xxv. 1. *om.* et sponsae (*hiat* r_1) $= δ$.
    9. †nobis *pro* uobis *sec.*
    15. †alio (*bis*).
    18. †habens *pro* abiens . $r_1\ r_2$ *om.* abiens $= a\ b\ c\ d\ ff_1$.
    20. tradidisti mihi . r_1 mihi dedisti $= b\ ff_1\ q$.
    21. †at *pro* ait.
        dominus suus (*hiat* r_1) $= d\ ff_1\ h$.
        om. in. (*hiat* r_1).
    22. *om.* autem (*hiat* r_1).
        acceperat $+$ similiter.
        dixit $= d\ f$.
        mihi tradidisti $= $ d $g_1\ h\ δ$. r_1 mihi dedisti $= ff_1\ q$.
        †alio.   } *om.* vv. 22, 23 $r_2 = a$
        superlucratus (*hiat* r_1) $= d\ f$.
    23. serue bone $= b\ c\ d\ f\ ff_1\ g_1\ q\ δ$.
        om. in.
        om. tui.
    26. †mala . $r_1\ r_2$ nequam (*ride sup.*).
        om. et *pri.*
        †metuo.
    29. *om.* ab eo (*hiat* r_1).

Matt. xxv. 30.　sernum nequam . r_1 r_2 nequam seruum$=a\,b\,c\,h\ q$.

32.　*om.* eos.

quemadmodum *pro* sicut$=$Cyp. i. 100, 112, 391.

separat pastor . δ pastor separat vel segregat.

33.　quidem oues$=\delta$. r_1 *om.* quidem$=b\ c\ d\ f\ f\!f_1\ h$ Cyp. i. 100, 112, 391.

34.　percipite *pro* possidete$=$Cyp. i. 100, 112, 391, 430.

ab initio *pro* a constitutione . r_2 ab origine$=c$ d $f\!f_1$ δ Cyp. i. 100, 112, 391, 430.[1]

38.　*om.* autem$=\delta$ Cyp. i. 100, 112, 391 . r_1 aut *pro* quando autem te uidimus.

40.　†respondit (*hiat* r_1).

43.　nudus eram (*hiat* r_1)$=h$. r_2 nudus fui$=$Cyp. i. 112.

carcere fui.[2]

xxvi. 6.　iesus esset$=f\!f_1$.

7.　accedens.

9.　*om.* istud . r_1 [h]oc$=d$; r_2 haec (*ms.*)$=h$.

13.　ut ubicumque.

21.　me traditur *pro* traditurus est me (*hiat* r_2) . r_1 tradet me$=a$ d h δ.

22.　contristati sunt (*hiat* r_2).

24.　+ et *ad init.* (*hiant* r_1 r_2)$=c\ q$.

tradetur *pro* nadit (*hiat* r_2) . r_1 nadet.

om. de illo (*hiat* r_2) . r_1 [de] eo$=a$ d $f\ q$.

26.　*om.* et pri (*hiat* r_2).

et *pro* ac (*hiat* r_2)$=c\ h$.

et dedit (*hiant* r_1 r_2)$=a\ c\ f\ q\ \delta$.

29.　diem illum cum illud (*hiat* r_2)$=b\ c\ f\!f_1\ h$ (illum diem) q　r_1 illud diem cum illud.

32.　†om. postquam autem (*hiant* r_1 r_2).

33.　dixit (*hiat* r_2)$=a\ c\ d\ h$. δ ait uel dixit.

om. illi (*hiant* r_1 r_2)$=b\ c$.

si *pro* etsi (*hiant* r_1 r_2)$=a\ b\ c\ d\ q\ \delta$.

ego enim nunquam (*hiat* r_2) . h ego autem numquam.

35.　si *pro* etiamsi (*hiat* r_2).

38.　+ iesus *ante* tristis (*hiant* r_1 r_2)$=a\ f\ h\ \delta$.

39.　cecidit (*hiat* r_2)$=d$.

quod *pro* sicut (*bis*) (*hiat* r_2)$=$Cyp. i. 133.

40.　discipulos suos (*hiat* r_2)$=a\ b\ c\ d\ f\ f\!f_1\ g_1\ h\ q$.

dixit (*hiat* r_2)$=a\ g_1$. r_1 ait$=b\ c\ f\ q$.

42.　abiit hautem iterum (*hiant* r_1 r_2).

om. si (*hiat* r_2)$=a\ h$.

om. hic (*hiat* r_2).

transire a me (*hiat* r_2 ; r_1 [? ms.]$=$A)$=f\ q\ \delta$.

om. tua (*hiat* r_2).

43.　*om.* et pri (*hiat* r_2).

44.　relinquens eos (*hiat* r_2)$=d$.

om. dicens (*hiat* r_2)$=a$.

45.　eis$=d\ q$.

47.　ex *pro* de$=a\ f$.

multitudo *pro* turba.

48.　quem *pro* quemcumque$=d\ f\ g_1\ h$.

51.　extendit . . . et (*hiat* r_1).

52.　in gladio (*hiat* r_1)$=h\ \delta$.

53.　exibet . r_1 r_2 exiberet.

57.　conuenerunt (*hiat* r_1)$=g_1\ \delta$.

58.　in atrio sedebat.

59.　*om.* autem.

61.　templum hoc dei$=b\ c\ d\ h$. r_1 (?) r_2 t. dei hoc.

62.　testificantur aduersus te.

64.　ad dexteram$=a\ b\ c\ f\ h\ q$.

---

[1] So also Lebar Brecc, p. 450: Bernard in *Trans. R.I.A.*, xxx. p. 323.

[2] So Lebar Brecc, p. 431: *Trans. R.I.A.*, xxx. 323.

Matt. xxvi. 65.   blasfemat.
             quid nunc adhuc.
      67.   cæderunt ($hiat$ r_1) . r_2 cedentes.
             eius pro ei$=c$ h . r_1 $om.$ ei (?) . r_2 $om.$ alii $usque$ dederunt$=a$ b δ.
      69.   illi et tu . r_2 ei et tu$=n$ ($corrector$).
      72. $om.$ et.
             iuramento+dixit . r_1 r_2 dicens$=b$ c f h.
      75. $om.$ et $sec.$ ($hiat$ r_1).
   xxvii. 1.   cum factum esset ($hiat$ r_1)$=h$.
       3.   damnatus est ($hiat$ r_1)$=b$ c d g_1 q δ . f ad iudicium ductus est ; h
               iudicatus est.
       5.   processit . r_1 r_2 secessit$=a$ b c h q.
             suspendit se$=d$.
       7.   †ex illis hautem.
     17. $om.$ ergo . r_1 r_2 autem pro ergo$=a$ b c d f g_1 h q.
     19. $om.$ enim ($hiat$ r_1).
     22.   †qui pro quid.
     23. $om.$ illis$=\delta$.
             pilatus pro praesis.
     24.   fier. in populo$=b$.
             dicens coram populo.
     28. $om.$ exuentes eum ($hiat$ r_1)$=a$ b c d q . r_2 cum spoliassent eum.
     29. $om.$ et $pri.$
             adorabant pro inludebant . r_2 deludentes . a b c h q deludebant.
     31.   calamidem cocciniam . h chlamydem et uestem purpuream.
             $om.$ et $tert.=d$. r_2 $om.$ et duxerunt $usque$ $fin.$ $vers.$
             +eum ad $fin.$ ($hiat$ r_1) . a b cruci eum figerent ; f eum cruci-
               figerent.
     32.   tollere pro ut tolleret.
     36.   obseruabant ($hiat$ r_1)$=\delta$. r_2 seruauearunt.
     37.   illins pro ipsius.
             inscribtam . r_2 scriptum est.
     38.   alterum pro unus $sec.$. r_1 r_2 unum$=f$ h q . a alter.
     39.   tunc euntes pro praetereuntes autem . r_1 r_2 transeuntes autem
               $=a$ b c d h q.
     40.   distruebas$=b$ ff_1 h δ . r_2 distruas$=f$ (-es.)
     42.   es discende.
     43.   confidat.
             dominum . r_1 deo suo . r_2 deum$=c$ d f g_1 δ . ff_1 domino.
             iam liberet eum.
     46.   circa hautem horam ($hiat$ r_1)$=c$ h ; r_2 circa uero horam   d circa
              . . . . autem horam ; q δ circa autem . . . . horam.
             $om.$ nonam.
     48.   arundinem . r_1 in harundin [. .]$=a$ h.
     49.   sinete ($hiat$ r_1)$=\delta$.
     51.   usque ad.
             terrae motus factus est magnus$=h$. a terrae motum factum est
               magnum.
     52. $om.$ multa.
     57.   esset factum.
     58.   +iesu ad $fin.$ ($hiat$ r_2).
     65.   sicut ipsi scitis ($hiat$ r_2).
     66. $om.$ abeuntes ($hiat$ r_2).
             lapidem+et discesserunt ($hiat$ r_2).
  xxviii. 3.   hautem pro enim ($hiat$ r_2)$=a$ b c d e f ff_1 g_1 n q δ . r_1 et erat$=h$.

An inspection of this list brings to light both Italian (xxiv. 24) and
African (xxiv. 35 ; xxv. 32, 34, 38 ; xxvi. 39) readings, the latter bearing about the same proportion to the former as in the preceding table.
The only reading supported by d alone of our selected MSS. is *cecidit*,
xxvi. 39. Moreover, we observe that nearly half the individual read-

ings of μ (60 out of 129) are supported by other Old Latin MSS., and may accordingly be probably assumed to be genuine readings, and not mere later corruptions of the text.   This is in itself sufficient to show that even readings in which μ stands alone against, or at least without the support of, $r_1 r_2$ may be of high value.   It is interesting, more- over, to mark that in a few instances (xxiv. 30 (43) ; xxv. 22, 23, 33, 43 ; xxvi. 40, 67 ; xxvii. 40, 43 ; xxviii. 3) readings of μ attested by other Old Latin texts are set over against rivals of r_1 or r_2 with similar support.   This appears to suggest that there may have existed side by side in Ireland two or more recensions of the Evangelical text, closely similar, and yet appreciably differing from one another.   Three of the individual readings of μ (xxiv. 15, $autem = \aleph^c$ L, etc. ; xxvi. 42, $om.$ hic $= V$, etc. ; xxvii. 17, $om.$ ergo $= 243$) have Greek support They may possibly be due to a revision of the text by the aid of MSS. of the original.

It seems unnecessary to burden these pages with tables showing the individual variants of r_1 and r_2.   It will suffice to state results. In r_1 there are about 110 such readings.   Of these about 55 have other Old Latin attestation : two bear marks of African origin, xxiv. 20, ne ($= e$ Cyp. i. 336), xxiv. 32, $fuerit\ tener$ ($= e$) ; one, in itself of but little account, is supported by f alone among the primary manu- scripts, xxvi. 29, $quia$; while d alone countenances xxiv. 31, $summum$ for $terminos$, and xxv. 34, $praeparatum$.   In r_2 we find about 175 individualisms, of which some 75 have Old Latin attestation ; about 6 being African—xxiv. 21, $sed\ neque$ ($= e$ Cyp. i. 336), xxiv. 27, apparet ($= e$ Cyp. i. 336), xxiv. 28, ubi ($= e$ Cyp. i. 336), xxiv. 30, $om.$ tunc ($= e$), xxv. 43, $nudus\ fui$ ($=$ Cyp. i. 112), $uenistis\ ad$ ($=$ Cyp. i. 100, 112, 392) ; and perhaps xxv. 45, $istis$ ($=$ Cyp. i. 101 [A]) ; one or two Italian—xxv. 36, $co\text{-}operuistis$ ($= f$), and perhaps xxiv. 41, $altera$ ($f\ alia$) ; while two are supported by d only, viz., xxiv. 34, $generatio$ $haec$, and xxv. 34, $ab\ origine$.

§ 3. *Readings in which $\mu\ r_1$ agree (St Luke)*.

The Lucan fragment gives less material than the Matthean for such an inquiry as we have just now made, r_2 having here deserted us. Some results, however, may be obtained.   The length of the passage and the largely increased deviation of μ from the Vulgate make it undesirable to give full lists of the readings.   Of the 360 or 370 variants in which $\mu\ r_1$ are together, 45 coincide with e, which is fortunately available for nearly the entire passage, against $b\ f$, and may therefore be esteemed as African.   They are the following :—

Luc. iv. 13.   ab eo $= a$ d e : ab illo $b\ f$.
　　　36.   quis est iste sermo $= e$ (quid): d quis est hic sermo ; $a\ b\ f$ quid (quod f) 　　　　　　　est hoc uerbum.
　　　43.   ad hoc enim ; d e in hoc enim : a quia ob hoc ; f quia ad hoc ; 　　　　　　　b quia ideo.

Luc. v. 14.   *om.* ipse = *e* : *a b d f* ipse.
      22.   mala = *e* : d iniqua ; *om. a b f.*
            ad eos = *e* : d eis ; *a b f* ad illos.
      24.   grabatum = *d* : *a b f* lectum ; *om. e, sed in vers. sequ. add.* gra-
            battum *post* tulit.
      33.   orationes = *a e* : *b f* obsecrationes ; d praecationes.
      36.   conueniet = *a d e* : *b f* conuenit.
Luc. vi.   8.   surrexit et = *e* : *a b d f* surgens.
      20.   ad *pro* in = *e* : *a b d f* in.
      29.   ei = *e* : *b f* eum ; *a d* ab eo.
      33.   ipsud = *e* : *a b d f om.*
      34.   eis = *a e* : *b f* his ; *om.* d.
      37.   dimittetur uobis ; *e* dimittitur nobis : *a b d f* dimittemini.
   vii.   4.   *om.* ad iesum = *a d e* : *b f* ad iesum.
       6.   ibat autem cum illis iesus = *a* d (eis) *e* (abiit itaque) : *b f* iesus
            autem abiit (ibat *f*) cum eis (illis *f*).
      12.   mortuus = *a* d (mortuum) *e* : *b f* defunctus.
      30.   doctores = *a d e* : *b f* periti.
      42.   amabit (-anit μ) ; *e* amat : *b* dilexit ; *a* diliget ; d *f* diligit.
      43.   respondit = *e* : *a b d f* respondens.
      47.   illi = *d e* : *a f* ei ; *b* tibi.
  viii.   4.   qui = *a d e* : *om. b f.*
       8.   bonam et optimam = *a e* : d bon. et uberam ; *b f* bonam.
       9.   similitudo = *e* : *a b* d *f* parabola.
      11.   similitudo = *e* : *a b* d *f* parabola.
      14.   suffocantur (*om.* euntes) = *e* : *b* euntes simul suf. ; *f* euntes suf. ;
            d abientes suf., *a* ingredientes suf.
      15.   audiunt . . . et ([aud.] . . . et r_1) = *e* : *a b d f* audientes.
            tenent = *e* : *a b f* retinent ; d continent.
      17.   est enim = *d e* : *a b f* enim est.
            absconsum = *d e* : *a b f* occultum.
      19.   eius et fratres = *d e* : *b f* et fratres eius ; *a* et fratres illius.
      22.   nauem = *d e* : *a b f* nauiculam.
      24.   discipuli = *a* ; *e* discentes (*ante* dicentes) : *om. b* d *f.*
      26.   in = *a d e* : *b f* ad.
      28.   exclamauit . . . dicens = *e* : *a b f* exclamans . . . dixit ; d excla-
            mauit . . dixit.
      49.   eo = *a d e* : *b f* illo.
   ix.   3.   non (*quater*) = *e* : *d* non . . neque . . neque . . neque ; *a b f* neque
            (*quater*).
            habueritis = *e* : *a f* habeatis ; d habere ; *hiat b.*
      11.   eum = *a d e* : *b f* illum.
            eis = *e* : *a b d f* illis.
      24.   hic = d *e* Cyp. i. 345 : *b* ille ; *om. a f.*
      32.   cum eo erant = *a d e* : *b* cum illo ; *f* cum illo erant.
      47.   iesus autem = *a d e* : *b* ad iesus ; *f* et iesus.
      49.   magister = *a d e* : *b f* praeceptor.

In twenty-one of these readings *e* alone of the group *a b d e f* supports μ r_1. Thus the anticipation which our experience led us to
entertain, that the African element would be fairly conspicuous, is
verified.

In the enumeration which follows we have of Italian readings 30
in all, or 16 if we include only those which have the support of *f*
alone.

Luc. iv.   5.   iterum = *f* : *e* secundo ; *om.* (*a*) *b d.*
       7.   me = *f* : *a b* ante me ; d *e* in conspectu meo.
   v.   6.   ita ut rumperentur = *f* : d ut etiam . . . rumperentur ; *c* ut
            dirumperetur ; *a b* rumpebantur (-atur *b*) autem.

Luc. v. 8. rogo te $=f$: d rogo ; *e* oro te ; *om. a b.*
     19. et per tegulas $=af$: *e* et per teculatum ; *b* et discoperuerunt tectum et ; *d* et detegentes inbrices ubi erat.
     36. parabolam $=a$ d f : *b e* similitudinem.
  vi. 10. sicut et altera ; *f* sicut altera : *b* d sicut (+ et d) alia ; *om. a e.*
     16. fuit traditor $=f$ (+ eius): *b* fuit proditor ; *a* erat proditor ; *d* etiam et tradidit eum ; *e* tradidit illum.
     20. spiritu $=af$: *om. b* d *e.*
     29. praebe + illi $=df$: *a b e* ei.
     40. erit si sit $=af$: *b* erit ut sit ; *d* erit ; *e* erits.
  vii. 3. qui cum audisset $=f$: *b e* et cum audisset ; d et audiens ; *a* audiens autem.
     14. iesus $=f$: *om. a b* d *e.*
     17. in omnem regionem $=f$: d in omni regione ; *a* in omni finitima regione ; *b* omni confinio regionis illins ; *om. e.*
     22. iesus $=f$: *om. a b* d *e.*
     24. iesus dicere ; *f* dicere iesus : *a b* d *e* dicere.
     42. illum $=af$: *b* d *e* eum.
     43. autem (? *sec. man.* r_1) $=af$: *om. b* d *e.*
 viii. 21. at ille $=df$: *a b* qui ; *e* ille autem.
     52. enim $=a$ d f : *om. b e.*
  ix. 5. de pedibus uestris $=f$: *a b* uestrum de pedibus ; *e* uestrum a pedibus uestris ; *d* pedum uestrorum.
     16. dedit $=f$: *a* d *e* dabat ; *b* distribuit.
     24. eam (*bis*) $=df$: *a b e* illam.
     39. ab eo $=df$: *a* ab illo ; *om. b* ; *claus. om. e.*
     41. incredula $=df$: *a e* incredibilis ; *b* infidelis.
     42. eum *sec* $=f$: *om. a b* d *e.*
     45. hoc uerbum $=f$: *a* d uerbum hoc ; *b* uerbum istut ; *e* uerbum illud. intellegerent (intellex. μ) $=af$: *b* d *e* sentirent.
     50. sinite eum et $=f$: *a* sinite illum et ; *om. b* d *e.*
     51. in hierusalem $=a$ d f : *b* hierusalem ; *e* ad hierusalem.

In 11 readings we find coincidences with d alone :—

Luc. v. 9. timor : *a f* pauor ; *b* miratio ; *e* stupor.
     20. nidens autem iesus fidem eorum (illorum r_1) : *a* et nisa fide illorum ; *b* quorum ut uidit fidem ; *e* ille autem cum uidisset fidem illorum ; *f* et nidens fidem eorum.
     24. grabatum : *a b f* lectum ; *om. claus. e.*[1]
 viii. 4. talem ad eos (illos r_1) : *b* ad illos talem ; *e* talem ; *om. a f.*
     14. adferent (μ -unt) fructum : *a f* dant fructum ; *b* referunt fructum; *e* fecundantur.
     15. fructificant : *a* fructum dant ; *b e f* fructum adferent (*f* -unt.)
     17. occultum : *a b f* absconsum (-ditum *f*) ; *e* celatum.
  ix. 10. ei : *a b e f* illi.
     19. ex *pro* de : *a b f* de ; *om. e.*
     45. coopertum : *a f* occultum ; *e* absconsum ; *hiat b.*
     47. eorum : *a b e f* illorum.

The only unsupported readings of μ r_1, so far as I have observed which can be claimed as bespeaking, and that more than doubtfully, a reviser who consulted the Greek text, are v. 36 *scindetur* $=$ R ; vii. 38 *tersit* $=$ ℵ* A D, etc. ($\dot{\epsilon}\xi\acute{\epsilon}\mu\alpha\xi\epsilon\nu$).

§ 10. *Individualisms of* μ r_1 *in St Luke.*

We come now to tabulate the African, Italian, and d readings found among the individual variants of our two manuscripts. It is curious

---

[1] But see above, p. 139.

to notice that while, as we might expect, the number of African variants in the two manuscripts is nearly equal, the Italian readings of μ exceed those of r_1 in the ratio of 4 : 1.

African readings in μ.

Luc. iv. 11.   quia=e : b d et ; f et quia ; *om.* a.
  v. 7.   cum uen. (*om.* et *quart.*)=e : $a f$ et uen. et ; d uenientes ergo ; *om.* b.
  14.   uade et=a d e : $b f$ uade.
  15.   de eo=a d e (deo) : $b f$ de illo.
  31.   respondit . . . et ; e respondit et : a b d f respondens.
  36.   *om.* et *pri.* =e : a b d f et.
      eos=a d e : $b f$ illos.
  vi. 9.   aut *pri. et tert.*=d e : $b f$ an ; *hiat* a.
  20.   dixit (*hiat* r_1)=e : a b d f dicebat.
  31.   nobis faciant=e : a b d f faciant (-ciam d) nobis.
  37.   iudicetur de uobis=e : b de nobis . . . iudicabitur ; a d f iudicemini.
      ne condempnemini=e Cyp. i. 139 : a d ut non cond. ; b et non condemnamini ; f et non condemnabimini.
  45.   bona=e : a b d f bonum.
  47.   sit similis=a e : d est similis ; $b f$ similis (-e b) est.
  vii. 12.   sequebatur cum ; e consequebatur : d cum . . erat ; a $b f$ cum.
  22.   et *tert.*=e : *om.* a b d f.
  25.   uestitum=e : a $b f$ uestimentis indutum ; d uestimentis uestitum.
  28.   quia=e : d quoniam ; *om.* a $b f$.
      illo est=a d e : $b f$ est illo.
  36.   recubuit=d e : a $b f$ discubuit.
  40.   dicere aliquod ; e dicere aliquid : a $b f$ aliquid dicere ; d quod dicere.
  viii. 10.   non est datum sed=e (nisi) : *om.* a b d f.
      similitudinibus ; e similitudinem (*sic*) : a b d f parabolis.
  14.   per sollicitudinem ; e per sollicitudinis (*sic*) : a b d a sollicitudinibus ; f a sollicitudine.
  16.   *om.* ponit *sec.* =e : a b d f ponit.
      omnibus luceat=e : a b f intrantes uideant lumen ; d qui intrant uideant lumen.
  21.   respondit=e : a b d f respondens.
  27.   exit . . et ; e cum exisset ; d exierunt . . et : $b f$ cum egressus esset ; a gresso . . . illo.
  28.   *om.* is=a d e : b is ; f qui.
  29.   alligabatur=a e : d f ligabatur ; b uinctus.
  49.   *om.* ei=e : a $b f$ ei ; d illi.
  51.   puellae et matrem=d e : a $b f$ et matrem puellae.
  ix. 14.   eos=d e : a $b f$ illos.
  25.   ipsum hautem=d e : $a f$ autem ipsum ; b autem.
  41.   *om.* et peruersa *post* incredula=a e : b d f et peruersa.
  47.   adpræhendit . . et=e : b d f adpraehendens ; a adpraehensum.

African readings in r_1.

Luc. iv. 6.   dixit=a d e : $b f$ ait.
  10.   te conseruent=e : $b f$ conseruent te : a d custodiant te.
  17.   erat scriptum=a d e : $b f$ scriptum erat.
  23.   ad illos=a e : $b f$ illis ; d ad eos.
  35.   et nihil=e : b nihilque ; a d f nihil.
  v. 7.   paene=d e : *om.* a $b f$.

Luc. v. 8. quod cum uidisset=*e* (*om.* quod) : *b f* quod cum uideret ; *a* hoc niso ; *om.* d.

quoniam=*d e* : *a b f* quia.

12. *om.* rogauit eum (*e spat.*)=*d e* : *b* rogabat eum ; *f* rogauit eum ; *a* orabat illum.

15. audire . . . curari=*a* d *e* : *b f* ut audirent . . curarentur.

18. [in]ferre eum=*e* : *b f* eum inferre ; *a* inferre illum ; d inducere eum.

28. surrexit et=*e* : *a b* d *f* surgens.

38. seruantur=*a* d *e* : *b f* conseruantur.

vi. 2. quid=*a e* : *b* ad eos quid ; *f* illis quid ; d ei ecce quid.

3. ad illos=*e* : *a b f* illis ; d ad eos.

21. et sitiunt iustitiam=*e* : *b* et sitiunt ; *a* et sititis ; *om.* d *f*.

35. quo[niam]=*a* d *e* : *b f* quia.

46. me uocatis=*a e* : *b f* uocatis me ; d mihi dicitis.

48. [est]enim=*e* : *a b* d *f* enim erat.

49. domum=*a* d *e* : *b f* domum suam.

vii. 6. dicens illi=*e* : *a* d *f* dicens ei ; *b* dicens.

22. renuntiate=*a e* : *b f* nuntiate ; d dicite.

34. uinarius=*e* : *a b f* bibens uinum ; d uinipotator.

37. uas=*e* : *b* d *f* alabastrum ; *a* ampullam.

42. ambobus=*e* : *a b* d *f* utrisque.

43. et dixit=*e* : *a b* d *f* dixit.

dixit=*e* : *a b f* dixit ei ; d dixit illi.

45. osculando=*a e* : *b f* osculari ; d osculans.

viii. 17. nihil=*a e* : *b* d *f* non.

19. ad eum *pri.*=*d e* : *a b f* ad illum.

24. accesserunt . . . et=*e* : *a b* d *f* accedentes.

magister=*a e* : *b f* praeceptor ; d domine domine.

25. iesus=*e* : *om. a b* d *f*.

ix. 3. non calciamenta=*e* : *a b* neque cal.; d *f om.*

3. et . . exite=*a* d *e* : *b* et . . . proficiscimini ; *f* donec exeatis.

11. excipiens=*a e* : *b f* excepit . . et ; d suscipiens.

12. deserto loco=*a* d *e* : *b f* loco deserto.

22. quo[niam]=*a* d *e* : *b* quod ; *f* quia.

32. cum eo *sec.*=*d e* : *b f* cum illo ; *a* ei.

39. subito=*a e* : d desubito ; *b f* et subito clamat.

50. *om.* ad illum=*d e* : *a f* ad illum ; *b* ad illos.

54. eos=*a* d *e* : *b f* illos.

Italian readings in μ.

Luc. iv. 5. in montem excelsum ualde [1] ; *f* in montem excelsum : d in montem altum ualde ; *e* supra montem ; *om. b.* ; *a* hierusalem.

mundi=*d f* : *a* orbis terrarum ; *b e* orbis terrae.

41. eos=*f* : *e* ea ; *om. a b* d.

19. eum cum lecto=*f* : *a* eum cum lectulo ; *b* illum cum lecto ; *e* illum . . . cum grabattum ; d grabattum cum paralytico.

24. dimittendi=*f* : *a* remittendi ; *b* d dimittere ; *e* dismittere.

31. eis=*f* : *a b e* ad illos ; d ad eos.

vi. 7. in sabbato=*f* : *a* (*e spat.*) *b* d *e* sabbato.

23. calumniantibus uobis=*f* : *b* d cal. uos ; *a* his qui calumniantur uos ; *e* eis qui uobis iniuria faciunt.

42. perspicies (*hiat* r_1)=*a f* : *b* respicies ; d *e* uidebis.

vii. 10. qui languebat=*f* : d aegrum ; *om. a b e*.

15. protinus (*hiat* r_1)=*f* : *om. a b* d *e*.

21. *om.* in *ad init.*=*a f* : *b* d *e* in.

26. dico nobis etiam ; *f* ita d. u. etiam : *a* d etiam d. u.; *b* utique d. u. et ; *e* ita d. u. et.

---

[1] Here, as in other cases to be mentioned presently, we have a conflate reading, one member of which is found in d.

Luc. vii. 36. in domum=$a\,d\,f$: $b\,e$ domum.
48. peccata + tua =f : *om.* b d e.
viii. 2. ab *sec.* (*hiat* r_1)=f : *om.* b d e ; *claus. om. a.*
11. haec est autem=f : a b d est autem haec ; e est autem . . . haec.
12. cecidit=f : b seminati sunt ; e seminatum est ; *om. a* d.
15. cecidit (*hiat* r_1)=f : *om.* a b d e.
18. et *sec.* =$a\,d\,f$: b etiam ; *om. e.*
29. eum=$d\,f$: a b e illum.
49. ad principem=f : a b a principe ; d ab archisynagogo ; e puer principis.
ix. 5. excutite puluerem=$d\,f$: a b e puluerem . . . excutite.
illis=$a\,f$: b d supra (-per d) illos ; e super eos.
39. eum *pri.* =f : a b d e illum.

Italian readings in r_1.

Luc. v. 14. mundatione=f : b e emundatione ; d purificatione ; a purgatione.
vi. 38. cumulatam=$a\,f$: b confersam ; d inpletam ; *om. e.*
viii. 14. cum audierint=f : a b audiunt et ; d e audierunt et.
ix. 13. iesus=f : *om.* a b d e.
18. discipuli eius=f : b d e discipuli ; a discipuli sui.
19. respondentes=a d f : b e responderunt.
54. uidentes=a d f : b e cum uidissent.

We must now give a list of individual readings of μ and r_1 in which the d element appears. It will be found specially remarkable in μ. In this manuscript we observe in the first place a constant tendency to substitute the oblique cases of "is" for those of "ille." In many instances the resulting reading is found in d alone of the group $a\,b\,d\,e\,f$. Examples will be found at iv. 9, 39; vi. 7, 17; vii. 12, 36; viii. 18, 22, 30, 40; ix. 2, 3, 13, 33, 42. Omitting these, we discover sixteen d readings. The list follows:—

d readings in μ.

Luc. iv. 7. *om.* procedens : a b f procidens ; e prostratus.
21. *om.* quia : b e f quia ; a quoniam.
36. in omnes : b f in omnibus ; a e super omnes.
v. 18. inducere : a b e f inferre.
37. utres ueteres *sec.* : *om.* ueteres a b e f.
vi. 26. homines : a b e f omnes homines.
vii. 10. in domum : a b e f domum.
viii. 10. scire : b f nosse ; e cognoscere ; *om. a.*
16. cooperit : a e f (-riet a) operit ; *om. claus.* b.
37. rogauerunt autem : b f et rogauerunt ; a et rogauit ; *hiat e.*
46. scio (sciui d) : a b f cognoui ; *hiat e.*
49. magistrum : a e illum ; f eum ; *om.* b (?).
56. expauerunt [1] (*hiat* r_1) ; *om.* a b e f.
ix. 19. ex profetis prioribus [2] ; d ex profetis : a b f propheta . de prioribus ; e profetarum.
27. filium hominis (+ uenientem d) in gloria sua : a b e f regnum dei.
51. conpleretur : a b f conplerentur ; e supplerentur.

[1] Apparently a conflation in μ.
[2] Again, it would seem, a conflation.

The list for r_1 is not so long. It comprises, in addition to substitutions of the parts of 'is' for those of ille' at iv. 21, 38, viii. 45 (*ms.*), the following :—

d readings in r_1.

Luc. iv. 24. amen amen : *a b e f* amen.
  vi. 14. primum simonem : *om.* primum *a b e f*.
   35. [iniq]uos (?*ms.*) : *a e* nequas ; *b f* malos.
  vii. 12. adpropiasset (·aret *d*) : *a b e* adpropinquaret; *f* adpropinquauit.
  viii. 3. illis : *a* illi ; *b* ei ; *e f* eis.
   39. in *sec.* : *a b f* per ; *hiat e*.
  ix. 10. r_1 seorsum + in nioum[1] ; d seorsum + in castellum (*om.* in locum desertum) : *om.* in nioum *a b e f*.
   33. faciamus (facio d) hic : *om.* hic *a b e f*.

Finally, a comparison of the lists now given for St Luke with those previously made for St Matthew brings to light the following facts. Allowing for the difference in length of the passages, and for the very small portion of the Matthean fragment for which African evidence is available, we find that the number of African variants in St Luke, attested by both μ and r_1, is as nearly as possible what our experience of St Matthew might have led us to expect. The same remark may be made of the comparatively small group of *d* readings ; though the examples of this class of variants are more satisfactory in the third than in the first Gospel. As regards these two constituents, the Irish Old Latin text appears to be homogeneous in the two passages. On the other hand, we observe in St Luke a very remarkable increase in the number of Italian variants. When we consider those readings in which μ is unsupported by r_1, or r_1 by μ, our results are not quite identical. We find a large increase in the African element of μ, while in r_1 the African readings have increased even more notably, being about four times as numerous as might have been anticipated from St Matthew. The Italian element in μ has become very considerable, though still less important than the African ; in St Matthew it was very small indeed. The Italian element in r_1 and the *d* element in both μ and r_1 are insignificant in both Gospels.

---

[1] A conflation.

CHAPTER VII.

THE LAST PAGE.—I. THE LITURGICAL FRAGMENT.

WE have already seen, in the second chapter of this work, that the last few verses of St John, followed by the colophon, are written on the recto of the final leaf of our manuscript. We have seen too that the task of deciphering the faded letters of the latter portion of the colophon is no easy one. When we turn the leaf and enter upon the study of its verso, our difficulties increase. At the first glance no more than a word or two appear to be legible. After I had spent some weeks upon it, however, some scarcely visible marks began to shape themselves into letters, and finally I have been able to read almost the whole page.

It was obvious to hope that chemical re-agents might restore some letters which, without the use of restoratives, were illegible. I accordingly sought permission of the Board of Trinity College to apply sulphide of ammonium to the faded writing. My request was granted. Professor Emerson Reynolds brushed the page with this application—usually so potent—and Professor Gwynn kindly undertook to watch the effect. The result has been disappointing. Photographs taken for me by Mr Greenwood Pim have enabled me to read (somewhat doubtfully) four letters which had previously escaped me, and I was made confident of one reading, about which I had had some hesitation. But with these exceptions I have been obliged to content myself with what my eyesight could reveal to me, assisted only by good light and some little patience.

Two facts at once strike us when we proceed to examine this page of the manuscript,—*first*, that the writing is in the same hand as the main portion of the book ; and *secondly*, that it follows the colophon. Combining these two facts, and assuming the correctness of the hypothesis which I have advanced as to the origin of the manuscript,[1] we are entitled to infer that, unlike the biblical text, this page has no claim to represent an exemplar coeval with St Molling of Ferns, but that it was written *by an inmate of his monastery*, about the close of the eighth or beginning of the ninth century.

Of the contents of the page Mr Westwood writes,[2] "There is (1) an inscription on the verso of the last page (*sic*), in the same hand as the text, containing the Magnificat, part of the Sermon on the Mount, Apostles' Creed, 'Patricius Epis', and (2) a circular table

---
[1] Above, p. 17.
[2] *Palæographia Sacra*, Irish Biblical MSS., ii. p. 5.

with inscriptions." The first of these we now proceed to examine, the other we reserve for the next chapter.

Of the liturgical fragment Mr Westwood's words are an approximation to a correct description, but they are no more. The document *contains* neither Magnificat nor Apostles' Creed, though both are referred to; it *does* contain "Patricius Episcopus," though a word of explanation was needed in the case of this somewhat mysterious title; and finally, it refers to several other pieces of interest which Mr Westwood has not mentioned. All this will be evident from the transcript which I now give. The document is written in one column of about thirteen or fourteen lines, each containing some thirty-five letters, towards the left of the page, as if room were left for a second narrower column to the right, which has not been added.[1] The exterior margin is very narrow. In the transcript, I have italicised letters which are not distinct enough to be read with entire confidence. Those which have been conjecturally supplied are enclosed in square brackets. The title (if any existed) is illegible, with probably a line or so of text.

```
– – – – – – – – – – – – – – – sent. al
– – – – – – – – – – – – – . .—Magnificat.
– onformn. Benedictus usq; ioh[annem babtis]ta
p̄cursore d̄ni] Uidens h̄ ih̄s turbas ascendit   t
[ī monte]m . b – – e – – n X̄PS illum conrici
[dead Ī] memoria ætna Patricius ēpis orat
[pro nobis omnibus] ut deleantur protinus peccata
[quæ commisimus] INuitiata ꝓ feramus pec
[tora Exaudi donec d]icis peccata plurima.—
[Maiesta]t[em]q; imensam corici dead et conglu
[ria Uni]tas [u]sq; i finem.Credo i dm pat
[noster – – – –     ] . .—
```

l. 1. "al" perhaps = "alleluia." There are apparently two letters in the right margin between ll. 1 and 2.

l. 3. After "f" we seem to have either "o" followed by six, or "a" followed by five vertical strokes. The latter are some combination of the letters "i," "r," "m," or "n." The letter "t" at the end of the line is in the margin, and does not appear to be part of the text.

l. 4. The line over "dni" and perhaps the "so" of "precursorem" are legible.

l. 10. The last letters are very difficult to read : see below.

l. 11. There is possibly one letter between "[Uni]tas" and "[u]sque" (?="i": see below).

For the benefit of those who, like myself, are ignorant of the Irish tongue, I may note that the Rev. T. Olden tells me that "conrici dead" = usque in (literally, 'donec attingat') finem.

---

[1] The length of a line of writing is 5·8 cent., the breadth of the page being about 10·5 cent.

A glance through this document will suffice to show that it is liturgical in character, and that the ecclesiastical office which it represents contained at least the following parts : (1) "Magnificat"; (2) . onf . . . ; (3) "Benedictus", etc. ; (4) "Uidens autem", etc. ; (5) "Christus illum", etc. ; (6) "[. .]memoria", etc.; (7) "Patricius episcopus", etc. ; (8) "Inuitiata quod", etc. ; (9) [. . .]icis peccata plurima ; (10) "[. . .]q ; inmensam", etc. ; (11) "[. . .]tas," etc. ; (12) "Credo", etc.

Can any of the parts thus described be identified ? Some with the greatest ease. For example, that which is called "Magnificat" (1) is beyond doubt the hymn of the Blessed Virgin, as used at Vespers in the mediæval Church of England, and at Evensong according to the Reformed Anglican usage. That this Canticle was used in the early Irish Church we need no further assurance than that which its presence in the *Liber Hymnorum*[1] affords. Again, "Uidens autem", etc., (4) is obviously a lection from St Matt. v., "Jesus" being inserted after "autem" in agreement with the majority of MSS. of the Irish recension, including the Book of Mulling itself. Once more, "Credo", etc., (12) is the Apostles' Creed, which we know to have been commonly employed in Celtic worship.

One word more before we leave l. 11 as to its last word. It is natural to read "pat̄" as the fourth word of the Creed "patrem." And this is not impossible, for the abbreviations in our MS. are sometimes quite arbitrary. Thus "patrem" is represented by "pā" at Matt. xv. 4, 6, while the same letters stand for "patri" in the intervening verse, not to mention other instances. But, on the other hand, t̄ is almost always used for "ter." I have therefore ventured to regard "pat̄" as the first word of the Lord's Prayer (13) and to conjecture "noster" as the first of the illegible words in l. 12. That the Credo should be followed by the Pater Noster is just what we might expect. The same sequence occurs in the Book of Dimma, the Visitation of the Sick in the Book of Mulling, the Antiphonary of Bangor, and the Book of Hymns f. 30v, i.e., apparently in all the Celtic offices, not strictly Eucharistic in character, in which the Creed is found;[2] the Book of

[1] *The Book of Hymns of the Ancient Church of Ireland, edited from the original manuscript in the Library of Trinity College, Dublin, with translation and notes*, by James Henthorn Todd ; Dublin, Fasc. i. 1855, Fasc. ii. 1869. Dr Todd collated a second copy of the Book of Hymns, then in the Library of St Isidore's at Rome, but the opportunity of doing so did not occur till too late to enable him to make any considerable use of it in the two published fasciculi of his edition of the Book of Hymns. It is now preserved in the Franciscan House, Merchants' Quay, Dublin, and I have occasionally referred to it as the "Franciscan Copy." A new and complete edition of the *Liber Hymnorum* is being prepared by Professors Bernard and Atkinson, and will, it is hoped, be shortly issued to members of the Henry Bradshaw Society. In the references to the printed editions of this book throughout the present chapter I denote them by the letters *L.H.* The figures following these letters give the pages of Todd's edition. With them I supply (enclosed in brackets), by the kindness of the editors, the references to the corresponding pages of the Bradshaw Society edition.
[2] Compare the old Irish Tract *De Arreis*, edited by Mr Kuno Meyer (*Rev.*

Deer[1] being, of course, no exception. The word "noster," especially if written n͞i, would fill only a small part of the vacant space in l. 12, which appears to have contained twelve or fourteen letters. What may have followed we can only guess. But we shall possibly guess correctly, if we take for our guide a hitherto inedited page (f. 30*v*) of the *Liber Hymnorum* to which Professor Bernard has called my attention.[2] We there find the words "Credo in deum patrem omnipotentem. usque in finem. et pater noster., Ascendat oratio," etc. It is quite possible that the formula, here indicated by its first words "ascendat oratio," may have followed the Creed and the Lord's Prayer in our fragment as well as in the Book of Hymns, and that in it we have hit upon number (14). I therefore print it here, as it is found in the Stowe Missal.[3]

Ascendat oratio nostra usque ad tronum caritatis tuae, domine, et ne uacua reuertatur ad nos postulatio nostra, per.

After these, perhaps the piece most easily recognised is that commencing "Patricius episcopus orat" (l. oret)—(7). This was written in full, and enough remains legible to place beyond question its identity with one of the couplets added in the Antiphonary of Bangor (f. 15*v*), and in the copy of the Book of Hymns preserved in the Franciscan Monastery, Merchants' Quay, Dublin, to the Hymn of Secundinus in honour of St Patrick. The couplet runs as follows [4] ·—

Patricius æpiscopus oret pro nobis omnibus
ut deleantur protinus peccata quæ commisimus.

The identification of these lines leads to the anticipation that the Hymn of St Secundinus itself, to which they are subjoined as an appendix in the only other MSS. which are known to contain them, may form one of the earlier parts of the office. And this anticipation will be strengthened when we remember that we are dealing, probably, with a *monastic service* and recall the contemporary words of the Book of Armagh,[5] "Patricius s͞c͞s e͞p͞s honorem quaternum *omnibus monasteriis et aeclessiis* per totam hiberniam debet habere III. Ymnum eius per totum tempus cantare . . ." If this "Hymn of St Patrick" forms part of our office, it will most probably be "Christus illum," etc. (5), or the following number. Now at first

Celtique, Oct. 1894), in which the recitation of Paters is frequently enjoined without the Credo (capp. 1, 3, 10, 13, 20. 31, 33),while the Credo never stands alone, being always either followed (14 [*cet credo* is here left untranslated], 26), or preceded (21) by a Pater.
[1] Warren, *The Liturgy and Ritual of the Celtic Church,* p. 166.
[2] *L. H.* (i. 156).
[3] Warren, *op. cit.* p. 227.
[4] I quote from the Antiphonary, with which our MS. agrees. In the Franciscan Book of Hymns there are some variations:—
Patricius sanctus episcopus oret pro nobis omnibus
et miseriatur protinus peccata quæ commisimus.
[5] F. 16. a. 1 (Stokes, *Tripart. Life,* ii. p. 333).

view it may appear impossible that it should be (5) ; for on a reference to the *Liber Hymnorum* we discover that neither the Hymn of Secundinus, nor, indeed, any other poem in the whole collection commenees with these words. The supposition, however, must not be at once set aside, for we find that the *third last stanza* of the hymn, which is alphabetical, begins with the very words of which we are in search. No other liturgical form which I have come across commences with the words " Christus illum " ; these words occur in our office just at the very place where we might expect to have the Hymn of Secundinus, or possibly an extract therefrom ; we may feel fairly confident therefore that in the concluding stanzas of this hymn,[1] which I now transcribe, we have discovered (5) of the office.

Xp̄s illum sibi legit in terris uicarium
qui de gemino captiuos liberat seruitio
plerosque de seruitute quos redemit hominum
innumeros de zabuli obsoluet dominio.

Ymnos cum apocalipsi psalmosque cantat dei
quosque ad edificandum dei tractat populum [2]
quam legem in trinitate sacri credit nominis
tribusque personis unam docetque substantiam.

Zona domini precinctus diebus et noctibus
sine intermissione deum orat dominum
cuius ingentis laboris percepturus premium
cum apostolis regnabit sanctus super israel.

We must now pause for a moment to consider a possible objection of a sceptical critic. Is it possible, at least is it likely it may be asked, that the last three stanzas of a popular hymn should be chanted in an office such as that which we are considering, apart from the preceding portion? The likelihood does not appear to be increased by the circumstance that the verses when separated from their context do not make very obvious or very good sense.

A complete answer to this difficulty is found in a story given by Dr Todd, in his notes to the *Liber Hymnorum*, from the Lebar

---

[1] *L. H.*, i. 21 (i. 44).

[2] On the words " dei populum " the Lebar Brecc has the gloss " popuitrine," which Dr Todd, (*L. H.*, i. 22) takes to mean " popuil trine, the people of the Trinity or the people of God, as in the Latin." This note receives confirmation from, while at the same time it illustrates, a phrase in the collect, " Creator naturarum," preserved in the Book of Mulling (Warren, p. 172), viz, : " has *trinitatis populi tui* . . . preces." In the Book of Deer (fol. 28b, Warren, p. 164) this runs " *trementis populi tui.*" Probably the Book of Mulling gives us the earlier form of the collect, composed by one who thought, if he did not write the rough draft, in Irish, and translated into too literal Latin an idiom of the vernacular speech, which has been removed in the recension given in the Book of Deer. The change would be facilitated by the close resemblance of the two words " trementis " and " trinitatis " in the minuscule Irish character.

Brecc.[1] The story is interesting, albeit somewhat frivolous ; moreover, it not merely serves our immediate purpose of annihilating the sceptic, but throws out a hint which we shall find valuable by and by. I need scarcely apologise therefore for quoting it almost at full length.

St Secundinus (or as the narrator calls him, Sechnall) had read his adulatory hymn to St Patrick, in whose honour it had been written. "When the recitation of the hymn was concluded, Sechnall said, 'I must have reward for it,' said he. 'Thou shalt have it,' said Patrick, 'the number of days that are in a year, the same number of souls of sinners shall go to heaven, for the making of this hymn.' 'I will not accept that,' said Sechnall, 'for I think that too little, and the praise is good.' 'Thou shalt have then,' said Patrick, 'the number of the hairs that are on the casula of thy cowl, the same number of sinners to go to heaven, for the hymn.' 'I will not accept it,' said Sechnall, 'for who is the believer who would not take that number to heaven, although he were not praised by myself, nor by anyone, as thou art.' 'Thou shalt have,' said Patrick, 'seven every Thursday, and twelve every Saturday, to go to heaven, of the sinners of Erinn.' 'It is too little,' said Sechnall. 'Thou shalt have,' said Patrick, 'every one to go to heaven *who sings it lying down and rising up.*' 'I will not accept that,' said Sechnall, 'for the hymn is too long, and it is not every one that can commit it to memory.' '*Its whole grace then,*' said Patrick, '*shall be upon the last three stanzas of it.*' 'Deo gratias,' said Sechnall.[2]

"The Angel promised the same thing to Patrick upon the Cruach, viz., heaven to every one who shall sing *the last three stanzas of it at lying down, and at rising up,* as is [said by the poet],

"A Hymn, which, if sung when alive,
Will be a protecting Lorica unto all."

The interview of St Patrick with the Angel on Croagh Patrick, alluded to in the last sentence, is recounted elsewhere in the Lebar Brecc,[3] but, oddly enough, without the words here quoted from it. But when we turn to the eleventh century *Tripartite Life* we find both stories. The former is abbreviated, but the final saying attributed to St Patrick occurs in it in an even more extravagant form : "'Whosoever of the men of Ireland,' saith Patrick, 'if the *three last chapters or the three last lines, or the three last words,* shall come at death with a pure intention, his soul shall be prepared.'"[4]

[1] *L. H.* i. 33. See also Whitley Stokes, *Tripartite Life,* ii. p. 398 *sqq.*
[2] The introduction to the Hymn of Secundinus is wanting in the Trinity College Book of Hymns, a leaf having probably been lost at the beginning of the MS. The Franciscan copy, however, has an introduction, in which this story is told in a somewhat abbreviated form—the latter portion, on which our argument is built, being identical with what we find in the Lebar Brecc (see Whitley Stokes, *Tripartite Life,* p. 382 *sqq.*)
[3] Stokes *op. cit.,* p. 476 *sqq.*
[4] *Ib.,* i. p. 246 *sq.* On the same page of the *Tripartite Life* demons are represented as saying that a certain "rich countryman . . . . used to repeat two or three stanzas of Patrick's hymn . . . . it was rather a satire than a panegyric on Patrick. Nevertheless by this we have been vanquished."

The other is given at full length, and in a form which satisfies the reference just cited.[1] St Patrick had, by means of his bell, succeeded in ridding Ireland from demons for "seven years and seven months and seven days and seven nights. Then the Angel went to console Patrick." His consolation consisted in offering him a number of boons from heaven in order to induce him to leave the Rick (Croagh Patrick). The conversation between the Angel and the saint is much too long to quote, but a few sentences are here printed.

"'Is there aught else He granteth to me?' saith Patrick. 'There is,' saith the Angel: 'every one who shall sing thy hymn, *from one watch to the other*,[2] shall not have pain or torture.' 'The hymn is long and difficult,' saith Patrick. 'Every one who shall sing it *from Christus illum to the end* . . . . his soul shall not go to Hell.'"

I do not guarantee the historical character of these tales. They demonstrate, however, two facts to which I ask special attention:—
1. That it was customary to substitute for the hymn of Secundinus its last three stanzas, exactly as appears to have been done in our office. 2. That the usual time for reciting the hymn, in whole or in part, was before retiring to rest at night, and after rising in the morning.

We have now advanced so far as to have identified (5) and (7) with the hymn of Secundinus, and a supplementary stanza or antiphon added thereto in two manuscripts. It is natural to guess that the intervening number is another similar addendum to the hymn. Four such supplementary couplets are known,[3] and one of them, found both in the *Lebar Brecc* and the *Liber Hymnorum* (T.C.D. MS.), is sufficiently attested by the few letters still remaining legible to have stood at this place in our MS. The couplet is as follows:—

> In memoria eterna erit iustus
> ab auditione mala non timebit.

The Book of Hymns has done us excellent service. We call it in to help us once more in identifying "Inuitiata quod," etc. (8). No hymn in the book has these for its first words. But we discover that of which we are in search in the *three last stanzas* of the hymn of St Cummain Fota,[4] which are as follows:—

> Inuitiata quo (*sic*) feramus pectora
> regi regnanti ab aeuo in secula
>   alleluia.

[1] Stokes, *Tripartite Life*, p. 114 *sqq.*
[2] A phrase which I do not venture to interpret.
[3] The variety which exists among the five authorities for these four stanzas is remarkable. Numbering those in the Trinity College Book of Hymns 1, 2, 3 respectively, and "Patricius Episcopus" 4, they are given in the following various relative positions in the authorities. *T. C. D. Book of Hymns*, 1, 2, 3 ; *Antiphonary of Bangor*, 2, 4 (the order here is not quite certain) ; *Lebar Brecc*, 1, 2 ; *Franciscan Book of Hymns*, 2, 3, 4 ; *Book of Mulling*, 1, 4.
[4] *L. H.* i. 80 (i. 21).

> Gloria patri atque unigenito
> simul regnanti spiritu cum agio
>   alleluia.
>
> Nimis honorati sunt amici tui deus [1]
> nimis confortatus est principatus eorum
>   alleluia.

Again, be it noticed, the last three stanzas stand in lieu of the whole hymn,—a striking confirmation of the conclusion which has been already reached in the case of St Secundinus' poem. The most sceptical will scarcely take refuge in the supposition that three verses as a substitute for the whole was an indulgence permitted only in the case of a single lorica, and not extended to less famous compositions.

As to the identity of number (9) "[. . . .]icis peccata plurima," to which I now proceed, I have no doubt. Its position, following the concluding stanzas of the hymn of Cummain Fota, renders it probable, if any other indication is found pointing the same way, that it is one of the collects written at the end of this poem in the MSS. And such an indication we have in the words "peccata plurima," which stand as the concluding words in the antiphon [2]—

> Exaudi nos deus per merita apostolorum optima
> ut deleantur pessima nostra peccata plurima.

Our only difficulty is to explain "icis." If my conjecture is correct, these must be the concluding letters of a phrase equivalent to "as far as." "Donec dicis" (a construction quite common in mediæval Latin prose), seems a not improbable guess, though it would have been more satisfactory if it had fitted the space better. The traces of the letter preceding "icis," which still remain, suit "d," and I have therefore inserted these words in my transcript. However the letters "icis," be explained, it is interesting to observe that our MS. here agrees with the Franciscan Codex in omitting the collect "Per merita," etc., which follows "Exaudi nos" in the T. C. D. Book, though the form of expression—"[. . .]icis peccata plurima," for "conrici dead," or "usque in finem"—seems to indicate a consciousness on the part of the scribe that in some copies a second collect or some other subsidiary matter, was found in addition to "Exaudi nos."

Why St Cummain's hymn should have been recited in St Molling's

---

[1] Dr Todd points out (*L. H.*, i. 80) that the last stanza is unmetrical, and is merely Ps. cxxxviii. 17, with one various reading, and therefore cannot have been intended by the author as part of the hymn. It was certainly so regarded, however, by the scribe of the *Lib. Hym.*, as Dr Todd shows, and also, if I have reasoned correctly, by the scribe of the Book of Mulling, whose evidence is probably older by some centuries (see Whitley Stokes, *Goidelica*, 2nd ed., p. 61; *Tripartite Life*, p. ci. *sq.*).

[2] *L. H.* i. 80 (i. 21).

monastery is not very clear, as there appears to be no notice in historical documents connecting him either with Molling or with the district in which he lived. He was, however, famous throughout Ireland, and an elder contemporary of our saint (ob. 661. *Annal. IV. MM.*).[1]

Number (10)—"[. . .]que īmensam," etc.—has next to be considered. We have to look for a stanza whose second word is "immensam," and we at once perceive that the stanza of which we are in quest cannot be the first of a poem. No hymn could have for its first word a substantive followed by the conjunction "que," and in this place q; can scarcely stand for the relative "quæ." Thus we have one further proof, if such were needed, of the custom of reciting the last stanzas of a canticle in place of the whole. A search through the Book of Hymns will quickly convince us that number (10) is an extract from the poem "Ymnum dicat,"[2] ascribed to Hilary of Poictiers.[3] Here are its *last three stanzas* :—

---

[1] We have here, it will be seen, a confirmation of the hypothesis that the page under review, and therefore also the Biblical portion of the MS. as we have it, was written, not by St Molling, but by a scribe who lived a century after Molling's death. It is unlikely that the fame of Cummain should have led to the recitation of his lorica within thirty years of his death, in a monastery with which he had no direct connection ; still less likely that the principle of three stanzas for the whole should have been applied to his poem so soon.

[2] This poem appears to have been used as a lorica. See Whitley Stokes, *Lives of Saints from the Book of Lismore* (*Anecdota Oxoniensia*, 1890), p. viii. *sqq.*, a reference which I owe to Professor Bernard. Compare also the Book of Leinster, fol. 282a (quoted by Dr MacCarthy, *Trans. R.I.A.*, xxvii. 183), and the ancient tract *De Arreis* published in the *Revue Celtique* for Oct. 1894, capp. 26, 32. In both these passages from the Treatise *De Arreis*, the Hymn of St Hilary is enjoined for recitation with the "biait," which Mr Kuno Meyer (p. 492) takes to mean Ps. cxviii. (A.V. cxix.). In this he follows Mr Whitley Stokes (*Book of Lismore*, p. 406). But throughout this treatise the Psalms are regularly cited by their first words *in Latin* (capp. 10, 18 [Ps. l., A. V.li.], 33, etc.) ; and to understand "biait" of this Psalm seems very unhappy in cap. 3—"lauda ⁊ biait ⁊ pater after each psalm." Here we should have Ps. cxviii. referred to by an *Irish* title in the same sentence with "lauda" and "pater," and the direction, in itself improbable, that Ps. cxviii. should be recited after every psalm. If "biait" in capp. 26, 32 were equivalent to the Beatitudes of St Matt. v. (cf. *Book of Lismore*, p. 323), we should have "Ymnum dicat" in juxtaposition with this passage (together with Credo and Pater in cap. 26) as in our fragment. The "chapters" of the "biait" *De Arreis*, 32, *Book of Lismore*, p. 180, may seem to favour the application of the word to the psalm : but the "chapters" may mean either a verse of a psalm or a single beatitude. Thus in the Preface to Ultan's Hymn (*L. H.* i. 60 [i. 14]), as frequently elsewhere, the word "chapters" is applied to the stanzas of the poem—"There are three chapters in it, and four lines in each chapter." If this view of the meaning of "biait" be accepted, an even more remarkable parallel to our office than the passages just mentioned in the treatise *De Arreis* presents itself in the eleventh century "Second Vision of Adamnan" (Lebar Brecc ; see the *Rev. Celt.* xii. 433) : "In the time that is given to God for fasting and prayer it is wrong to think of aught save the benefit of the soul both by preaching and celebration, to wit, a hundred genuflexions with a Biait, a *Magnificat*, a *Benedictus*, and a *Miserere mei Dominus*, and a cross-vigil, with Patrick's Hymn, and the Hymn of the Apostles [*i.e.* the hymn given in the Bangor Antiphonary, f. 4v sqq., or that of Cummain Fota ? see *L. H.* i. 83 (i. 18)], and smiting of hands, and a *Hymnum dicat*, and Michael's Hymn, . . . and they strike their breasts . . . and all say, 'May mercy come to us.'"

[3] *L. H.* ii. 151 (i. 36).

Maiestatemque immensam concinemus iugiter
ante lucem nuntiemus christum regem sacculo.

Ante lucem decantantes christo regi domino
et qui in illum recte credunt regnaturi cum eo.

Gloria patri ingenito gloria unigenito
simul cum sancto spiritu in sempiterna secula.

It will be observed that·what we reckon—in this following both
MSS. of the Book of Hymns and the majority of copies of the *Ymnum
Dicat*—as the last stanza is a doxology. This doxology is in reality
not part of the hymn, as the scribe of the Bangor Antiphonary seems
anxious to hint to us by his punctuation (f. 4*v*). And indeed the same
thing is evident from the fact that two other hymns in the Antiphonary
close with the same words, namely, "Ignis Creator," f. 11*r*,[1] and
"Media noctis," f. 11*v*. A St Gall manuscript of the Hymn, in fact,
omits the doxology, as Professor Bernard, to whom I am indebted for
much of my knowledge of this poem, has been good enough to inform
me.

To make up the customary three stanzas, however, it is necessary to
include it ; and this appears to be the explanation of the words which
I have read "et conglu[ria]." The letters are difficult to decipher
partly because of imperfect formation in the case of the first two or
three, and partly because of a rent in the vellum which crosses the
last three letters of l. 10. It is thus *possible* that for *c* we should
read *a* or *o*, for *o*, *a*; *n* may just as well be *r*; *g* I had for some time
read as *t*, and *u* *may* be *h*. Nevertheless, I am pretty confident that
the reading in my transcript is correct. By way of explanation it is
only necessary to say that "con"="with,"[2] and that "gluria"—
"gloria" by a common substitution of *u* for *o*.[3]

We have already seen that the Hymn of Secundinus is followed by
two antiphons. In like manner the antiphon "Exaudi," etc., follows
the Hymn of Cummain Fota. It may therefore be regarded as not
improbable that number (11) is one of the antiphons belonging to
the Hymn of Hilary (10). Now three such antiphons are known to
exist, and all of them are preserved in the Trinity College Book of
Hymns. They begin respectively, "Te decet ymnus," "Canticis
spiritualibus," "Unitas in." The Franciscan copy has the first two
of these, while, as Professor Bernard tells me, no other known MS.

---

[1] Mr Warren writes (*Ant. of Bang*or, ii. 46), "It will be noticed that this
doxology [to 'Ignis Creator'] is written in fresher ink and by a different hand
from the rest of the hymn." If this be correct my argument is strengthened ;
but it does not seem to be borne out by the facsimile.

[2] Whitley Stokes, "Calendar of Oengus," (*Transactions R.I.A.*, Irish Manuscript Series, vol. i.), p. ccxxxviii.

[3] *Cf.* for this substitution Gilbert, *National Manuscripts of Ireland*, part i.
p. vi. Many examples might be cited from the Book of Mulling, the most
noticeable being the name of the scribe, the first syllable of which is elsewhere
commonly written Mol. "Gluria" seems not to occur elsewhere in the MS.

of the Hymn gives any antiphons. We may fairly expect—though, of course, it must not be assumed as certain—that number (11) is one of the three just mentioned. In deciding among them we have not much to guide us. The space before "usque" is occupied with letters for the most illegible. However, the letter "t" is fairly distinct, and is followed by (apparently) two letters, *forming part of the same word.* This last consideration disposes of the claim of "Te decet." Both the remaining antiphons have the letter "t" in a suitable position, but the preference must be given to the latter, as the marks following "t" may well represent "as," but can scarcely be "icis." If, as is possible, another letter is obliterated between "[Uni]tas" and "usque" it was probably "ı"=in. I am inclined, therefore, to believe that number (11) is the antiphon which I now transcribe [1]:—

Unitas in trinitate te deprecor Domine ut me semper trahas totum tibi uotum uouere.

Of number (2) I can say no more than that it appears to be an Irish rather than a Latin formula. It has a parallel in "Don-fair trocaire" ("May mercy come to us") etc., of the Second Vision of Adamnan.[2]

I have left for the last number (3) "Benedictus," etc., because I cannot be quite confident that my identification of it is correct. At first, one might feel inclined to assume that it is the canticle still usually designated by this name, and used in the ancient Irish Church.[3] This supposition, however, is rendered untenable by the words "usque ioh . . . ," *i.e.,* as far as the word "iohannes," or some case of this word, or the line beginning therewith. For, though the Benedictus has St John the Baptist for its subject, he is not mentioned in it by name. I would suggest that what is meant by the words which I have noted is an extract from the Hymn, attributed to St Columba, beginning "Noli Pater."[4] It consists of seven stanzas, the fourth, fifth, and sixth of which I transcribe.

> Benedictus in secula recta regens regimina
> iohannes coram domino adhuc matris in utero
>
> Repletus dei gratia pro uino atque siccera
>
> Elizabeth et Zacharias uirum magnum genuit
> iohannem baptizam precursorem domini.

The words of the last line, allowing for customary abbreviations, would about suit the spaces of lines 3 and 4 of my transcript, and,

[1] *L. H.* ii. 161. (i. 42). On the extreme rarity of this Antiphon see Warren, *Antiphonary of Bangor,* ii. p. 38.
[2] See p. 153, note 2. Similar forms are found in the treatise *De Arreis,* 12, 21 (*Rev. Celt.,* 1894, p. 495 *sq.*).
[3] *L. H.* ii. 190 (i. 57).
[4] *L. H.* ii. 262 (i. 88).

if they are inserted there, we have an exact description of these stanzas. Again, as before, three stanzas for the whole is the principle of selection. All this points to the correctness of our hypothesis that we have in these stanzas the passage referred to in number (3).[1] One difficulty only has to be met. In all the other cases in which three stanzas were chanted as a substitute for the entire hymn the three last were chosen ; and in the case of the hymn of St Secundinus, the legend to which I have already appealed implies that this was the regular and customary practice. Is it likely that the usage was different with the " Noli Pater "?

I answer that, whether *a priori* likely or not, a departure from this usage does appear to have taken place in the present instance. For the words " Benedictus usque ioh . . ." imply that only a portion of a canticle was to be sung, and that this portion did not conclude with the last verse of the hymn. Had it been so, the ordinary formula which occurs elsewhere in the office *conrici dead*, or its equivalent *usque ī finem*, would have been used.[2] And, moreover, good reason can be given why precisely the portion of the hymn " Noli Pater " above quoted should be sung in preference to the last three stanzas. It is possible that for once the compiler of our office may have paid attention rather to the meaning of the words which he put into the mouths of those who used it than to traditional custom. At least this much is clear : the three stanzas just cited make good sense, and are in themselves a complete poem on St John the Baptist. They are, moreover, the only stanzas in which he is mentioned. Had the last three stanzas been chosen, the extract would have begun in the middle of a sentence and have been absolutely unmeaning as regards its first three lines, while the last stanza would have introduced an entirely new thought, apparently altogether unconnected with what immediately precedes it, and in the hymn itself (supposing that we have it in its original form) more closely associated in its idea with the opening verses. This last the MS. stanza runs thus :—

> Manet in meo corde dei amoris flamma
> ut in argenti uase auri ponitur gemma.

I think, then, that the probability is that the hymn described as " Benedictus usque ioh . . ." is stanzas 4, 5, and 6 of St Columba's " Noli Pater." The probability will be either destroyed or transformed into certainty when (if ever) a few more letters of can be read. Meanwhile we must be content to guess.

---

[1] It ought to be added that the combination of letters which I have read as " tã " is not exactly similar to anything which I have observed elsewhere in the manuscript. For this reason no argument can be based upon it. I have not noticed any other place in which "tam" occurs at the end of a line : but *cf.* the combinations used for "tio," Mar. vii. 8, xv. 41 ; "triam," Mar. vi. 1 ; "tia," Mar. ix. 20 ; "tiam," Matt. xii. 42, Joh. i. 16 ; "sti," Matt. xxv. 24, xxvi. 25, etc.

[2] Yet see p. 152.

Assuming then, for the present, the correctness of our guess, we turn now to the introduction to "Noli Pater"[1] in the *Liber Hymnorum*, in order to discover what the compiler of this collection has to tell us of its origin and use. He ascribes it to the time when King Aedh granted to St Columba the site of a church at Derry. No sooner had the gift been presented than "the town was burned, with everything that was in it. . . . The fire, however, in consequence of its greatness, threatened to burn the whole Daire, so that it was to save it, at that time, that this hymn was composed. Or it was the day of Judgment he had in view, or the fire of the festival of John." Rather a liberal choice! and none the less so because the only allusions to fire in the entire hymn are the word "fulgure" in the first, and "amoris flamma" in the last stanza. It is obvious that all this is mere criticism and guess-work. Clearly the only thing in it all which rests on tradition is the ascription of the poem to St Columba. But we stand on firmer ground in the next sentence, in which the writer tells us of the customs of his own day, and which quite accounts for his anxiety to discover or manufacture allusions to fire in the hymn. "And it is sung," he adds, "[as a protection] against every fire, and every thunderstorm, from that time forth; and whosoever sings it *at bed-time and at rising*, it protects him against lightning, and it protects the nine persons whom he desires [to protect]." It was, then, a lorica, and it was used night and morning.

We have now acquired some general information as to the character of the office which forms the subject of our consideration—not such information as we might have desired, or as we may perhaps hope for in the future, but still sufficient to make a further question worth asking: What was the purpose of the office? when was it used?

If we could restore the first line or two of the page, speculation would probably be needless. The title would supply us at once with the knowledge which we seek. Meanwhile, it will have been noticed that the story from the Lebar Brecc, which I have cited in connection with the hymn of St Secundinus (5), as well as the note with which it concludes, with regard to the angel at the Cruach, and the parallel passages from the *Tripartite Life* convey definitely the information that the hymn was to be said, as a lorica, *at bed-time and rising*. A similar statement, as we have just seen, is made in the *Liber Hymnorum* about the "Noli Pater" (3). These two hints are sufficient to lead to the conclusion that the office was said daily, either at bed-time, as was Compline in the mediæval Church, or in the early morning, like Matins, or rather perhaps, at both these times.[2]

[1] *L. H.*, ii. 259 (i. 87). The introduction in the Franciscan copy is in some respects different. But it has the important words, "Whosoever repeats it on lying down and rising up it saveth him from every fire" (Stokes, *Tripartite Life*, p. civ.). The story is preserved, with the mention of lying down and rising up as the special times of recitation, in the Edinburgh MS. of St Columba's Life. Skene, *Celtic Scotland*, ii. p. 482 *sq.*

[2] Possibly, however, in private. Mr Warren regards this as the more probable view. "I am inclined to think," he writes in the *Academy*, Jan. 26th, 1895,

For this conclusion we find some confirmation from the " Ymnum Dicat " of St Hilary (10). This hymn is marked off by its concluding stanzas as one eminently likely to have been used at an early morning service. The two immediately preceding the doxology, with their twice-repeated " ante lucem," have been quoted above. Before them come the following, not less appropriate for morning use :

> Ante lucem turba fratrum concinnemus gloriam
> qua docemur nos futuri sempiterna secula
>
> Galli cantus [1] galli plausus proximum sentit diem
> nos cantantes et precantes quae futura credimus.

It is therefore no more than one might expect that, in the Book of Cerne, the *Ymnum Dicat* is one of two poems which follow a collection of fourteen prayers and hymns, expressly stated to be intended for use in the morning. And that the hymn was used in the morning may further be implied by the rubric prefixed to it and " Aeterne rerum " in a manuscript cited by Thomasins, " Incipiunt hymni nocturni post mediam noctem ad primum gallicantum." [2]

Evidence, however, which seems at first view to indicate that this poem was used at another time of the day, must not be overlooked. In the Trinity College Manuscript [3] two accounts of the composition of the poem are given. The first, which is somewhat obscure, is as follows :—"Hilarius . . . fecit hunc ymnum xpo ın monte gargani, *after eating dinner* (naprainne = prandium) illio in the robber's house. And after giving thanks to God, the sons of life dwindled post till they were not bigger than infants, as that seemed unto the priest who was with them. An angel came and said to them, Nisi penitentiam egeritis in infernum ibitis. egerunt ergo penitentiam et dedit deus indulgentiam eis per istam laudem *sic nobis conuenit canere post prandium.*" The last words may seem to indicate that it was customary to sing this hymn, after the supposed example of Hilary of Poictiers, at the conclusion of a meal, rather than at bed-time or

p. 83, " that we have here a collection of formulæ . . . intended for private use by a sick person as a sort of compound *lorica* or charm." He thus connects our fragment with the Office of the Visitation of the Sick. Against this view I have given what appear to me decisive reasons in the *Academy* of Feb. 2nd, p. 106, viz. : that it is written at the end of St John's Gospel, the *Visitatio* following St Matthew, and being written by a different scribe. I may now add one or two words. It seems probable, as has just been pointed out, that the Office was intended for *daily* use. This is scarcely consistent with its being said only by the sick. And we find in its various parts nothing specially appropriate to sickness. The hymn "Noli Pater" was a lorica against fire and lightning. Why was protection against these more needed by a sick man than by one who was in good health ?

[1] On the meaning of this phrase see Warren, *Antiphonary of Bangor*, ii. p. 60.

[2] Warren, *op. cit.*, ii. p. 37. It must be remarked, however, that this rubric may suggest rather midnight than the early morning: see Warren as referred to in the last note.

[3] Stokes, *Goidelica*, 2nd ed., p. 93. *L. H.*, ii. 151, 162 (i. 35).

in the early morning.[1] This, however, must not be too readily assumed, for several reasons. *First*, there can be no doubt that the passages already cited in connection with numbers (5) and (3) bear witness to an established usage. To me it seems that the sentence just quoted does not go so far as this. It does not so much justify what *is* done, as state what, in the writer's opinion, *ought* to be done (*conuenit*). It has rather the sound of an apology for the practice of a few persons of special piety, than of a defence of a settled monastic rule. *Secondly*, it is a little doubtful how we are to understand the word "cancre." It may seem natural to take it transitively and supply "istam laudem" (*i.e.*, the hymn of St Hilary) from the preceding clause. It is, however, equally possible that it is used intransitively, in which case no reference whatever is made to the recitation of our hymn. And so Dr Todd appears to render it.[2] *Thirdly*, it is to be noted that the Trinity College copy here lacks the support of the Franciscan manuscript. And *lastly*, admitting that we have here proof of the recitation of the hymn of St Hilary "post prandium," as a regular practice, this does not in any way conflict with the supposition that it was chanted at other times as well.

And, in fact, we have definite proof that this was the case. The poem is mentioned in stanza xxiv of the metrical rule of Ailbe of Emly as follows [3] :—

> "The *Hymnum Dicat* should be sung
> At striking the bell for Canonical Hours,
> All wash their hands carefully,
> The brethren assume their habit."

Thus the regular use of the hymn was not restricted to the conclusion of meals. It does not, indeed, seem very likely that it was recited before every hour, as the first two lines here quoted seem to imply. The mention in the third and fourth lines of the monks performing their ablutions and donning their habit points rather to the first office of the day. And with this the context agrees. The stanza (xxii) next but one before that just quoted runs ·—

> The perfect observance of the Canonical hours
> Is reckoned the chief rule ;
> Correct *Matins*, according to the Divines,
> *End of night, beginning of day.*[4]

---

[1] It might be argued on similar grounds that the Hymn of Secundinus was recited *before* meals. *Trip. Life*, ii. 399.

[2] "Thus it is our duty to sing after dinner :" to which he appends the note, "It (*i.e.* the story) does not appear to have much connection with the duty of *saying grace* after dinner, which, nevertheless, seems to be intended as its moral, from the words 'sic' etc." *L. H.*, ii. 162.

[3] *Irish Ecclesiastical Record*, vol. viii. p. 183. The rule is preserved in a 17th century manuscript at Brussels : Stokes, *Martyrology of Gorman*, p. x.

[4] So, as Mr Stokes kindly informs me, the last line should be rendered. The writer in the *Irish Ecclesiastical Record* has it, "Is at the close and the beginning of day."

Then, in stanza xxiii, the direction is given that no one is to speak
" till the hour of one." This leads us to interpret stanza xxiv as
referring to the "striking of the bell" for the first Canonical hour,
viz., Matins. And, in accordance with this, we have in stanza xxix,—

> It is not permitted to the brethren to depart
> Until the hour of Tierce, etc.

What seems to be meant is that, at the sound of the bell, the
monks recited the *Ymnum Dicat,* and then assembled in the Oratory
for Matins, and that they remained there till Tierce had concluded.
Thus we have here further reason for believing that the hymn of St
Hilary was used after rising from bed in the morning. Would it be
too much to draw the additional conclusion that our office was meant
to be used by the monks in private, in their several cells, before they
met in the Oratory for united worship at the first Canonical hour?
However this may be, our conviction as to the time of recitation of
our office, in spite of the statement in the T.C.D. manuscript, may
remain unshaken.

Setting aside the question of the time, there is one particular in
which all the passages which have been cited agree. They all go to
show that the office, whether used in the morning, after meals, or in
the evening, was said *daily.* And this appears to receive some confirmation from two considerations which I shall now mention.

1. Allusion is made by Adamnan (*Vit. S. Col.*, ii. 9.) to a certain
" hymnorum liber septimaniorum sancti Columbae manu descriptus."
This according to Reeves (*ad loc.*), was " a volume containing hymns
for the various services of each day in the week."[1] If this be so, we
may infer that the daily services consisted in large part of hymns or
canticles. And the inference is borne out by another passage in the
same work. St Columba, as is well known, died just after the bell
for matins had rung. The service proceeded as usual. And then we
are told (iii. 23; Reeves, p. 239),—"*hymnis* matutinalibus termin-
atis"—the body of the saint was borne to the hospice. Again it is
implied that a daily service consisted mainly of hymns. Such is the
character of the office which we are considering, and so far our supposition is confirmed that it was intended for daily use in the monastery.

2. In the life of St Molling, preserved in Marsh's Library, Dublin,
and dating, according to Reeves, from the 14th century, the following
narrative occurs.[2] " The King [Fianachta, from whom St Molling
had procured the remission of the Borromean tribute by a trick] sent

---

[1] According to the Lebar Brecc Preface to the *Altus*, St Columba received from
Pope Gregory the Great " the Hymns of the week, that is [a book with] hymns
for each *night* of the week " (Reeves' *Vit. Col.*, p. 318 *sq.*), which is not without
its bearing on the question of the time of day at which our office was used. The
Preface in the *Liber Hymnorum* (*L. H.*, ii. 221 [i. 63]) omits the latter clause.
[2] I quote from *The Ancient Life of St Molyng, being translation of an old
Manuscript preserved at Marsh's Library, Dublin, with Notes and Traditions,* by
P. O'L. Dublin, James Duffy and Sons, p. 19 *sq.* A description of the so-called

the army with anger after St Molyng to kill him together with his people. The holy senior Molyng, knowing this, bade his own people to proceed more speedily on their way, praying to the Lord ; and he himself began a sacred poem in the Scotic (Irish) language, in which he named many saints, praying to them and singing their praises, commencing with a virgin and finishing with the same—that is, first making mention of the most Blessed Virgin Brigid, and at the end using the name of Mary the Mother." A little further on the writer adds, " That sacred canticle of St Molyng is always kept with honour in Ireland, and men of good will, undertaking a journey, sing it ; and through the favour of St Molyng, and the rest of the saints whose memory is sung in it, the Omnipotent God sets them free from divers dangers." [1]

If the hymn was, as the writer of this Life asserts, kept in honour throughout the whole country, it must have been above all sung in St Molling's own monastery at St Mullins. Why, then, is no mention made of it, so far as can now be discovered, in our office ? Perhaps because it was in the Irish tongue, which may have been sufficient to exclude it from the service of the Church.[2] A more probable reason, however, may be assigned. It was a lorica intended, not for daily, but for occasional use, namely, at the commencement of a journey. It would therefore be excluded from a daily office. Such then, we again infer, was the nature of the service which we have been considering.

To sum up. We have recovered in these obscure, scarcely legible lines of the Book of Mulling a sketch of—or, to use a more technical word, a kind of directory for—what appears to have been a daily office used night or morning in the monastery of St Molling of Ferns, in the early part of the 9th century. It is, I believe, the only sample of a daily service of the Ancient Irish or Scottish Church known to exist. It, is, undoubtedly, unlike the Irish Missal, of home manufacture. It certainly does not inspire us with much respect for the liturgical instinct of our fathers in the Faith, but it

---

" Book of Kilkenny," of which this Life forms a part, may be found in a paper by the late Bishop Reeves, in the *Proceedings of the Royal Irish Academy*, second series, vol. i.—Polite Literature and Antiquities, p. 339, " On a MS. volume of Saints—chiefly Irish—now in Primate Marsh's Library, Dublin, commonly called the Codex Kilkenniensis." See also his *Life of St Columba*, p. xxv. *sq.*, where it is dated " thirteenth century."

[1] The Hymn is given in the Book of Leinster (facsimile edition, p. 308) and has been printed by Mr S. H. O'Grady in his *Silva Gadelica*, vol. i. p. 389 *sq.* Mr Whitley Stokes has published a translation of the first stanza in the *Revue Celtique*, t. xiii. p. 117, and the concluding stanza (misplaced in the Book of Leinster) he has been good enough to put into English for me. These stanzas in their English dress are as follows :—
O Brigit, bless our way, that evil come not to us on our journey,
O nun from full Liffey, may we safely reach home by thine aid '

Come to protect us, O Mary, O Mother of the King [of heaven]
O E'mnat, O splendid Fidnab, O fair Colmnat and O Brig !

[2] Cf. Warren, *Liturgy and Ritual*, p. 155 *sqq.*

has its interest as one of the not numerous examples of their work in this department.

It may be well to add a scheme of this service, so far as I have succeeded in restoring it. It consists of the following parts (following an illegible portion at the beginning) :—

1. The song of the B.V.M. (*Magnificat*).
2.   ?
3. Stanzas 4, 5, and 6 of the Hymn of St Columba (*Noli Pater*).
4. A lection from the beginning of St Matthew v., followed apparently by a formula not yet identified.
5. The last three stanzas of the Hymn of St Secundinus (*Audite Omnes*).
6 and 7. Two stanzas supplementary to this hymn (*In memoria* and *Patricius Episcopus*).
8. The last three stanzas of the Hymn of Cummain Fota (*Celebra Juda*).
9. The Antiphon "Exaudi," etc., appended to this hymn.
10. The last three stanzas of the Hymn of St Hilary of Poictiers (*Hymnum dicat*).
11. The Antiphon "Unitas in Trinitate," etc.
12. The Apostles' Creed.
13. The Lord's Prayer, followed possibly by
14. The Collect "Ascendat oratio," etc.

All the parts of this office, so far as they have been identified (with the exception, of course, of 4), are found in the *Liber Hymnorum*, while, of 14 Latin Hymns in the two fasciculi of this book published by Todd, at least five are recited : a valuable proof of the use of the collection in Ireland at least a century or two before either of the MSS. of it now extant was written.[1] At the same time, the copies used at St Mullins in the 9th century must have differed considerably from both of those which we now possess. Thus, our manuscript agrees with the Franciscan copy against its rival in the insertion of "Patricius episcopus" (though with a different text) after the Hymn of Secundinus, while it sides with the T. C. D., and against the Franciscan copy, in adding "In memoria." Again, with the Franciscan copy it omits "Per merita," etc., after the Hymn of Cummain Fota, while it differs from both, but most widely from the Franciscan, in giving "Unitas in Trinitate" as the *only* Antiphon after the Hymn of St Hilary.

One or two words may be added before leaving our Liturgical Fragment. It will be observed that I argue for the existence of a practice in the ancient Celtic Church of singing three, usually the last three, stanzas of certain hymns in place of the whole. And I imagine the proof already given is sufficient; but I am tempted to conclude this chapter by quoting some further passages, which not merely corroborate my reasoning, but themselves receive a fresh meaning when the prevalence of the practice referred to is borne in mind. The first of these is from the Preface to the Hymn of Ultan

[1] For their date see Stokes, *Trip. Life*, vol. i. p. ci *sq.*

in praise of Brigid.[1] "Audite virgines laudes," says the writer, "is its beginning. The alphabetical order is in it. . . . Dicunt alii, that this hymn was originally long, but (that) there remain here only four chapters of it, viz., the first chapter *and the last three chapters*, causa brevitatis." [2] This is exactly as it should be. The first "chapter" would be cited, no doubt, as giving the title; the last three as being, in some sort, equivalent to the whole.

That this was actually the case we are further assured when we glance at the hymn as printed by Dr Todd.[3] First come three stanzas beginning respectively with the letters X ("Xps in nostra insola") Y Z, and then the stanza—

> Audite uirginis laudes sancta quoque merita
> etc.   etc.

This stanza Dr Todd gives excellent reason for believing not to have belonged to the original poem, in spite of the assertion of the scholiast that some reported it to be the original first verse. How, then, are we to account for its presence here? Most readily. The end of a poem in the Book of Hymns is regularly indicated by repeating under its last line the first word or two of its first stanza. Thus, after the stanza "Zona," etc., of the Hymn of Secundinus are written the words "Audito omnes," [4] separating the poem itself from the supplementary verses which follow. In like manner, the close of Ultan's Hymn would be marked in the MSS. by writing "Audite," with or without some of the following words of the first stanza, under the last line. When the custom of reciting only the last three stanzas produced its natural result, and the scribes only wrote, and finally only knew, these stanzas, in all likelihood the words "Audite" or "Audite virginis" would still be preserved as indicating the title of the hymn. Some scribe, seeing the words in his exemplar, and knowing another poem beginning with the same words[5] (though not written with the same metre or assonances), supplied, as he supposed, the missing portion of the stanza by tacking on to the phrase which remained words from the other hymn.

Dr Todd, it is true, will not admit this explanation. "The suggestion," he says (p. 58), "of the scholiast's preface, that the hymn

---

[1] *L. H.*, i. 60 (i. 14).

[2] In the Franciscan copy the first two sentences are found as here quoted, but the last sentence is omitted. Whitley Stokes, *Tripartite Life*, vol. i. p. civ. *sq.*

[3] *L. H.*, i. 57 (i. 14)

[4] The Franciscan copy has the one word "Audite."

[5] Hymns beginning with "Andito" were not uncommon. Out of twelve poems in the Antiphonary of Bangor, two begin with this word, and another has it for the first word of its second verse, the first verse being prefatory (ff. 13 *v*, 15 *v*, 17 *v*). These three hymns are the only strictly alphabetical compositions in the book, for that on f. 36 *v* is scarcely an exception. *Cf.* Mone, *Lateinische Hymnen*, iii. 242, "Mehrere irische Hymnen fangen mit Audite an. S. *Muratori* anecdota 4, 136 flg., vielleicht nach Deuteron. 32, No. 671, 1." Other examples are given by Warren, *Antiph. of Bang.*, ii. p. 52.

originally consisted of a capitulum for every letter of the alphabet, is
unnecessary." He forgets that the scholiast, by his "dicunt alii,"
informs us that he is not making a suggestion, but handing on a
tradition. And the tradition, especially when supported by the considerations which I have already adduced, is excellent evidence for
the fact. At the very least, the passage cited shows this, that to the
writer of the Preface there was nothing strange in a poem being
abbreviated by the very peculiar method which we know was applied
to St Secundinus' Hymn.[1] The statement[2] that "Alphabetical poems
containing stanzas for the last three letters of the alphabet only were
common" does not in the least invalidate this testimony, unless we
have direct evidence that these are complete, and not merely "abbreviated" hymns. It is, indeed, very likely that many of them are
in their original form; but this is exactly what one might expect, for
when it became fashionable in repeating the hymns to neglect all the
stanzas but three, the fashion would very quickly follow among hymn-
writers of economising labour by writing no more than the three
stanzas which were all they could expect to be sung. The very
existence, in fact, of a large number of hymns, such as Dr Todd
refers to, is a signal confirmation of the thesis which I have endeavoured to establish, rather than an argument on the other side.

But Dr Todd's main proof, that the writer of the preface was
incorrect in his account of Ultan's Hymn, is of much interest—none
the less so because it completely breaks down in view of the results
at which we have arrived. He appeals (p. 55) to the Basle MS. A.
vii. 3,[3] in which occurs what "is probably a part of an ancient
office" in which St Ultan's Hymn was recited. After two hymns
recited in the office have been given at full length, the words
follow :—

item xps in nostra insola que uocatur. ·

This is proof, according to Todd, that by the compiler of the office
the line "Christus in nostra insula" was regarded as the beginning of
the hymn. Those who have assented to my reasoning with reference

---

[1] Todd seems to have been nearer the true explanation of the phenomena of
Ultan's Hymn and others of the same class than he was himself aware. He
remarks (p. 55, note 2), "The indulgence granted to the repetition of the
Hymn of St Patrick was ultimately conceded to the last three verses of it," and
then he asks, "Was it on this principle that the Hymn to St Brigid contained
only the verses beginning with the last three letters of the alphabet?" If for
"contained" he had written "was represented by" the question might have
been answered in the affirmative.

[2] For the correctness of which some evidence would have been welcome. The
only instance given by Dr Todd is a hymn which contains five stanzas. No
instance, so far as I have observed, is met with in the Bangor Antiphonary or
(with the exception of that now before us) in the Book of Hymns.

[3] This manuscript is also described by F. Keller in his *Bilder und Schriftzüge*,
published in the *Mittheilungen der Antiquarischen Gesellschaft in Zürich*, vii.
bd. iii. heft, p. 86, by Bishop Forbes, *Arbuthnott Missal*, p. xli. *sqq.*, and by F.
E. Warren, *Liturgy and Ritual*, p. 185. Some interesting remarks upon it will
also be found in Berger's *L'Histoire de la Vulgate*, p. 115.

to the use of the hymns of SS. Secundinus, Columba, Cummain, and Hilary, in our office, will at once perceive that this argument is absolutely worthless. All our experience tends to show that it is quite unsafe to assume that hymns, when used in the Offices, were recited in their entirety.[1] And in fact we have here a fresh and most unexpected instance of the principle for which I have been contending. The hymn of Ultan is represented in the Office preserved in the Basle MS. by its *last three stanzas only.*

Having gone so far, it is worth while to notice how closely our Office and that of the Basle MS. agree in character. Both consist principally of hymns; in both we find three stanzas of a hymn used instead of the whole; in both the hymns are followed (in some cases at least) by appropriate collects; and in both there are lections, in ours from Holy Scripture, in the other from the apocryphal Epistle of Christ to Abgarus. Our Office, however, is clearly the fuller and more elaborate of the two.

Our second illustrative passage shall likewise be taken from a preface in the Book of Hymns. In that which is prefixed to the hymn of St Columba, written, as we are told, to supply the deficiencies of his celebrated "Altus" and beginning "In te Christe," our attention is arrested by these words :—[2]

Columcille made this hymn. . . . But some say that it was not Columcille at all that composed it, [except] from "Christus redemptor" to (?) [the words] "Christus crucem," and that is the reason why many repeat that part.

The portion, which we are here informed was alone repeated by many stands as follows[3] :—

> Christus redemptor gentium christus amator uirginum
> christus fons sapientium christus fides credentium
>
> Christus lorica militum christus creator omnium
> christus salus uiuentium et uita morientium
>
> Coronauit exercitum nostrum cum turba martirum
> christus crucem ascenderat christus mundum saluauerat.

These *three stanzas*, therefore, according to the testimony of the scholiast, were in his day recited by many in place of the entire hymn. Once again, however, Dr Todd rejects the assertion of the writer of the preface. "Perhaps," he somewhat strangely remarks,[4] "the meaning may be" the stanzas which we have copied, together with the two which follow them and form the conclusion of the poem. But when a man makes a plain statement, why should he mean some-

---

[1] This applies also to Psalms. See the tract *De Arreis* (*Rev. Celt.*, Oct. 1894), cap. 13, where the words "In manus usque veritatis" are doubtless a description of the single verse Ps. xxx. 6 (A. V. xxxi. 5).

[2] *L. H.*, ii. 252 (i. 84). W. Stokes, *Goidelica*, 2nd ed., p.103. Square brackets enclose words the original of which is illegible in the manuscript.

[3] *L. H.*, ii. 257 (i. 85). [4] *L. H.*, ii. 253.

thing entirely different? It will certainly be wiser to accept the scholiast's account of the customary practice with regard to the recitation of the hymn, while we feel quite at liberty to dispute the theory held by him or others as to the origin of this practice. It seems far from improbable that, according to prevalent usage, the three stanzas printed above were regarded as the equivalent of the poem, and that *as a result* of the special honour thus assigned to them they alone came to be regarded as St Columba's composition. But however this may be, there can be little doubt that we have here another instance of the substitution of three stanzas for the whole. And it is an instance of peculiar interest from the circumstance that the three stanzas selected are not those with which the hymn concludes. This is a strong confirmation of our identification of the third element of our office with three stanzas—but not the last three—of the hymn " Noli Pater." In the case of the " In te Christe," the selection of three medial stanzas is established. And the coincidence is perhaps worth remarking, that for both of these poems Columban authorship is claimed by the scholiast.

Finally, we may be allowed to add two or three extracts, the meaning of which certainly needs elucidation. The gloss which the investigation now brought to an end enables us to put upon them will, it may be hoped, be obvious. The first is from the *Annals of the Four Masters*[1] (A.D. 978):—

Mugroin, Abbot of Hy, scribe and bishop, *skilled in the three*[2] *verses* [died].

The second is from the " Colloquy of the Ancients," a story preserved in several manuscripts, and among them the Book of Lismore[3]:—

To stay him therefore came Finn, in whose manner of staying an *óglaech* were special properties, one of them being that if on the mutineer he made *but three quatrains* he would incontinently become reconciled.

With this sentence we may well compare the account of the battle of Cúil Dremne in the same book, a portion of which is thus paraphrased by Mr Whitley Stokes[4]:—

The hostile armies meet at Cúil Dremne, and Diarmait's wizard makes an *airbe druad* ("druid's fence") between the two armies. *Colomb cille chants three stanzas* . . . . and one of his men overturns the druid's fence, leaps across it, and is at once killed. Battle is then joined, and Diarmait is beaten.

[1] O'Donovan renders the italicized words "the most learned of the three divisions" : the " three divisions" being Ireland, Mann, and Alba.
[2] Reeves (*Ecclesiastical Antiquities of Down*, etc., p. 134) supplies after " three " the words "kinds of."
[3] S. H. O'Grady, *Silva Gadelica*, ii. p. 202.
[4] *Lives of Saints from the Book of Lismore*, p. xxviii. sq.

NOTE TO CHAPTER VIII.

After these sheets had been printed off the writer received a kind communication from Miss Margaret Stokes, who has recently examined the device treated of in the following chapter. She has discovered near the Cross of Christ and His Apostles what seems to be an indication of the entrance to the cashel, reminding us, as she remarks, of the words "I am the door." This is a signal confirmation of Mr Olden's theory of the meaning of the device. A paper was lately read by Miss Stokes before the Royal Irish Academy on this device, and will appear, together with a facsimile (which will of course supersede the rough sketch on the opposite page), in the *Proceedings* of that Society.

CHAPTER VIII.

THE LAST PAGE—II. THE CIRCULAR DEVICE.

" The circular device with inscriptions" mentioned by Mr West-wood in his description of the Book of Mulling is the subject of the chapter upon which we are now entering. It occupies the lower part of the page, the upper portion of which contains the fragment discussed in the last chapter. Let me premise that about this circular device I have little to say beyond describing it as accurately as possible, and suggesting one or two questions, which I shall be obliged to confess my inability to answer satisfactorily.

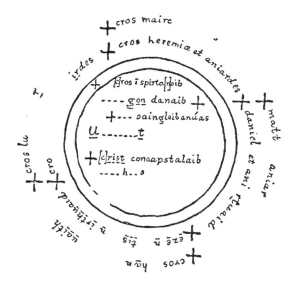

Unlike the Liturgical piece which we have been considering, this device was clearly intended to occupy the whole width of the page, the common centre of the two circles, which are its most prominent feature, being only about ½ centimetre to the left of the middle of the page. In the diagram which I now give, the dimensions of the original are preserved. It must be understood, however, that it is only a diagram, and not a facsimile, though no doubt it will be found sufficiently accurate for practical purposes. I have replaced the Irish characters by letters of a more familiar form, and in the writing outside the circles have inserted no letters or marks which I have not actually read, with more or less certainty.

In the manuscript the diameter of the inner circle is 3·6 centimetres, of the outer, 4·2 centimetres.

I now transcribe the various lines of writing, numbering them for convenience of reference, and conjecturally supplying illegible letters where it seems certain that such letters existed.

1. (Outer circle of writing).	+cros mairc　　[ande]s　　+matt　　　aniar +cros [io]han　　[h]uaith　+cros lu[c – –] [anoi]r
2. (Inner circle of writing).	[ano]irdes+cros heremiæ et aniardes+daniel et aniartuaid+eze[c]h[iel –]tis[– – a]n[o]irthu- aid +cros [esaiæ]

Taking next the lines within the circles in their order we have—

3. +[c]ros I spirta [n]oib
4. – – – – – gon danaib+
5. + – – oaingleib anúas
6. U – – – –t.
7. +[c]rist conaapstalaib
8. – – – –h – – s

l. 1. At the word [ande]s is a rent in the vellum, which the binders have remedied (?) by pasting a piece of paper over the word. It consists of about five letters and the tail of í (s) is distinct. In very good light the last five letters of [h]uaith are almost certain.
l. 2. There are five or six letters after "ezechiel," but "tis" is most uncertain, especially the two last letters; t may be c. See further below.
l. 5. The correct reading of the legible words was first given by Mr Whitley Stokes in the *Academy*, August 1, 1896, p. 82. I think I can see the cross at the beginning of the line, followed by about three letters now illegible: but these must be regarded as very uncertain.

The following is a translation :—

1. +Cross of Mark　　　　south　　+Matthew　　　　　　west
　　+cross of John　　　　north　　+cross of Luke　　　　east
2. On the south-east+cross of Jeremiah, and on the south-west+Daniel, and on the north-west+Ezekiel [– – –], on the north-east+cross of [Isaiah].
3. +Cross of the Holy Spirit.
4. – – – – – – – – – with gifts+
5. + – – with angels from above.
6. ?
7. +Christ with his apostles.
8. ?

The most obvious thing to remark about this device is that it is a map or plan of some kind. This is made quite clear by the writing outside the circles, in the inner line of which the positions of the pairs of crosses are marked as south-east, etc., while in the outer the cardinal points are noted. That our figure, then, is a map or plan appears to be certain, and this is almost the only fact which one can hold to have been established with any strong probability as to its purpose and character. I mention it here for the sake of its bearing on a problem which at once suggests itself. At what point ought we to begin to read the two outer circles of writing (ll. 1, 2)?

In answer to this question, we observe, first of all, that two starting points are excluded : those, namely, which are marked as S.W. and N.W. respectively. The word " and," which in each of these cases precedes the designation of the position of the cross, at once disposes of their claim. Our choice, therefore, is limited to the S.E. and N.E. points. Taking the former, in reading line 1, we begin with the cross of Mark, and find the evangelists named in the order, Mark, Matthew, John, Luke. In the other case the order will be Luke, Mark, Matthew, John. Now in the Book of Mulling itself the Gospel of St John was certainly intended to be placed last, as we know from the fact that it is followed by the colophon. This may seem to decide in favour of beginning the reading with the cross of Luke, and it may appear, moreover, to yield evidence on the question of the order of the Synoptic Gospels in the Book of Mulling—of which, apart from this, we know nothing.

On the other hand, it must be observed that if this conclusion be correct, the order of the Gospels in our manuscript is most unusual [1]—absolutely unique, I believe, among Irish codices, which, with the exception of the Codex Usserianus, agree in this particular, in all recorded cases, with the A.V. Again, we must bear in mind that the device under consideration is a plan, and that the crosses marked on it, no doubt, represent actual stone or wooden crosses erected on the ground. Now it is probable that these crosses were planted in the order which the person who erected them was accustomed to regard as the correct order of the evangelists after whom they were named. But it is quite possible that, in setting up his crosses, he proceeded from right to left, while the scribe who indicated their places on his map could only write from left to right. If we reckon from right to left we get the conventional order Matthew, Mark, Luke, John, which appears much more likely than the other to have been that adopted by the scribe of our manuscript. The result of our argument, then, is this : The question to which we addressed ourselves is left unanswered ; it is impossible to decide whether the scribe began ll. 1, 2 at the S.E. or N.E. point ; but on the more important problem of the order of the Gospels in the Book of Mulling we have shed some little light : it must either have been Luke, Mark, Matthew, John, or Matthew, Mark, Luke, John, and more probably the latter I shall presently adduce evidence which will, as I think, convert this probability into something very nearly approaching to certainty.

One other fact may be noted with reference to ll. 1, 2. It is

---

[1] The order, Luke, Mark. Matthew, John, is not mentioned by Gregory, *Prolegomena to Tischendorf's N.T.*, p. 137 *sq.*

obvious that some sort of parallelism is suggested between the four evangelists and certain Old Testament worthies—probably the four greater prophets. It is not very easy to guess what may have been the special features which suggested a comparison between St Mark and Jeremiah, between St Matthew and Daniel; but that the fashion of pairing together saints of different eras, " who were of one manner of life," was congenial to the Celtic mind is manifest from the lists preserved in the Book of Leinster and elsewhere.[1] In these lists prominent Irish saints are compared with saints of the Universal Church, especially those mentioned in the New Testament.[2] It is quite possible that similar comparisons may have been instituted between saints of the Old and New Covenants, and that of these comparisons the device before us supplies one example.[3] Possibly those who are versed in the literature of the early Celtic Churches may be able to cite other similar instances.

I must content myself with a reference to one passage for a due appreciation of the importance of which the preceding paragraphs will have prepared us. It is the prayer of Colga Ua Duinechda, given in the Yellow Book of Lecan (T.C.D. H. 2. 16), col. 336.[4] This manuscript belongs to the fourteenth century, but the prayer is much older—probably contemporary with its reputed author, not long after whose death the Book of Mulling was written. This at least appears to be the view of Dr MacCarthy,[5] who gives the following translation [6] of its first two clauses:—

> I beseech with Thee, O Jesus holy, thy four Evangelists who wrote thy Gospel divine, to wit, Matthew, Mark, Luke, John.
> I beseech with Thee thy four chief prophets who foretold thy Incarnation, Daniel, and Jeremias, and Isaias and Ezechiel.

The whole structure of the prayer makes it clear that, by naming in succession the evangelists and the major prophets, the writer intended to suggest a parallel between them. The prayer is, in fact, made up of a long series of pairings of the same kind. Thus, in the three following clauses we have the nine grades of the heavenly

---

[1] First printed by Todd, L. H., i. 69 sq. Compare Olden, The Church of Ireland, in the "National Churches" series, p. 425; Stokes, Martyrology of Gorman, p. xvii.

[2] It is worthy of remark that one Old Testament saint—"Job of the Patience" —is mentioned.

[3] It must not, however, be supposed that comparisons between the evangelists and the major prophets are peculiarly Celtic. Examples are in fact numerous in mediæval art. See Berger, L'Histoire de la Vulgate, pp. 210, 248, 296; and especially Mrs Jameson, Sacred and Legendary Art, 7th ed., vol. i. p. 140. Cf. also Ebner, Quellen und Forschungen zur Geschichte und Kunstgeschichte des Missale Romanum in Mittelalter; Iter Italicum, p. 407, sqq.

[4] The Prayer is found also in the Brussels MS., 5100-4. Stokes, Martyrology of Gorman, p. ix.

[5] Trans. R.I.A., xxvii. 156.

[6] Ib., p. 178 Mr Whitley Stokes (ub. sup.) translates the first clause somewhat differently: "I appeal to Thee, thou holy Jesus, by the four evangelists," etc. But our argument is not affected by the variation in rendering.

and earthly churches set over against each other, and immediately afterwards the twelve patriarchs, the twelve minor prophets, and the twelve apostles, etc.

Next let us observe that the evangelists are named in the usual order, which we have already concluded to be probably that of the Book of Mulling, viz.: Matthew, Mark, Luke, John. Moreover, the prophets are named in the order, Daniel, Jeremiah, Isaiah, Ezekiel. This can only be because, the evangelists being compared individually with the prophets, Matthew corresponded to Daniel, Mark to Jeremiah, Luke to Isaiah, and John to Ezekiel; or because, the two groups being compared together as groups, Daniel, Jeremiah, etc., was the customary order of the greater prophets in Bibles of the period. In either case, Daniel standing under Matthew in our figure and Jeremiah under Mark, we may safely infer that Isaiah stood under Luke and Ezekiel under John. When we turn back to the MS. we find this conjecture verified in the case of Ezekiel (as shown above l. 2), though none of the letters of this name could have been read without the assistance of the hint derived from Colga's Prayer.

But further, this prayer helps us a good deal towards understanding the purpose of the exterior pairs of crosses. They must be equivalent to an invocation of prophets and evangelists. On the hypothesis that the device is a plan, we may well believe that the erection represented by the circles and the interior crosses was, as it were, placed under their protection by planting round it crosses in their honour. And here it may not be amiss to quote, by way of illustration, the closing words of the Prayer of St John the Evangelist [1]: "amen matheus marcus lucas iohannes." On which Dr Todd remarks, "This is a curious example of the ancient custom of invocating the names of the Evangelists, as a protection against evil."

Yet again, there can now remain no doubt as to the order in which the crosses were erected: whoever planted them proceeded "left-wise"—i.e., in a direction contrary to the diurnal course of the sun.[2] We should certainly not have expected this. The Cathach of the O'Donnells was to be "sent thrice *right-wise* round the army of the Cinell Conaill" in order that they might be assured of victory in battle.[3] And, to take an instance which, as will presently appear, is even more to our purpose, when the angel Victor marked out the site of the future Church of Armagh "He went *right-hand-wise* round the rampart, and Patrick behind him with his Bachall Isu in his hand, and Ireland's elders a-chanting around him."[4] But, indeed, refer-

---

[1] *L.H.*, ii. 270 (i. 91).
[2] A fact which was pointed out to me by the Hon. John Abercromby.
[3] O'Donnell, quoted by Reeves, *Vit. Col.*, p. 250.
[4] Lebar Brecc Homily on St Patrick, Stokes, *Tripartite Life*, ii. p. 472 *sqq.* Mr Stokes' account of the practice here exemplified is scarcely justified by the evidence. He seems (*op. cit.*, i. p. clxxii) to class it as a method of showing

ences to the right-hand turn in Irish literature are very numerous.[1]
The left-hand turn is less frequently alluded to, but some examples
may be cited.

In the story of Cuchulainn's death [2] we are told that "Cuchulainn
went to him (his horse). And *thrice did the horse turn his left side*
to his master . . . Then Cuchulainn reproached his horse, saying that
he was not wont thus to deal with his master . . . And Leborcham
met him and besought him not to leave them . . . But he *turned his
chariot to the right*" and proceeded on his way. Further on, somewhat similar omens of his approaching death are related.

Again in the "Seél Baili Binnbérlaig" [3] we read : "They saw the
horrible apparition(?) of a man coming towards them from the south
. . . *His left was towards the land.*"

Once more, the Book of Ballymote, f. 361a, has the following
story [4]:—"Through pride, once on a time Boann (well knowing the
well's virtue) said that there existed not any occult power able to
deform her beauty, and so visited the spring : thrice she walked left-
handed round it ; whereupon out of it three volumes of water spout
forth over her and despoil her of a thigh, an arm, and one eye ; then
to hide her disgrace she turned away and fled sea-ward, the water
following her to the estuary of the Boyne."

Fourthly, the Book of Rights [5] mentions as one of the five prohibi-
tions of the King of Laighin (Leinster), "To go round Tuath
Laighean left-hand-wise on Wednesday."

And lastly, in the narrative of the Siege of Howth [6] we find the
reverence, and says that it consists in walking "with the right hand towards the
person or thing *to be honoured.*"

[1] Besides those mentioned in the text I have observed the following : The
right-hand circuit of Ireland is mentioned in *Egert.* 1782 (O'Grady, *Silva Gadelica*,
ii. 86), in the Book of Ballymote (*O'Grady*, ii. 374) in the poem "The Circuit of
Ireland by Muircheartach MacNeill," and in the legendary tale prefixed to it in
O'Donovan's Edition, p. 21 ; a saint walks right-wise round an army to give it
victory, Stokes' *Lives of Saints from Book of Lismore*, p. 240 (*cf.* the hag's song
in *Egert.* 1782, O'Grady, ii. p. 434, and that of Caeilte in the Book of Lismore,
O'Grady, ii. 210) ; Senan and the angels consecrate an island by going round it
right-hand-wise (Stokes, *op. cit.*, p. 214). While apparently the right hand *turn*,
as distinct from the right hand circuit is referred to in the Yellow Book of Lecan,
col. 690 *sq.* (*Revue Celtique*, ii. 198), in the "Voyage of Snedgus and Mac Riagla"
from the same book (*Rev. Celt.*, ix. 19), in the "Colloquy of the Ancients" from
the Book of Lismore (O'Grady, ii. 262), in the Life of Findchua from the same
(Stokes, *op. cit.*, p. 236), in the Tripartite Life of St Patrick (Stokes' *Tripartite
Life*, p. 39) and in the parallel passage of the Lebar Brecc Homily on St
Patrick (Stokes, *op. cit.*, p. 453). On the whole subject see Sir Samuel Ferguson,
On the Ceremonial Turn called "Desiul" (*Proceedings R. I. A.*, 2nd ser., Ant. I.
p. 355), and Stokes, *Lives of Saints from Book of Lismore*, pp. 348, 405 *sq. Cf.*
also W. Simpson, *The Buddhist Praying Wheel*. No doubt many other instances
might be added.
[2] Abridged from the Book of Leinster by Mr W. Stokes, *Revue Celtique*, iii. 175.
[3] From Harl. 5280, f. 48a ; *Rev. Celt.*, xiii. 224.
[4] S. H. O'Grady, *Silva Gadelica*, ii. p. 520. The same story is narrated in the
Bodleian *Dinnshenchas*, 36 (*Folk-Lore*, vol. iii. p. 34).
[5] O'Donovan's Edition, p. 3. So in the Edinburgh *Dinnshenchas*, 68, one of
the "three tabus of Tailtiu" is "looking at it over one's left shoulder when
coming from it" (*Folk-Lore*, iv. 69).
[6] From the Book of Leinster, pp. 114b-117a ; *Revue Celtique*, viii. 49.

following: "In Ireland there dwelt a hard, merciless man, to wit, Atherne the Urgent of Ulster . . . He was so called from going by Conor's counsel, on a (bardic) circuit. This is the way he went at first, *left-hand-wise about Ireland* till he made the round of Connaught," etc.

These passages may suffice to show that the left-hand circuit was regarded as presaging evil. Our attempt, whatever it may be worth, to explain the fact that it is depicted in our manuscript must be postponed to a later stage of the present inquiry.

A slight difficulty remains to be noticed. The extract from Colga has enabled us to read the name of Ezekiel under that of St John ; but we might have expected to find the word Ezekiel without any addition, just as we have Daniel and Jeremiah. On the contrary, between "ezechiel" and "anoir" there are about six letters, namely, 't' (or 'c') and (but these are very doubtful) 'is'—this group of three being preceded and followed by one or two which are illegible. This may be the name of a second person coupled with Ezekiel, or more probably a descriptive epithet of the latter. What the epithet may be I am unable to guess.

But to proceed. We have seen that the device under consideration is a map or plan. But a map, we at once ask, of what? To this question I can give no answer which commends itself to me as altogether satisfactory. A suggestion, however, which has been made to me by Mr Olden is plausible, and at least deserves mention. He is inclined to think that the circles represent the Rath of St Molling, within which were his ecclesiastical buildings ; the concentric circles perhaps indicating a double or even triple rampart, as in many royal residences. The settlement of an ecclesiastic, he says, his "city" (*cathair, civitas*), was exactly like that of a native chieftain, except that it would be furnished with crosses as an indication of its purpose. In support of this statement he kindly refers me to the *Life of St Fintan or Munnu*, in which we read that, when the Saint was in the woods (in the Barony of Forth, Co. Wexford), he saw three men, clothed in white garments, who told him, "Here will be your city," and they marked out in his presence seven places, in which afterwards the chief buildings of his city should be erected, and Fintan placed crosses there.[1]

All this is very interesting. It suggests that the crosses in our diagram mark the sites of monastic buildings [2] at St Mullins ; and if this can be established, the diagram itself will, it would almost seem, lead to the further inference that the buildings within the rampart were dedicated, like modern churches, to the Persons of the Blessed Trinity, or to the Saints.

[1] *Dict. of National Biography*, xix. p. 43, *cf.* Olden, *Church of Ireland*, p. 57.
[2] It is no argument against this theory that one of the buildings (represented by the cross in l. 3) must have been actually in the vallum. See the curious plan of the monastery on Oilen-Tsenach in Lord Dunraven's *Notes on Irish Architecture*, vol. i., p. 38.

Let us endeavour then to test the hypothesis by any evidence which may be available in addition to the Life of St Fintan to which allusion has been just now made.

The first remark to be made is that the theory which it suggests as to the meaning of the interior crosses is confirmed by several passages which appear to indicate that it was quite usual to mark the site of a church by a cross, either incised in stone, or erected in the ground, exactly as Fintan is represented to have done. According to the life in the Book of Lismore, this would seem to have been the ordinary habit of St Columba, though the sentences now to be quoted[1] are not free from ambiguity. It will be noticed that the number of crosses sained by him is exactly equal to the number of churches which he founded.

"Many then were the churches he (Colum Cille) marked out, and the books he wrote, to wit, three hundred churches and three hundred books . . Colomb founded a church in the place where Swords standeth to-day. And he left an ancient man of his household there, even Finan the Feeble, and he left the gospel which his own hand had written. Then he marked out the well named Sord, that is 'pure,' and sained a cross. For it was his wont to make crosses, and writing-tablets, and book-satchels, and other church-gear. Now he sained three hundred crosses, and three hundred wells and a hundred tablets, and a hundred croziers, and a hundred satchels."

St Patrick's practice, as early tradition represents it, appears to have been similar to that of the later Saint. Let us take for instance the following from Tirechan's collections in the Book of Armagh [2] :—

"Et perrexit Patricius ad fontem qui dicitur Mucna, et fecit Cellam Senes quae sic uocatur. Et fuit Secundinus solus sub ulmo frondosso separatim. Et *est signum crucis in eo loco* usque in hunc diem."

The last sentence seems to refer to a cross marked on the ground as an indication of the site of the church which was afterwards to be built. And in this interpretation of the words we are confirmed by several passages in the Tripartite Life and Book of Armagh, of which I quote one,[3] giving the references to the others in the footnote.[4]

"Then Patrick founded a cloister at A'th Maigne in Asal. A merciless man resisted him there . . Patrick marked out with his crozier a cross in the flagstone, and cut the stone as if it were soft clay."

Sometimes, however, the Saint erected a standing cross. Witness this passage from Tirechan [5] :—

"Et ecce quidam uir uenit ad illos, nomine Mace Dregin, cum filís septem gentilibus . . . et elegit unum filium ex ipsís cui nomen erat

---

[1] Stokes, *Lives of Saints from the Book of Lismore*, p. 176 *sq.*
[2] Stokes, *Tripartite Life,* ii. p. 321. The story is told also in the Tripartite Life (i. p. 111.).
[3] Stokes, *op. cit.*, i. p. 79.
[4] Stokes, *op. cit.*, p. 137, 337.
[5] Book of Armagh, f. 14 b. 2 (Stokes, *op. cit.* ii. p. 326).

Macc Ercae . . . Extendit manum et indicauit ei locum in quo sunt ossa eius procul, et digito suo signauit locum et *crucem posuit* ibi."

To which may be added, perhaps, a passage in the Tripartite Life[1] in which it is stated that in each of two places where St Patrick intended that monasteries should be established he " set a stake."

Then, when we turn from the interior to the exterior crosses, we find, in the first place, evidence that crosses were actually planted without the rampart in ancient ecclesiastical establishments. Thus we learn from the late Sir W. R. Wilde[2] that at St Kieran's Church, three miles from Kells, in the County Meath, there were five termon crosses remains of which are still preserved *in situ*, while tradition adds that there were originally eight. Four of those which survive are at the cardinal points, and we may infer that some store was set by this arrangement of the crosses, as that one which stood to the north of the Church was actually planted in the bed of the river. The Church of St Kieran must have presented a very remarkable analogy to that of St Molling with its eight exterior crosses carefully set at such points of the compass as to divide the circular rath into quadrants—if indeed our circular device really represents the monastery at Tech Molling.

From the Four Masters (A.D. 1070) we gather that Clonmacnoise also, St Kieran's principal foundation, had its exterior crosses.

And that the custom exemplied in these instances prevailed widely is shown by the direction of the *Hibernensis* : [3] " Terminus sancti loci habeat signa circa se . . . Ubicunque inveneritis signum crucis Christi, ne laeseritis."

Once again, that some of these exterior crosses should have been dedicated to the Evangelists agrees exactly with what we know from other sources. I cannot indeed produce evidence of as early date as the Book of Mulling, but the last entry under the year 1225 in the Annals of Lough Cé [4] is worthy of our attention :

" Maelbrighde O'Maicin, abbot of Tobur-Patraic, in Christo quievit. He was a virgin and sage ; and it was by him the church of Tobur-Patraic was begun, and its sanctuary and crosses were diligently finished, in honour of Patrick, and Mary, *and the Apostle John.*"

And so too at Iona many crosses have been destroyed, and yet among the four which remain, two are named after the evangelists St Matthew and St John. [5]

In one other respect these exterior crosses agree with the analogy supplied by the remains of a monastic establishment. There exist

[1] Stokes, i. p. 149 sq. For a different explanation, see Olden, *Church of Ireland*, p. 57, and compare O'Curry, *Lectures*, p. 59.
[2] *The Beauties of the Boyne and Blackwater*, p. 138 *sq.* This passage and several of those which are cited hereafter were brought under my notice by Mr Olden.
[3] xliv. 3. Wasserschleben, *Die Irische Kanonensammlung*, Leipszig, 1885, p. 175.
[4] Hennessy, i. p. 291.
[5] Reeves, *Vit. Col.*, p. 419 *sqq.*

in the island of Ardilaun or Ardoileán, off the coast of Galway, some very interesting ruins, surrounded by a cashel, unfortunately in a very imperfect state. Thirty years ago, however, when it was examined and described [1] by Mr G. Henry Kinahan, it was much more nearly in its original condition, and Mr Kinahan has placed it on record that the rampart had three doorways, facing respectively south-east, north-east, and south-west.[2] Of course it is possible, and one is inclined to think probable, that there had also been a north-west doorway, which in the broken state of the cashel Mr Kinahan was unable to observe. We return now to our diagram, and we find its four pairs of protecting crosses exactly at these points of the rampart. May we suppose that these also were the entrances to the enclosure? Certainly nothing could be more natural than that at the very gates of the monastery should be placed the protecting crosses dedicated to the four evangelists and the four prophets. St Fechin of Fore was probably not singular in having a cross at the door of his church.[3]

Up to this point all the evidence adduced has gone to support the hypothesis of Mr Olden. It has been shown that the external crosses are in their number, dedication, and position, just such as might have been found outside the rath of an ancient Celtic monastery. It has been shown too that there is nothing impossible in the supposition that the interior crosses indicate the positions of the monastic buildings within the enclosure.

Nevertheless, before producing what appears to us a further very striking and cogent argument in favour of it, we may be allowed to suggest a slight modification. In all that has been said we have assumed, or as we may perhaps rather affirm, by all that has been said we have proved that the exterior crosses do *not* represent buildings, but actual crosses of wood or stone erected on the ground. Now it must be regarded as *primâ facie* likely that the crosses outside and inside the circles denote similar objects. Why then assume that those found within the circle represent buildings? We have certainly proved that this is possible, but we have not proved that it is probable. It may just as well have been that they were simply standing crosses erected for any of the other purposes, for which in ancient times crosses were used—such as to mark a grave,[4] or to serve as a memorial of some striking event.[5] That crosses stood thus in ancient monasteries we cannot doubt.[6]

And now, this being said, it remains to point out that Mr Olden's conjecture has received a very considerable accession of probability

[1] *Proceedings of the Royal Irish Academy*, x. p. 551 *sqq.*
[2] So too Dundesert cashel had "two complete entrances, one north-west, the other south-east": Reeves, *Ecclesiastical Antiquities*, p. 181.
[3] See Colgan, as referred to in note 6.
Stokes' *Tripartite Life*, p. 325 (Book of Armagh, f. 14 a. 1.).
[5] Stokes, *op. cit.*, p. 276 (Book of Armagh, f. 3 a. 1.), Reeves' *Vit. Col.*, pp. 88, 231.
[6] See Colgan, *AA.SS.* Jan. 22, cap. 23, p. 135, quoted by Petrie, *Round Towers*, p. 172; Reeves' *Vit. Col.*, p. 269; Stokes' *Calendar of Oengus*, p. 4.

since it was first proposed. For at that time line 5 of the writing had not been read. Mr Whitley Stokes, with an acuteness which one who has made many vain attempts to discover their meaning can thoroughly appreciate, informs us that the much worn letters spell the words "conaingleib anúas"="with angels from above." I fancy I can now see before this phrase the traces of a few letters and the faint marks of a cross. At any rate, it is most reasonable to surmise that if, as we have shown, our device is a map, these words indicate the spot where an apparition of angels was seen. Fortunately we know of two visions of angels, both of which occurred in the very place which *ex hypothesi* the device represents, and either of which was of quite sufficient importance to be dignified with a memorial cross if any tradition existed as to the spot where it occurred.

In proof of this statement let me ask attention to two passages, the first translated by Mr Whitley Stokes from the Book of Leinster,[1] the other kindly rendered for me by Mr Olden from the Brussels life of St Molling.[2] They run thus :

"Find [*i.e.* Mac Cumall] arose and his warriors along with him. And they set forward with their left hand to [the river] Barrow to the point of Ross Bruicc[3] over Barrow. The royal champion sat down on a ridge[4] over the wood (*ross*). He beheld a host melodious, floating, in bands ascending to heaven and descending (Gen. xxviii. 12). What host is yon? say the Fian. Those are angels (says Find) even the household of the King of heaven and earth, and shavelings (*talcind*) will come here in the place in which yon angels are." Subsequently a warrior named Enan has a vision in which he sees the clerics just referred to, namely "[Saint] Molling with his community afterwards."

"He (Molling) went to Sliabh Mairge and from that went southward and beheld a watch of angels on the point of Ross Brocc over the stream pools of the Barrow."

If either of these visions of angels gives the key to the meaning of the fifth line of our inscription, we have proof that the structure of which a plan lies before us was situated on a ridge at St Mullins, and that the spot to which this line refers was within the rath of St Mólling's monastery. And indeed, apart from the passages quoted, a similar explanation of the words "with angels from above" might have

---

[1] *Revue Celtique*, xiii. 45, 49.

[2] Cf. *Dict. of Nat. Biog.*, xiii. p. 380.

[3] "The wood of the badger," another name for the place now known as St Mullins.

[4] The expressions here used exactly describe the site of St Molling's monastery. It is situated in the angle formed by the junction of a small stream with the Barrow. This is no doubt the "point of Ross Brocc." The existing ruins are crowded together on an elevation at a considerable height above the river and about 150 yards from it, fitly described as the "ridge over Barrow." See Ordnance Survey Map, Co. Carlow, Sheet 26. It will be observed that almost identical phrases are found in the two passages given in the text.

been suggested, since stories of the places in which monasteries were to be erected being indicated by angelic visitations are not uncommon. An example which readily occurs to one is the story of Iarlaithe, to whom the "place of his resurrection" was pointed out by St Brenainn. "Then," we are told,[1] "the twain made this lay between them, while gazing at the grave-yard and the train of angels manifestly (rising) from it. And Brenainn spake the first five stanzas, and then Iarlaithe spake :

"Lofty the grave-yard of the splendid angels."

We are now perhaps in a position to make some attempt to explain the left-hand circuit of St Molling, or whoever else planted the crosses in honour of the evangelists, which has already attracted our attention as a difficulty to be solved. We have advanced so far as to be able to regard the supposition that our figure represents a monastery as at least on the level of a working hypothesis. That being so we might have expected St Molling to proceed, like the Angel Victor and St Patrick at Armagh, "right-handwise round the rampart;" why did he go in the opposite direction? A sufficient answer may possibly be suggested by the able paper of Sir Samuel Ferguson "on the Ceremonial Turn called *Desiul*" already referred to.[2] That writer quotes some perplexing words from the twenty-eighth book of Pliny's *Natural History*, of the meaning of which commentators had failed to give a satisfactory account : "In adorando dextram ad osculum referimus totumque corpus circumagimus, *quod in lævum fecisse Galli religiosus credunt.*" Are we to take this as a statement that the Gauls practised the left-hand turn in religious ceremonies, and so differed from the Romans? If so Pliny's evidence contradicts what we know from other sources. Accordingly, Sir Samuel Ferguson interprets the word "religiosus" in the sense of "unlucky, ominous, inauspicious, forbidden, uncanny," and translates : "which the Gauls deem it a direful thing to do left-hand ways." "In other words," he proceeds, "the turn which was usually practised towards the right by the Romans, was sometimes, on occasions of imprecatory or malignant appeals to the gods, practised by the Gauls to the left."[3] Perhaps this is the meaning of the left-hand circuit of St Molling. The monastery is placed under the protection of the Apostles and Evangelists by the erection of the crosses, while vengeance is called down upon those who may violate it by the procession

---

[1] Stokes, *Lives of Saints from the Book of Lismore*, p. 251 *sq. Cf.* also pp. 164, 285 *sq.* Another instance will be found in the *Prophecy of Art Son of Conn* (*Proceedings of R. I. A.*, 1895, p. 533). Con sees "the going and coming of the angels up and down" at Trevit. Following up this vision he predicts the foundation of a monastery there by St Lonan.

[2] Above p. 172, note 2.

[3] Compare Brown's *Life and Legend of Sir Michael Scott*, Edinburgh, 1897, p. 182.

against the course of the sun.[1] But whether Sir Samuel Ferguson's explanation of Pliny's remark is correct or not, the remark itself may be cited as a parallel to that which has caused us difficulty, and so as removing the difficulty, so far as is necessary for our purpose that it should be removed.

But now what appears to the writer a more serious difficulty must be dealt with. Is it probable, it may be asked, that the monastery would be exactly circular, as on the supposition that our diagram is its ground-plan it must have been?

Now, I am well aware that by many the difficulty here stated will not be felt to be a difficulty at all. Eminent and accurate writers have made the general assertion[2] that the vallum in Irish monasteries "was of a circular figure." Those who accept this statement will, of course, reply to the question just now proposed that the circles in our diagram are exactly what might have been expected. So far from being a difficulty to be overcome, they are an argument in favour of Mr Olden's hypothesis. It is necessary for us, therefore, at once to state, and to give some reasons for, our belief that in most cases Irish monasteries were not circular in shape.

Literary evidence on such a subject is, naturally, not abundant. And to examine with any degree of fulness that which is supplied by the remains still existing of ancient ecclesiastical establishments is, in the space at our command, impossible. It may suffice to accept the evidence adduced by the learned writer of *The Ecclesiastical Architecture of Ireland.* "It is clear," he says,[3] "that in the earliest monastic establishments in Ireland, the abbot, clergy, and monks had each their separate cells, which served them as habitations, and that such other houses, as the house for the accommodation of strangers, the kitchen, etc., were all separate edifices, surrounded by a cashel or *circular wall,* and forming a kind of monastery or ecclesiastical town, like those of the early Christians in the East, and known among the Egyptians by the name of *Laura.*" A few pages further on[4] he proceeds, "In the western and southern portions of the island, in which the custom of building with stone seems to have prevailed far more generally [than elsewhere], we have still remaining abundant examples, not only of such detached monastic habitations, but of all the other buildings necessary in these early establishments." Several of the pages of the section of Mr Petrie's great work, from which these sentences have been extracted, are occupied with descriptions of some of the ancient monastic remains—five in number—which had come under

---

[1] Compare the Annals of the Four Masters, A.D., 1162. "Caiseal-an-urlair was erected by the successor of Columcille, *who pronounced a curse against anyone that should come over it.*"

[2] Reeves' *Vit. Col.,* p. 361 ; Petrie, *Ordnance Survey of the County of Londonderry,* i. 213 ; Stuart, *Book of Deer,* p. cxlv.

[3] P. i, *Ecclesiastical Architecture,* p. 416.

[4] P. 418.

his own observation. The first of these is the monastery on Ardoileán, or High Island, an island in the Atlantic, about two miles from the coast of Connemara. "This monastery," says Dr Petrie,[1] "is surrounded by an uncemented stone wall, *nearly circular*, enclosing an area of one hundred and eight feet in diameter." On the same page he speaks of it as "the great circular wall;" and similar language has been used quite recently by Mr R. A. S. Macalister.[2] Fortunately, however, the cashel had been inspected by Mr O'Donovan, and his words,[3] though somewhat contradictory *inter se*, have the merit of substituting accurate figures for general descriptions: "The large round wall . . . . is nearly an oblong, measuring in length from north to south 38 yards, and in breadth, from east to west, 23 yards . . . . The most perfect part of it [is] near the N. W. corner." (!) A wall with such measurements can be termed cirenlar only by an abuse of language. It certainly could not be represented by a circle in a plan.

Dr Petrie's second instance of a "circular enclosure," of which remains existed in the early years of this century, is that in the great island of Aran. Its shape he does not mention, possibly because at the time of his visit this could not be ascertained on account of the ruinous condition of the cashel.

He next refers to the cashel surrounding the ecclesiastical establishment of St Molaise in the island of Inishmurry. This, he tells us,[4] "is of an *irregular* round form, and nearly 200 feet in its *greatest* internal diameter." From this it is clear that it could not be represented in a plan by a circle. It is, in fact, more truly described as pear-shaped than as circular.[5]

Of the remains of the monastery at Glendalough, Dr Petrie says,[6] "Of the cashel, or wall itself, which enclosed the monastic establishment, there are but slight vestiges remaining, but these are sufficient to show that it was built without cement, and of a very irregular figure, in consequence of the inequality of the surface along which it passed, and the great extent of the area which it enclosed." And he then passes to the establishment at Clonmacnoise, on which he remarks that "from a ground-plan preserved among Sir James Ware's MSS. in the British Museum, we find that the wall which surrounded the churches and cemetery at Clonmacnoise was equally irregular in its figure as that at Glendalough; and from a similar cause,—the inequality of the surface over which it passed; but as cement was used in its construction, there is little doubt that it was of much later age than that of Glendalough."

[1] *Op. cit.*, p. 420.
[2] *Journal of Royal Society of Antiquaries of Ireland* for 1896, p. 202.
[3] Ordnance Survey MSS., quoted by Mr Macalister, p. 209 *sq.*
[4] *Op. cit.*, p. 445.
[5] See the plan in Lord Dunraven's *Notes on Irish Architecture*, vol. i. p. 44. Lord Dunraven remarks (p. 45) that the irregularity in the shape of this cashel "is not to be accounted for by the nature of the ground."
[6] *Op. cit.*, p. 446.

Thus of the five examples of ancient cashels mentioned by Dr Petrie not one is proved to have been circular, and four were of a different figure. Other instances might be added, such as the monastery on Skellig Michael,[1] but what has been said is sufficient to show that circular cashels were not so common as has been sometimes assumed to be the case.[2] Are we then to infer that the circles in our figure cannot be supposed, after all, to represent the cashel of a monastery? By no means. For, whatever view may be held as to the normal shape of the vallum, I believe that several instances of monasteries which were undoubtedly circular, may be cited.

I do not care to press the case of the *civitas* of St Cuthbert, in Farne Island, which is described for us by Bede[3] in these words,— "Condidit civitatem suo aptam imperio, et domos in hac acque civitati congruas evexit. *Est autem aedificium situ pene rotundum*" etc. It manifestly approximated to the round form, but whether closely enough to warrant its representation by a circle we cannot say. Not much more to our purpose is the description of the Ferta laid out by St Patrick at Armagh, preserved in the Tripartite Life:[4] "The enclosure was 140 feet, the great house 27, the kitchen 17, and the oratory 7." For, notwithstanding the acute remark of Dr Todd, that both enclosure and buildings were of a form for the measurement of which one dimension was sufficient,[5] it scarcely follows that they were exactly circular. We must not attribute to the description the accuracy of an engineer's specification.

But a more cogent instance is at hand. Adamnan, in the title of

[1] Lord Dunraven's *Notes*, i. p. 30. Compare also the Cashel on Oilen-Tsenach, p. 38. Reeves (*Ecclesiastical Antiquities*, p. 196) mentions a triple oval cashel in Mahee Island, Strangford Lough, and (p. 182) the Cashel of Dun-Desert, which departed so far from the round form that it is described as only "nearly circular" by one who made his report sixty years after every trace of it had been swept away, and who does not seem to have been quite accurate in the few measurements which he gives. A Scottish example is the cashel in Skye, described by Dr J. Anderson in his *Scotland in Early Christian Times*, First Series, p. 94.

[2] In dealing with this question I have preferred direct investigation of the evidence to an appeal to authority: none the less so since the opinion of experts must be admitted to be far from being unanimously favourable to the view which I have ventured to express. I cannot, however, refrain from quoting a sentence or two from the essay with which Miss Margaret Stokes' sumptuous edition of the *Notes on Irish Architecture* of the late Earl of Dunraven concludes: "The resemblance," she remarks (vol. ii. p. 136), "between the pagan and ecclesiastical fort is so strong and so significant of the same primitive condition of knowledge in the builders, that some comparative study of both monuments is required before those points of difference are discovered which may prevent us from falling into the error of supposing that all the monastic forts were originally pagan and afterwards converted to Christian uses. . . . In the first place, the pagan fortress is composed of two and sometimes three areas or wards, the interior, or fort proper, being either an oval, a circle, or half an ellipse, but with no sign of variation in the ground plan which would suggest that it was meant to enclose structures already in existence; whereas the Christian fort deviates from the regular oval or circular form so as to take in the oratories and other buildings it is intended to protect."

[3] *Vit. Cuth.*, xvii.
[4] W. Stokes, p. 237.
[5] *St Patrick, Apostle of Ireland*, p. 478.

the fifteenth chapter of the third book of his *Vita Columbæ*, mentions a certain brother who fell "de monasterii culmine rotundi [1] in Roboreti Campo,"—from the roof of the *round monastery* at Durrow. In the account of the incident in the text (which is taken from Cummian), the brother is said to have fallen "de summo culmine magnæ domus . . . quæ his in diebus in Roboreti Campo fabricatur." The two phrases evidently describe the same building. What was it? Petrie,[2] followed by Reeves and Fowler,[3] has little doubt that it was the Round Tower of the Monastery. Mr Whitley Stokes,[4] on the other hand, and apparently with greater probability, identifies it with the *tech mor* or "great house." The three later writers, however, in this advancing a step beyond Petrie, identify the "magna domus" with the "monasterium rotundum." This is, I venture to think, unnecessary and unwarranted. Nowhere else in Adamnan is the word "monasterium" applied to a single building of the *civitas*, and du Cange gives no instance of the word used in this sense. Even at iii. 8 the "fratrum monasteria," which at first view might appear to mean the cells of the monks, are shown by the context to be several monasteries in the Island of Tiree, in one of which lived the "congregatio" of Baithene. "Monasterium," therefore, in the present passage must have the same meaning, unless it is impossible so to take it. I conclude that in "monasterii culmen rotundi," occurring as it does, in the heading of a chapter, where we might expect to meet compendious phrases, we have a short way of expressing "culmen domus quæ in monasterio rotundo est." The building so described was certainly high ("magna," "major," "altissima," "enormis," so high that a fall from it meant almost certain death; see Reeves, *ad. loc.*); it was probably or possibly round; but the thing which concerns us is, that the monastery at Durrow, with which it was connected, was round,[5] like the monastery, if such it was, depicted in our manuscript.

[1] With most unusual inaccuracy Reeves has in his glossary "monasterii culmen *rotundum*." He was probably misled by Petrie's argument: "Not certainly that the monastery itself had a rotund roof," etc. Certainly not, but there is no mention of a "rotund roof" in the Latin.
[2] *Ecclesiastical Architecture*, p. 382 *sqq.*
[3] *Adamnani Vita S. Columbae*, Oxford, 1894, p. 144.
[4] *Tripartite Life*, p. clv, *Lives of Saints from the Book of Lismore*, p. 329.
[5] A very kind and learned critic remarks, "You appear to take the word *rotundum* as descriptive of the particular monastery referred to. But as all monasteries were round, *i.e.* the Civitas or Fort, the word would convey no distinctive meaning." To this I make answer; (1) The argument for the circular form of the monastic *buildings* is as strong (one might rather say considerably stronger) as that for the circular form of the Civitas. If, therefore, "monasterium rotundum" indicates the *tech mor*, or the round tower, "rotundum" is at least equally devoid of meaning. But (2) whatever the *usual* form of the monasteries may have been, I think I have proved that they were not in *all* cases round; and (3) all that is implied by the use of the word "rotundum" is that the Durrow monastery was different in shape from that in which Adamnan wrote, and with which his readers were familiar, or, in other words, that the monastery at Iona was *not* exactly circular. This may well be granted, at least till contrary evidence is produced.

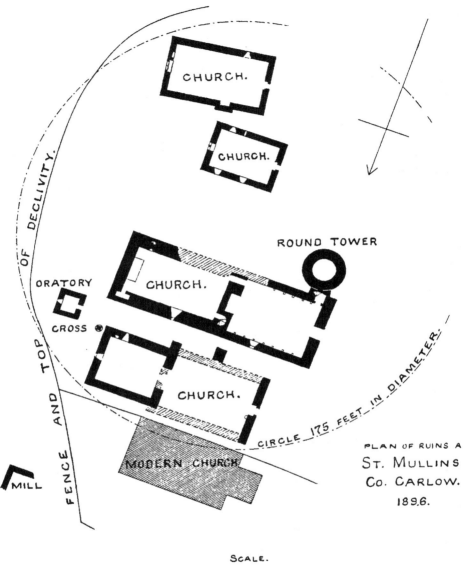

CHURCH.

CHURCH.

ROUND TOWER

OF DECLIVITY.

ORATORY

CHURCH.

CROSS ●

CIRCLE 175 FEET IN DIAMETER.

CHURCH.

TOP AND FENCE

PLAN OF RUINS A
ST. MULLINS
CO. CARLOW.
189.6.

MODERN CHURCH.

MILL

SCALE.

FEET 10 5 0   10   20   30   40   50   60   70   80   90   100 FEET.

And we may perhaps place along with the "round monastery" of Adamnan that which is spoken of in the following passage of Tirechan's Collections in the Book of Armagh:[1]

"Et crediderunt in Deo. Et consumpti sunt dies ululationis filiarum regis, et sepelierunt eas iuxta fontem *Clebach*, et fecerunt fossam rotundam (in) similitudinem *fertæ*, quia sic faciebant (Scotici) homines et gentiles. Nobiscum hautem reli(c) uocatu(r), id est reliquiæ, et feurt. Et immolata est (?*ferta*) Deo et Patricio cum sanctarum ossibus et haeredibus eius post (se in) saecula, et aecclessiam terrenam fecit in eo loco."

But this discussion has already exceeded its due limits. It must be brought to a close with the consideration of a question which every reader will ere this have asked: Do the remains still existing on the site of St Mulling's monastery yield any evidence for or against the hypothesis advanced by Mr Olden? Does our supposed plan suit the topography of St Mullins? Can we point to probable sites of ancient buildings or sacred spots marked by the crosses of our scribe?

These questions occurred to me the moment I received from Mr Olden the suggestion which has been considered in this chapter. And I anticipated that in seeking an answer to them much help would be derived from an excellent paper entitled "St Mullins, co. Carlow," with plans of the ruins as they were in 1892, published by the Rev J. F. M. ffrench in the *Journal of the Royal Society of Antiquaries of Ireland*, part iv. vol. ii., *fifth series*, p. 377. But actual trial quickly convinced me that this paper, by itself, does not supply sufficient material for our purpose. Very gladly, therefore, I availed myself of the kind invitation of Mrs Kavanagh of Borris Lodge to visit St Mullins and see with my own eyes the spot which has such interest for all students of the ecclesiastical history of Ireland. Shortly after Easter 1896, armed with Mr ffrench's paper and accompanied by my friend J. H. Cunningham, Esq., C.E., Fellow of the Society of Antiquaries of Scotland, I spent a few pleasant hours at Ross Broce. Our time was short, but Mr Cunningham's presence enabled me to make good use of it. At my request he made some measurements, and drew the plan which is reproduced on the opposite page. It is founded on that made by Mr Cochrane for Mr ffrench, but gives the results of excavations made since it was published, and marks some details which it did not record.[2] It is so

[1] Book of Armagh, f. 12, b. 1. Stokes' *Tripartite Life*, p. 317. We might add also, the cashels at Shankill in the Ards, and Killyhurragh in the parish of Ardclinis, Co. Antrim, mentioned by Reeves in his *Ecclesiastical Antiquities of Down, Connor, and Dromore*, pp. 23, 299. But the degree of precision with which he uses the word "circular" applied to both these must remain doubtful.

[2] Such are the western doorway in the building with which the round tower is connected, another doorway in the wall which divides it into two parts, the lower part of an altar at the east end of the same building, and a piscina in its south wall. Also a small window slit in the south wall of the small church lying next to it on the south.

placed that the points of the compass agree as nearly as possible with those indicated in the device reproduced from our manuscript on p. 167.

The first remark to be made is that the ruins are situated on the level top of a ridge (no doubt that which is mentioned in two passages which have been already cited[1]) which descends abruptly on its eastern, northern, and southern sides.[2] The limits of the monastery on these three sides are therefore pretty clearly defined. The fence marked in the plan indicates the place at which this sharp declivity begins to descend.

There is no sign of a rath, a circumstance which need cause us no surprise. Its absence, however, deprives us of the power of testing our theory in one important particular. But it should be observed that a circle of about 175 feet in diameter can be drawn lying almost wholly within the fence, and yet including all the existing ruins. Such a circle is indicated by the dotted line in the plan. A round monastery, therefore, of about the normal dimensions[3] may very well have at one time occupied the crown of the ridge.

When we seek to identify the crosses in our manuscript with sacred spots on the ancient site at St Mullins we are at once met by difficulties. With one exception,[4] all the existing buildings are evidently of much later date than the ninth century. It might be argued that the more modern structures were erected on the spots formerly occupied by buildings of the ancient *civitas*. But this is in itself disputable,[5] and in any case these earlier buildings were probably smaller than their successors, and it is, therefore, impossible to decide where the crosses representing them should be placed. The exception to the modern character of the buildings is that which is marked as

[1] Above p. 177.
[2] See the drawing of St Molling's Well which accompanies Mr ffrench's paper.
[3] The rath of St Patrick at Armagh, which was regarded as the standard, measured 140 feet, see above p. 181. It may be remarked that a circle of about 150 feet diameter, concentric with that in the plan, would include the oratory of St James and all the other churches, with the exception of small portions of those to the north and south. On the supposition that these later buildings stood on the sites of smaller chapels of early date, the latter might well have been included within a rath of this measurement.
[4] The building over the well with the antique appearance of which Mr ffrench was so much impressed (p. 384) does not appear to have any claim to be regarded as of very early date. The " inclining jambs " of its doorway both incline *in the same direction,* and the fact that its breadth at the sill is greater than at the top is due, not to the intention of the builder, but to the fact that the stone next the lintel on the right is not squared. These phenomena point to bad masonry, but all bad masonry is not old. And the projections of the side walls, on which Mr ffrench lays stress, are smaller than those described by Brash.
[5] In one case—that of the present Parish Church—this supposition seems to be almost demonstrably incorrect. It stands outside the cemetery. I was told by the forester on the Kavanagh estate that his father had assisted at the building of the church. According to his account an attempt was made to build the church partly inside the ancient graveyard. The peasantry, however, offered violent resistance, and in consequence it was placed wholly without the boundary. It is unlikely that one of the old churches was outside the burying ground, or that the people, who had already displayed such strong feeling, would have permitted such a building to be destroyed in order to make room for a Protestant church.

the Oratory. This little chapel appears to correspond in position to the cross at the beginning of the seventh line of our device, while the fragmentary cross[1] to the east of the *Teampul mor* may answer to that which had its place (if we may suppose that this was so) at the beginning of l. 8. But here we cannot speak with assurance : for another difficulty remains : the position of the ancient rath cannot be accurately determined, and we can therefore do no more than conjecture, with whatever degree of probability, how the oratory and the cross stood with reference to it.

To conclude, topographical evidence has not helped us much. It leaves Mr Olden's suggestion nearly as it was before—a hypothesis highly plausible in itself, not indeed altogether free from difficulties (more or less grave), but by no means improbable—yet still only a hypothesis : a theory which is not, perhaps cannot be, either proved or disproved. As a hypothesis it may well hold the field till something more probable is proposed to occupy its place.

And now the last line of this little book has been penned. To the writer its preparation has been a constant source of pleasure. It has for some years occupied hours of leisure snatched from the many cares of pastoral work in a large city. If it stirs up some student, with more time for research and greater skill for handling the subjects with which it deals, to keener interest in a too little known relic of the ancient Celtic Church of Ireland, its purpose will have been accomplished.

LAUS DEO.

[2] The sides of this cross are decorated with interlaced work, and not, as Mr ffrench says, with " a kind of lozenge pattern."

APPENDIX A.

THE OLD LATIN PORTIONS OF "THE GARLAND OF HOWTH."

FOR a description of the manuscript of the four Gospels known as the "Garland of Howth" (T.C.D. A.4. 6), and usually designated by the symbol r_2, the reader may be referred to Professor Abbott's *Evangeliorum Versio Antehieronymiana*, Præfatio, pp. xiv.–xviii. I have already given reasons for my belief that the latter portion of St Matthew, printed in this appendix, is the only fragment of genuine Old Latin text which the manuscript preserves.[1] Professor Abbott[2] regards the whole of the first gospel as pre-hieronymian in character. M. Berger, on the other hand, describes it as approaching nearer to the ancient version than, for example, the Book of Kells, but still only a mixed text.[3] It may be that both writers have been misled by failing to observe the abrupt change which, as has been pointed out, takes place in the latter part of the sixteenth chapter.

I have not thought it necessary to reproduce the text line for line from the manuscript, and for convenience of reference the numbers of chapters and verses have been added throughout. In expanding contractions I have printed the letters which had to be supplied in italics.

*   *   *   *   *   *

XVI. |homines d*icu*nt esse filium hominis [14] At illi dix[erunt io]- [f. 5 r. hanne*m* babtiza*m* Alii h*autem* heliam alii ucro heremiam aut unu*m* ex profet*is* [15] d*ixit* ill*is* ih͞s Uos h*autem* quem me *esse* dicitis [16] R[e- *spondiens*] simon petrus d*ixit* tu es x͞p͞s filius dei uiui [17] *Respondiens* h*autem* ih͞s d*ixit* ei beatus es simon bar iona q*uia* caro et sangis n*on* reuelauitibi *sed* pat*er* meus qui in caelis *est* [18] Ideo dico tibi tu es petrus et sup*er* hanc petra*m* ædificabo æclisiam mea*m* et porte inferni n*on* præualeabunt aduersus eu*m* [19] et tibi dabo claues regni caelo*rum* Et quicu*m*q*ue* ligaueritis sup*er* terram eru*n*t ligata et in caeli*s* et quicu*m*q*ue* solueritis sup*er* terram cru*n*t soluta et in caeli*s* [20] Tunc

[1] Above, p. 67.
[2] *Op. cit.*, p. xv.
[3] *Histoire de la Vulgate*, p. 42 ; *Revue Celtique*, vi. p. 355.
xvi. 17.   After ih͞s there seems to be a cross.

imperauit discipulis suís nemini dicirent quia ipse esset x̄p̄s̄ ²¹ EX[in]-
de coepit ih̄s̄ ostendere discipulis suís quod o[po]rtet eum ire in
hirusalem et multa pati asenioribus et principibus sacerdotum et
occidi et post tertium diem resurgam ²² Et adsumiens eum petrus
coepit increpare et dicire absit até domine nonerit istud ²³ Et ipse
coepit dicire conuersus ait Uade post me satanas scandalum es mihi
non enim sapis quæ dei sunt sed quæ hominum ²⁴ Tunc ih̄s̄ dixit discipulis suís Sí quis uult post me uenire abnegat se ipsum sibi ettollat
crucem suam etsequatur me ²⁵ Qui enim uoluerit animam suam saluam
facere perdet eam Qui enim perdiderit animam suam propter me
inueniet eam ²⁶ Et quod enim proderit bomini sí lucretur hunc mun-
d[um] animae uero suae detrimentum patitur Aut |quantum   [f. 5 v.
danit homo comotationem propter animam suam ²⁷ nam filius hominis
uenturus inmaiestate fratris sui cum angelís suis   Et tunc reddet
unicuique secundum opera sua ²⁸ Amen dico uobis quoniam sunt
aliqui destantibus istís qui non gustabunt mortem donec uidiant
XVII. filium hominis uenientem in regno suo ¹ Et factum est post dies sex
Adsumpsit ih̄m̄ petrum et iacobum et iohannem frater eius et duxit
illos in montem excelsum seorsum ² et splendiuit facies eius sicut sól
et uestimenta hautem eius factasunt sicut nix ³ Et ecce aperuit eís
moyses et helias cum eo loquentes ⁴ respondiens petrus dixit ad ih̄m̄
domine bonum est nobís hic esse sí uís faciamus hic trea tabernacula
tibi unum et moysi unum Et heliae unum ⁵ adhúc eo loquente Et ecce
nups abscondita obumbrauit eís Et ecce uox denube diciens hic est
filius meus dilectus inquo mihi bene conplacui Audite ipsum ⁶ Et
audientes caeciderunt in faciem suam et timuiarunt ualde ⁷ Et accediens eos tetigit eos et dixit surgite et nolite timere ⁸ eleuantes
hautem oculos suos Neminem uiderunt nissi ih̄m̄ solum ⁹ Et discen-
dentibus illis de monte praecipit eís ih̄s̄ nemini dxeritis uisum donec
filius hominis amortuis resurgat ¹⁰ Et inter rogauerunt eum discipuli
dicentes quid ergo scribe dicunt quod heliam oportet primum uenire
¹¹ ipse respondit ait helias quidem uenturus est restitu[et]|uere   [f. 6 r.
omnia ¹² dico hautem nobis quod helias iam uenit Et non cog-
nouerunt eum et fecerunt ei quanta uoluerunt ¹³ tunc intellexerunt
discipuli quod de iohanne babtista dixit illís síc et filius hominis necesse habet pati ab eís ¹⁴ Et cum uenisset ad turbam accessit adeum
homo genibus prouolutis ¹⁵ diciens domine misserere filio meo quia
lunaticus est et malae torquetur nam sepins in ignem cadit et aliquando
in aquam ¹⁶ Et obtulli eum discipulís suís et non potuerunt curare eum
¹⁷ Respondiens ih̄s̄ dixit O' generatio incredula et peruersa quo usque
patiar uós adferte illum ame ¹⁸ Et increpauit illum ih̄s̄ Et exiit ab eo
demonium et curatus est puer exilla hora ¹⁹ Tunc accesserunt discipuli
ad ih̄m̄ secreato Et dxerunt ei quare nos non potuimus ieccere eum
²⁰ dixit illís ih̄s̄ propter incredulitatem uestram Amen dico uobís sí
habueritis fidem sieut granum sinapis et dicitis monti huic transí
hinc transibit et nihil inpossibile crit nobís ²¹ hoc hautem geñus non
iecitur nissi per orationem et ieiunium ²² IPsís hautem conuersantibus

in galiliam D*ixit* illi ihs̄ futuru*m* *est enim* ut filiu*m* hominis tradet*ur*
inmanus hominum ²³ Et occident eum Et p*os*t *ter*tium diem resurgere
et contristatis*unt* uechimen*ter* ²⁴ Et cum uenisset ihs̄ incapharnaum
ac cessiar*unt* quide dragma | accessiar*unt* exigebant ad petrum   [f. 6 v.
et d*i*xer*unt* magis*ter* u*es*t*er* n*on*soluet dedragma ²⁵ ait utique et
intrauit indomum *per*uenit eum ihs̄ diciens quid t*i*bi uidet*ur*
simon reges*terre* accib*us* accipiunt tributum *uel* censum afilís suis
án abalienís ²⁶ at ille d*i*xit abalienis D*ixi*t illi ihs̄ ergo liberi s*unt*
²⁷ ut h*autem* scandalizemus eos uade admare Et mitte amum in
mari Et cum piscem qui primus ascenderit tolle et*ª*perto ore eius
VIII. inuenies ibistateram illa*m* sumiens da eís p*ro*me et té ¹ IN illa
die accesser*unt* discipuli adihm̄ dicentes quis putas maior est in
regno caelor*um* ² Et ihs̄ uocauit pueru*m* Et statuit eum inmedio
eor*um* ³ Et d*i*xit amen dico uobís nissi conuersi fueritis et efici-
amini sicut infantem n*on* intrabitis inregnum caelorum ⁴ Et qui
cum*que* humiliauerit se sicut puer iste hic maior *est* in regnum
caelorum ⁵ Et q*ui* acciperit ᴉɴfantem talem innomine meo me
accipit ⁶ Qui h scandalizauerit unu*m* depussillis istis qui in me
credunt expedit ei ut mola assinaria in collo *eius* suspendat*ur* Et
demergatur inp*ro*fundu*m* maris ⁷ uae huic mundo ascandalis necesse
est enim uenire scandala Uerum tam*en* dico nobis Uae homini p*er*
qu*em* scandalum uenit ⁸ q*uod* si manus tua *uel* pes tuus scandalizate
abscede ea*m* Et p*ro*iecce abste | bonum est tibi inuita*m* uenire   [f. 7 r.
debile*m* et clodum q*uam* duos pedes *uel* duas manus habente*m* mitti
in ignem aet*er*num ⁹ Sí oculus tuus ‴erue eu*m* scandalizat te etp*ro*iecce
absste Bonum *est* tibi unu*m* oculum habentem inuita*m* uenire q*uam*
duos oculos habente*m* mitti in gechenam ignis ¹⁰ Uidete necontemnatis
unum ex hís pussillís istis qui in me credunt Dico *enim* uobís
q*uonia*m angeli corum in˙ caelís uident faciem patris mei qui
in caelis *est* ¹¹ Uenit filius hominis saluare q*uod* perierat ¹² quid
nobis uidetur Sí fuerint alieni ·c· oues Et sí errauerit una ex eis
n*on*ne relinquet nonagenta noem in montib*us* et nadet q*ue*rere ea*m*
¹³ Amen dico nobis q*uod* gaudebit in ea*m* magis q*uam* nonagenta
noem qu*æ* n*on* periant quid nobis uidet*ur* ¹⁴ Síc n*on* *est* uoluntás
ante patrem m*eu*m qui in caelis *est* ut periat un*us* ex pussillis istís
¹⁵ Quod sí peccauerit inte frat*er* tuns uade corripe eum inte et ipsum
solum quodsí audierit te lucratus es fratre*m* tuum ¹⁶ sí h*autem* nonté
audierit adibe tecum adhuc unu*m* *uel* duos ut inore duorum testium
uel triu*m* stet omne uerbu*m* ¹⁷ Quod sí n*on* audierit eos defer æclisi*ę*
Sí nero nec aeclisiam audierit sit tibi sicut ethinus et puplicanus
¹⁸ Amen dico no[bis] quicu*m*que alligaueritis sup*er* terram eru*nt* liga-
| ta et in caelís Et quicu*m*que solueritis sup*er* terra*m* soluta et   [f. 7 v.
in caelo ¹⁹ Iterum dico nobís q*uasi* duob*us* conuenerit int*er* uós de omni
ré qu*æ*cumque petieritis fiet uobís apatre meo qui incaelís *est*
²⁰ Ubi s*unt* duo *uel* tres congregata innom*ine* meo ego in medio

xviii. 13.   In the right margin, opposite "magis," is written "eɪ[.]ıt"
(? = "erit").

corum [21] Tune accediens adeum petrus dicens ei domine sí peccauerit
in me frater meus quotiens demittam ei usque septies [22] Dicit illi ihs
non dico tibi usque septics sed usque septuagies etsepties [23] IDeo
dico nobís simile est regnum caelorum homini regi qui uolunt rationem ponere cum sernis suis [24] et cum coepiset rationem ponere
oblatus est ei unus qui debebat x· tallenta [25] cum non haberet unde
rederet iusit eum dominus uenundari et uxorem et filios eius Et
omnia quæ cumque habebat et reddi debitum [26] Procediens ergo sernus
ille orabat eum diciens patientiam habe in me domine Et omnia
reddam [27] Missertus est hautem dominus serui illius dimisit eum et
debitum dimisit ei [28] Egressus hautem sernus ille inuenit unum ex
conseruís suis qui debebat eum ·c· denarios Et adpræchendiens et
suffucabat eum diciens redde mihi quod debeo tibi [29] Procedens con-
sernus eius rogabat eum diciens patientiam habe inme reddam tib[i]
[30] Ille hautem noluit sed habiit et missit eum in carcerem donec
redderet debitum [31] Uidentes conserui

*   *   *   *   *   *   *

XIX. | possiuilia sunt [27] Tunc respondiens petrus dixit ei quid ergo erit [f. 9 r.
nobis ecce nos relincimus omnia et secuti sumus te [28] ihs hautem dixit eís
Amen dico uobís quod uos qui saccuti estis me ingeneratione ista Cum
sederit filius hominis inmaiestate sua sedebitis et uos super xii tribus
israhel [29] Et omnis quirelinquerit domum uel fratres aut sorores aut
matrem aut filios aut agros propter nomen meum centuplum accipiet
insaeculo isto Et uitam aeternam infuturo [30] Multi hautem erunt
XX. primi nouissimi et nouissim[i] primi [1] Simile est enim regnum caelorum
hom[ini pa]tri familias qui exiit primo mane conducere operarios
inmessem suam [2] conuentione hautem facta cum operarios exdinario
diurno missit inuiniam suam [3] Et egressus [diu]rno Et egressus circa
horam tertiam et inuenit alios stantes inforo otiosos [4] et [illi]s dixit ite
et uos inuiniam meam et quod iustum fuerit dabo nobís [5] Ali hautem
abierunt iterum [hautem exi]it circa horam nonam et fecit similiter [6] circa
undecimam horam Exiit hautem et inuenit alios stantes Et dixit illis
quid hic statis otiosos tota die [7] dicunt ei quia nemo nos conduxit ait
illís ite ad uniam me[a]m [8] Cum sero hautem fatum esset dicit dominus
uinie | procuratori suo uoca operarios et redde illís mercidem [f. 9 v.
INcipiens annouissimís usque adprimos [9] Cum uenissent hautem qui circa
undecimam horam uenerunt acciperunt singulos denarios [10] Uenientes
hautem et primi arbitrati sunt quod plus essent accepturi accipiarunt et
ipsi singulos denarios [11] accipientes murmurauerunt aduersus patrem
familias [12] hii nouissimi una hora fecerunt et patres illos nobís fecisti
qui portauimus pondus diei et estus [13] At ille respondiens uni eorum dixit
amice non facio tibi iniuriam nonne exdinario conuersisti mecum
[14] tolle quod tuum est et nade uolo hautem huic nouissimo huic dare.

xviii. 31. There is a hiatus here owing to the loss of one leaf (xviii. 31–xix.
26). There is also a misplacement of the remaining leaves, that containing
xxi. 11 sqq. being made by the binder to follow the present verse.
xix. 28· We should perhaps read "sederet."

O

sieut et tibi ¹⁵ non licet m*ihi* facere q*uod* uolo in e*í*s aut oculus tuus
nequam *est* q*uia* ego bonus sum ¹⁶ Sic er*unt* nouissimi primi et primi
nouissimi multi *enim* s*unt* uocati pauci u*ero* electi ¹⁷ Et ascendiens ih͞s
in hirusolim*í*s adsumpsit duodecim discipulos suos   Et ait ill*í*s ¹⁸ ecce
ascendimus hirusolima*m* et filius hominis trade*tur* principib*us* sacerdotu*m* et scrib*í*s et contempnabunt eum morte ¹⁹ et tradent eu*m*
gentib*us* ad deludendum et ad flagillandum et crucifigendum Et tertio
die resurget ²⁰ Tunc ait ad eum mat*er* filiorum sebedei cum duob*us*
fili*í*s adorans et petrus aliquid ab eo ²¹ ipse h*autem* d*í*x*it* ei quid
u*í*s at illa d*í*x*it* ei ut sedent hii duo filii|mei unus ad   [f. 10 r.
dext*er*am tuam et alius ad sinistram inregno tuo ²² res*pondiens*
h*autem* ih͞s d*í*x*it* nestis quid petatis potestis bibere calice*m* quem
ego bibiturus sum Et dicunt ei possumus ²³ calice*m* quide*m*
bibetis sedere h*autem* add*ex*teram u*el* adsinistram n*on*est meu*m* dare
nob*í*s *sed* quib*us* datum *est* apatre meo ²⁴ Et audientes ·x· contristati
sunt ad du[o]b*us* fratrib*us* ²⁵ ih͞s uocauit eos adse ait illis s[ei]tis q*uia*
principes gentium dominantur eoru*m* [et] qui dominant*ur* eorum Et qui
dominant*ur* [eoru*m*] potestates exercent in e*í*s ²⁶ n*on* itae*st* inter*uos* s[*ed
quicumque*] ²⁷ inter uos primus *esse* erit uester sernus ²⁸ Sicut [fi]lius
hominis n*on* uenit ministrari *sed* mini[st]rare et dare anima*m* suam
redemptione*m* pro mult*í*s   Uos h*autem* qu*er*itis depussillo crescere Et
demaiore*m* *esse* minoris intrantes h*autem* et rogati ad cena*m* nolite
recumbere in loc*í*s maiorib*us* neforte clarior sup*er* ueniat et a[c]cediens
quité ad cenam uocauit dicat tib[i] adhuc accede   Et confunderis s*í*
h*autem* in loco inferiore recumberi   Et sup*er* uenerit humil[i]ore té
dicet tibi qui te adcena*m* uocauit accede ad h*ú*c superius et erit hoc
tibi gloria ²⁹ Et egredientib*us* ill*í*s ad hericho saecutae s*unt* eum turbae
multae ³⁰ Et ecce duo caeci sedentes sup*er* uiam audientes q*uod* ih͞s
transiit Et clamauer*unt*|dicentes misserere ·n*ostri*· filii dauid   [f. 10 v.
³¹ Turba h*autem* increpabat eos ut tacerent at illi magis clamabant dom*í*ne
misserere ·n*ostri*· filii dauid ³² Et uocauit eos et ait illis quid uultis
utfaciam nob*í*s ³³ dicunt illi ut aperientur oculi ·n*ostri*· ³⁴ missertus h*autem*
ill*í*s ih͞s tetigit oculos coru*m* et confestim uidiar*unt* etsecutae s*unt* eum
XXI. ¹ Et adpropinquassent hirusolimam Et cum uenissent bethfage inmontem oliueti t*un*c missit duos exdiscipul*í*s suis ² dicienes ite [a]d
castellu*m* q*uod* contra uos*est* et confestim inuen*í*etis [a]sina*m* alligata*m*
et pullu*m* cum ea soluite et addu[c]ite mihi ³ Et s*í* quis nob*í*s aliquid
dixerit q*uia* dominu*s* [o]p*us* habet et confestim remittent uos ⁴ hoc
h*autem* factum *est* ut impleretur q*uod* dictum *est* p*er* essaia*m* profeatam
dicentem ⁵ dicite filiae si*ó*n Ecce rex tuus nenit tibi mansuetus et
sediens sup*er* assina*m* et pullum nouellu*m* sub iugale ⁶ Euntes h*autem*
discipuli feceru*nt* sicut pr*æ*cip*er*at illis ih͞s ⁷ et adduxer*unt* assina*m* et

xx. 25.   We should perhaps read "e*ó*s" for "e*í*s."
xx. 26.   The word "inter" (v. 27) begins a fresh line. The vellum is cut above
the final "s" of the previous line. It may have had a horizontal stroke over it.
Three or four letters are gone.   Hence I restore the reading "s̄ q̣ c̄ q:" — "*sed*
q*uicumque*."   What seems to be a portion of the first q remains.
xx. 28.   A slight space follows "superius," in which possibly something is
written.

pullum Et inpossuer*unt* sup*er* eum uestimenta etsedebat [s]up*er* eum
[8] Plurimi h*autem* strauer*unt* uestimenta sua in uia Alii h*autem* cedebant
ramos dearborib*us* etst*er*niebant inuia [9] turbae h*autem* qu*ae* procedebant et qui sedebant clamabant dicentes ossanna filii dauid Benedictus
qui uenit innomine d*omi*ni ossanna inexcels*ís* [10] Et cum intrasset hiruso-
limam commota *est* uniuersa ciuitás dicentes quis *est* hic |[11] multi [f. 8 r.
h*autem* d*i*xer*unt* hic *est* ih*s* anazareth galiliae [12] [et intrauit] ih*s* in
templum d*e*i et ieccit ih*s* omnes uenden[tes et e]mentes intemplo et
mensas numulariorum E[t cath]edras uendentium columbas euertit
[13] et d*i*xit s[crib]tum *est* domus mea domus orationis uocauit*ur* [uos]
h*autem* fecistis eam speloncam latronum [14] Et acce[dunt] adeum caeci
et claudi intemplo et sanabat eos [15] [ui]diens h*autem* princeps sacerdotum et scribe mirab[ilia] qu*ae* fecit ih*s* Et pueros clamantes et
dicentes [ossan]na filii dauid indignati s*unt* [16] et d*i*xer*unt* ei audist[i
quid] isti d*i*cu*nt* ih*s* h*autem* d*i*xit ill*ís* utiq*ue* n*on* legisti EXore in-
fa[ntium] et lactantiu*m* p*er*fecisti laudem [17] Et relictis illis ab[iit] foras
extraciuitatem inbethania ibiq*ue* mans[it [18] ma]ne h*autem* transiit
inciuitatem essuriit [19] Et uidien[s arbo]rem feci unam secus feci unam
uenit adeam E[t] n[ihil] inuenit ineam nissi folia tantu*m* ait adeam
[Nu]mqu*am* e[xte] fructus nasceretur in sempet*er*num et aruit con-
ti[nuo] ficulnia [20] Et uidentes discipuli mirati s*unt* quomodo [conti]nuo
aruit [21] res*pondiens* h*autem* ih*s* d*i*xit e*ís* Amen dico nob*ís* [si ha-]
bueritis fidem et n*on* essitaueritis n*on* solum difi[cul]nia facietis se*d*
mundi huic dxeritis tolle et iact[a te in] mare faciet [22] omnia
qu*ae*cumque petieritis inorat[ione] credentes accipietis [23] et cum ueniset
intemp[lum] Accessiar*unt* adeu*m* principes sacerdotum [et seni]oris
populi dicentis inqua potes[tate haec] facis Et quis tibi dedit h*aec*
potestatem [24] R[es*pondiens* ih*s*] |d*i*xit [illis] int*er*rogabo uós [f. 8 v.
et ego unum uerbum dicite m[ih]i Et ego uob*ís* dicam inqua
potestate h*aec* faci [25] babtismum iohannis unde nenit decaelo
an ex [h]ominib*us* illi h*autem* cogitabant intrasć dicentes [26] si
[di]xerimus decaelo dicet nob*ís* quare er*go* n*on* credidistis [ill]i S*í*
dixerimus ex hominib*us* timemus turbam omn*es* [enim] habebãt
iohannem sic*ut* profeatam [27] respondentes ad ih*m* d*i*xer*unt* nescimus
Ait ill*ís* ih*s* nec ego nob*ís* dico in qua [p]otestate h*aec* facio [28] quid
nob*ís* uidet*ur* homo quidam [h]abebat duos filios et accediens ad
primum [d*i*xit] filii uade hodie op*er*ari inuiniam meam [30] ille h*autem*
d*i*xit [eo] dom*i*ne et n*on* habiit Accessit h*autem* ad alium d*i*xit simi-
[liter] [29] ille h*autem* res*pondit* nolo et postea penetentia duct*us* Abiit
in uiniam [31] quis ergo ex duob*us* fecit uoluntatem patris dicunt nouis-
simus d*i*c*it* illis ih*s* Amen dico uobis qu*i*a puplicani et meritrices pra*e*-
[ce]dunt uos inregnum dei [32] Ueuit *enim* iohannis ad [u]os inula
iustitiae et n*on* credidistis ei puplicani h*autem* et meritrices
credidiar*unt* ei Uos h*autem* uidentes nec poenetentia*m* egistis qu*od*

---

xxi. 11. The page beginning with this verse is out of its place. See note to
xviii. 31.

xxi. 12. For "E[t cath]edras" we should pe*r*haps read "C[ath]edras."

credidistis ei postea [33]Alia*m* parabula*m* audite homo erat pat*er* famili-
[as] et plantauit ninias Et sepem circu*m* dediteu*m* [et] fodit in eam
torculár et edificauit turre*m* locauit ean colonis et pe*r*egre p*r*ofectus *est*
[34] C*u*m h*au*te*m* ad[p*r*o]p[in]casset fructu*m* tempus missit sernos suo[s]
ad [c]olonos ut acceperent defructib*us* suís [35] E[t]|coloni [f. 11 r.
ad*p*raechensís sernís unum coeder[*unt* a]lium lapidauer*unt*
alium ue*r*o occider*unt* [36] ite*r*u*m* missit alios seruos plures priori-
b*us* fecer*unt* illis similite*r* [37] nouissime h*au*te*m* missit illís filium
suu[m] unicum diciens uerebunt*ur* filiu*m* meu*m* [38] Coloni [h*au*te*m*]
uidentes filiu*m* d*i*xer*unt* intrase hic *est* heres uen[ite] occidam*us* eu*m*
Et habem*us* hereditate*m* ei*us* [39] et ad*p*raechensu*m* eu*m* occider*unt* et
deiecer*unt* extra uiniam [40] C*u*m ergo uenerit d*o*min*us* uiniae quid
faciet coloni[s il]lís [41] Et d*i*xer*unt* illi malos malae perdet et ueni[am]
locauit aliís colonís qui reddant ei fructus t[em]porib*us* suis [42] d*i*cit
illís ih*s* numq*uam* legistis inscript[u]rís Lapidem quem rep*r*obauer*unt*
ædificantes hic factus *est* in capud anguli ad*o*mino factus e[st] istud
hoc *est* mirabile inoculís nostrís [43] ideo dico nobís q*uia* auferetur a
uobís regnu*m* dei Et dabit*ur* genti facienti fructu*m* ei*us* [45] Et cum
audissent pri[n]cipes sacerdotu*m* et farissei fabulas cognouer[unt]
q*uod* deipsís diceret [46] et q*ue*rentes eu*m* tenere inuenier*unt* turbas

XXII. quonia*m* sicut p*r*ofeata eu*m* habeaban[t [1] Et] res*pon*diens ih*s* d*i*xit illis
inparabula*m* diciens [2] Simile [est] regnu*m* caeloru*m* homini regi qui
Nuptias filio suo [3] Et missit sernos suos uocare ad nuptias et noluer*unt*
uenire [4] Et iterum missit alios seruos diciens dicite inuitatís Ecce
prandiu*m* meu*m* parani tauri mei et saginata occissa Et|omnia [f. 11 v.
paratas*unt* uenite adnuptias [5] illi h*au*te*m* [n]eglexiar*unt* et abiar*unt*
alii in uillas suas alii ue*r*o ad negotione*m* sua*m* [6] caeteri h*au*te*m*
ad*p*raechensus illius contumilia adflictos occider*unt* [7] réx h*au*te*m*
audisset et iratus *est* Et missit exercitum suu*m* Et dispe*r*dit homicidas
illos et ciuitates eoru*m* succendit [8] tunc d*i*x*it* sernís suís Nuptiae quide*m*
parate s*unt* sed q*ui* uocatis*unt* nonfuiar*unt* digni [9] ITe ergo ad exitu*m*
uiarum Et quos cumq*ue* inueneritis uocate adnuptias [10] et egressi serui
illius inuias Et congregauer*unt* q*uot* q*uot* inueniar*unt* bonos et malos Et
inpletes*unt* nuptiae discumbentib*us* [11] intrauit autem réx ut uideret
discumbentes Et uidit ibi hominem ᴺᴼᴺ uestimentu*m* ueste nuptiale
[12] et ait illi ammiee q*uo*mo*do* huc uenisti n*on* habiens uestem nuptialem
At ille obmutuit [13] tunc réx missit ministros tollete eum manib*us* et
pedib*us* Et mitere eu*m* in tenebras exte*r*iores ibi erit fletus et stridor
dentiu*m* [14] Multi h*au*te*m* nocati pauci ue*r*o electi [15] Tunc abiar*unt*
farissei *consilium* fecer*unt* ut caperent eu*m* inuerbo [16] et misser*unt*
discipulos suos cum herodianís dicentes magiste*r* q*uia* uera n*on* *est*
tibi cura dealiquo n*on* *enim* respicis in pe*r*sonas hominum [17] q*uid*
uidet*ur* tibi sí licet censu*m* cessari á n*on* [18] cognoscens h*au*te*m*
ih*s* ᴺequitias eoru*m* d*i*xit Numquid me te*m*ptatis chypochrite
[19] Ostendite mihi nouisime censu*m* At illi optulle|r*unt* ei [f. 12 r.
denarium [20] ait illis ih*s* cuius *est* imago h[*aec*] et conscriptio

xxii. 17. "á" is probably a slip for "ā"=a*ut*.

²¹ dicunt ei cessaris Tunc dicit illís ihs reddite ergo quae sunt
cessaris cessari et quae sunt dei deo ²² Hiís auditís mirati sunt et relicto
eo recesserunt ²³ IN illa die accesserunt ad eum saducei qui dicunt
non esse resurrectionem Et interrogauerunt eum ²⁴ dicentes magister
moyses dixit sí quis mortuus illius fuerit nonhabiens filium adducat
fratrem uxorem illius et suscitet semen fratri suo ²⁵ Erant enim apud
nos ·ui· fratres Et primus uxorem duxit et mortuus est non habiens
semen reliquit uxorem suam fratri suo ²⁶ similiter et secundus et
tertius usque adseptimum ²⁷ nouissime hautem omnium et mulier
defuncta est ²⁸ IN resurrectione ergo cuius erit de ·uii· uxor omnes
enim habuerunt eam ²⁹ Respondiens ihs dixit errantes nescientes
scripturas neque uirtutem dei ³⁰ IN resurrectione ergo mortuorum
Neque nubunt Neque nubunt Neque nubuntur sed crunt sicut angeli dei
in caelo ³¹ Deresurrectione ergo non legistis quomodo dictum est nobis
adomino dicente ³² EGo sum deus abracham deus issác deus iacob non
est deus mortuor sed uiuentium ³³ Et cum audisset turbae mirabantur
indoctrinam eius ³⁴ farissei hautem audientes quod silentium inpossuit
saduceís congregatisunt aduersus eum ³⁵ INterrogauit eum unus
exeís legis doctor temptans eum Et dici∣ens ³⁶ magister   [f. 12 v.
quod mandatum maximum in lege. ³⁷ Et [a]it illi ihs dilegis
dominum deum tuum ex toto corde tuo Et in tota anima tua et
in tota mentatua ³⁸ hoc est mag[num] et primum mandatum
³⁹ secundum uero simile huic dileges proximum tuum tamquam te
ipsum ⁴⁰   IN hiis duobus mandatís tota léx pendet et profete
⁴¹ Congregatis hautem farisseís interrogauit eos ihs ⁴² diciens quid
nobís uidetur deoperibus fidelis est dicent ei dauid ⁴³ Ait illís ihs
quomodo ergo dauid dicit uocat eum dominum diciens ⁴⁴ Dixit
dominus domino meo sede adextrís meís donec ponam inimicostuos
scabellum pedum tuorum ⁴⁵ Sí ergo dauid inspiritu uocat eum dominum quomodo filius eius est ⁴⁶ Et nemo poterat respondere illi uerbum

XIII. Nec auus est quisquam exilla die quod eum amplius interrogare ¹ Tunc
locutus est turbís et discipulís suís ² diciens super cathedram moysi
sediarunt scribe et farissei ³ Omnia ergo quaecumque dixerunt nobís
facite et seruatae secundum nero facta corum Nolite facere dicunt enim
et ipsi non faciunt ⁴ Alligant enim honorograuia et inportabilia et
inponunt super humeros hominum digito suo noluit ea moueri ⁵ Omni
uero sua opera faciunt ut uidiantur abominibus dilatant enim filacteria
sua et magnificant fymbrias ⁶ Amant hautem primos discubitos in
conui∣uís et primas cathedras in sinagogís ⁷ et salutationes   [f. 13 r.
in foro et uocari ab hominibus rabbi ⁸ Uos ucro ne uocemini ab hominibus rabbi unus est enim magister uester xps Nam uós omnes fratres
estis ⁹ Et patrem nolite uocare nobís super terram unus est enim pater
uester qui in caelís est ¹⁰ Nec uocemini magistri quoniam magister
uester xps est ¹¹ qui uult maior inuobis esse erit nester minister ¹² Et

xxii. 24.   The word "et" is doubtful.
xxii. 40.   There is a space before "IN" in which a word (? Et) may perhaps be
written.

quicum*que enim* exaltauerit sé humiliabit*ur* et qui se humiliat exalt-
abit*ur* ¹³ Uae h*autem* nobis scribe et farissei chipochrite q*ui* cluditis
regn*um* caelorum ante homines Uos *enim* non*introitis* Nec introiuntes
sinitis introire ¹⁴ Ue nobis scribe et farissei chipochrite qui comeditis
domum uidbarum occassione longa orantes pr*opter* hoc accipietis
amplius iudici*um* ¹⁵ Uae uobís scribe et farissei chypocrite q*uia* cir-
cumitis mare et aridam ut faciatis unum pr*osilitum* Et cum factus
fuerit faciatis eu*m* fil*um* gechene duplo quam uos ¹⁶ Uae uobís duces
ceci qui dicitis qui cum*que* iurauerat intempl*um* nihil *est* qui h*autem*
iurauerit inaur*um* templi debitor *est* ¹⁷ stulti et cæci quid *enim* [maiu]s
est aur*um* án templum q*uod* sanctificat aur[*um* ¹⁸ et q]uicum*que* iurauerit inaltare nihil *est* Se[d qu]icum*que* iurauerat ineo q*uod est* super illud
debitor *est* ¹⁹ quid *enim enim* maius *est* donum *uel* altare q*uod* sanctificat
do|num ²⁰ Qui [eni]m iurauerat p*er* altare iurat p*er* eum et [f. 13 v.
p*er* omnia q*uae* sup*er* illud *sunt* ²¹ Et qui [iu]rauerat pertempl*um* iurat
in illo et in [eo] qui habitat in ipso ²² Et qui iurat p*er* cae[lum] iurat
p*er* thronu*m* dei et p*er* eu*m* qui sedit in ipso ²³ Uae uobís scribe et
farissei chypochrite qui· decimatis menta*m* et anniata*m* Et cyminu*m*
et reliquistis q*uae* grauiora s*unt* legis iudicium et misseric*ordiam* et
fidem pace*m* h*autem* oportuerat facere et illa n*on* omit*ere* ²⁴ duces
caeci excolentes calice*m* camellum h*autem* glutientis ²⁵ Uae uobís
scribae et farissei chipochrite qui mundatis quod deforis *est* calicis
et parapsidis intus h*autem* pleni rapina et iniquitate ²⁶ farissae caece
munda primu*m* q*uod* intus *est* calicis ut fiat id q*uod* deforis *est* mundum ²⁷ Uae nobís scribe et farisse q*uoniam* simile estis dealbatís
monumentís q*uae* aforis apparent hominib*us* speciossa intus ucro
pleana s*unt* os[sibus] mortuoru*m* Et omnes p[urcitia ²⁸ sic et] uos
quidem aforis par[etis hominibus] insti intus h*autem* pleni estis fi[cta
simulatione] et iniquitate ²⁹ U*e* nobís s[cribae et far]issei chypocrite
qui edificatis [sepul]chra pr*ofetarum* et ornatis monumenta [i]ustor*um*
³⁰ et dicitis q*uia* sí|fuissemus in dieb*us* patrum nostroru*m* [f. 14 r.
non [es]simus socii *e*orum insangine pr*ofetarum* ³¹ ita[que] testimonium p*er*ibetis nobís quia filii estis *e*orum q*ui* occideru*nt*
pr*ofeatas* ³² Et uos adinplete mensuram patrum uestror*um*.
³³ serpentes [ge]neratio uiperaru*m* q*uomodo* effugietis aiudicio
g[e]ene ³⁴ Ideo ecce ego mitto aduos pr*ofeatas* Et sa[pi]entes et
scribas et exillís occidetis Et crucifig[et]is et flagillabitis insinagogís
et p*er*sequemin[i] deciuitate inciuitatem ³⁵ Ideo uenit sup*er* uos omnis iustus sanguis q*ui* effuss*us est* sup*er* terra*m* asan[g]uine abiel
iusti usq*ue* adsanginem sacharie filii barachi[ae que]m occidistis
int*er*templu*m* et altare ³⁶ Amen [dico no]bis uenient h*aec* omnia
sup*er* generation[em istam] ³⁷ hirusalem hirusalem q*uae* occidis pr*o*-
feat[as] Et lapidas eos qui adte missi s*unt* quotiens uolui congregare
filios tuos sicut gallina congregat pullos suos sub alas suas Et

---

xxiii. 20. The reading "[eni]m" is perhaps doubtful.
xxiii. 28. The words "fi[cta simulatione]" are supported by *h*, and suit
the space.

noluisti ³⁸ Ecce relinqu*etur* uobis domus uestra deserta ³⁹ Dico h*autem*
uob*ís* q*uonia*m n*on* uidebitis me amodo donec dicatis b*e*nedic*tus* qui
XIV. uenit inn*omine* d*omi*ni ¹ Et ressus ih͞s det*e*mplo et ibat et accessiar*unt*
adeu*m* discipuli *eius* ut ostender*unt* ei fructura*m* templi ² Ipse
h*autem* res*pondiens* d*ixi*t uidetis h*aec* omnia Amen dico uob*ís* n*on* [re-]
lincet*ur* hic lapis sup*er* lapidem qui n*on*distru[atur] ³ Sedente h*autem*
illo inmonte oliueti accesser*unt* a[d eum] | discipuli [f. 14 v.
eius insaecriato dicentes d*í*c nob*ís* q*uando* er*unt* quod signu*m*
uentus tui et *con*summationem seculi ⁴ quib*us* respon[diens] · d*ixi*t
uidete Nequis uos seducat ⁵ Multi *enim* uenient inn*omine* meo
dicentes ego sum x͞p͞s et multos seducent ⁶ Audistis *enim* pugnas
et oppiniones bellor*um* s*ed* turbemini Oportet *enim* hoc fieri s*ed*
n*on*du*m* *est* finis ⁷ exurget *enim* gens *con*trag*entem* et regnu*m* *con*tra
regnu*m* et cr*unt* fames et t*er*re motus per loca ⁸ Omnia h*aec* s*unt* initia
dolor*um* ⁹ Tunt tradent uos intribulatione et occident uos et eritis
hodibiles gentib*us* pro*pter* nomen meum ¹⁰ Et t*unc* scandalizabunt
multi Et inuicem se tradent et occident se inuice*m* ¹¹ Et multi scodo-
pro*fete* exurgent Et multos seducent ¹² qu*i*a habundauit iniquit*ás* et
re[fri]gerescet carit*ás* multor*um* ¹³ qui h*autem* p*er*seuerauerit usq*ue* in
finem hic saluus erit ¹⁴ Et pr*ae*dicabitur h*óc* euangelium regni p*er*
totu*m* orbe*m* intestimonium omnib*us* gentib*us* Et t*unc* uenient finis
¹⁵ Cu*m* ergo uideritis abominationem desolutionis q*uod* dictu*m* *est* p*er*
danielum pro*fetum* stante*m* *in* loco s*an*cto qui legit intellegat ¹⁶ Tunc
qui in india s*unt* fugiant in montib*us* ¹⁷ Et q*ui* intecto s*unt* n*on*-
discendanttollere aliq*ui*d dedomo ¹⁸ Et q*ui* in agro s*unt* n*on* uert͞atur
tollere tonicas suas ¹⁹ Uæ h*autem* prignantib*us* et nutrientib*us* in
ill*ís* dieb*us* ²⁰ Orate h*autem* ut n*on* fiat fuga u*estra* cheme *uel* sabbato
²¹ erit *enim* tribulatio magna qualis n*on* fuit ab initio saeculi
usq*ue* modo s*ed*neq*ue* fiet ²² et nissi bre | uiati fuissent [f. 17 r.
dies illi n*on*saluasset omnis car[o sed] prop*ter* electos brebiabunt*ur*
dies illi ²³ Tunc si qui[s no]bis dixerit Ecce h*íc* ecce ill*íc* nolite
cred[ere ²⁴ su]rgent *enim* seodo x͞p͞i et seodo pro*fete* Et dabunt
sig[na] magna et prodigia ita ut inerrorem inducant*ur* s*í* fier[i]
pot*est* etia*m* electi ²⁵ ecce praedixi nob*ís* ²⁶ s*í* *enim* dixerint uob*ís*
ecce indeserto *est* Nolite credere ²⁷ sieut *enim* fulgor exiit aboriente
et apparet usq*ue* in occidente*m* ita erit aduentus filii hominis ²⁸ Ubi
fuerit corpus ill*íc* *con*gregabunt*ur* aquile ²⁹ Statim h*autem* post tribula-
tione*m* dieru*m* illor*um* s*ól* obscurabuntur et luna n*on* dauit lumen
suum Et stelle cadent decaelo Et uir[t]utes caelorum commoue-
buntur ³⁰ Et t*unc* apparebit signu*m* filii hominis incaelo et lamentabunt s*é* om[nes] trib*us* t*er*re et uidebunt filium hominis uenie*n*t[em]
in nubib*us* caeli cum uirtute multa et maiesta[te] ³¹ Et mittet angelos
suos cum uoce magna Et *con*[gre]gabunt electos suos aquatuor angul*ís*
uent[orum] assu*m*m*ís* caelor*um* usq*ue* adt*er*minos eorum Cum co[e

xxiv. 6. For "hoc" we should perhaps read "haec."
xxiv. 22. Fo. 17 has been misplaced by binder, and now follows that containing xxv. 34-xxvi. 18.
xxiv. 26. "*enim*" should perhaps be read "h*autem*."

[perint] *hautem* haec fieri respicite et leuate capud q*uonia*m adpro[piat]
redemtio uestra ³² Ab arbore *hautem* fici discite [para]bula*m* cu*m* ia*m*
ramus *eius* tener fuerit Et folia nata [fu]erint cognoscitis p*ro*pe e*ss*e
aestate*m* ³³ sic et uobis cu[m] uideritis *haec* omn*ia* scitote q*uonia*m
p*ro*pe *est* ianu*is* ³⁴ A[m]en dico uobis q*uonia*m n*on* p*ra*ete*r*ib*it*
generatio *haec* donec fiant [omn*ia*] ³⁵ caelu*m* et te*rra*m transib*unt*
Uerba *hautem* mea n*on* p*ra*eteribu[nt] | ³⁶ de die *hautem* [f. 17 v.
illa *uel* hora nemo scit nissi pat*er* solus ³⁷ S*icut* *enim* indieb*us*
noe. ita e*r*it aduentus filii hominis ³⁸ S*icut* *enim* erat in dieb*us*
ill*is* ante diluium manducabant et bibebant et nubebant uxores
ducebant usq*ue* indiem q*uo* int*r*auit noe i*n*arcam ³⁹ Et n*on*
senser*unt* donec uenit diluium ettullit omn*es* ita erit aduentus
filii hominis ⁴⁰ Tunc e*r*unt duo inagro un*us* adsu*m*metur et alius
relinq*uetur* ⁴¹ du*ę* molentes ad mola*m* una adsu*m*metur et alter
relinq*uetur* ⁴² Uigilate erg*o* quia nescitis qua die *uel* hora dom*i*n*us*
ues*ter* uenturus *est* ⁴³ illud *hautem* scitote q*uonia*m s*i* sciret pat*er*
familias qua hora f*u*r ueniet uigilaret utiq*ue* et *non* c*on*sentiret per-
foderi domu*m* sua*m* ⁴⁴ IDeo et uos estote parati q*uia* nescitis qua
hora filius hominis uenturus *est* ⁴⁵ Quis nam *est* fidelis ser*n*us et q*uem*
c*on*stituit dom*i*nus sup*er* familia*m* sua*m* ut det illi cybum intempore
⁴⁶ Beatus ser*n*us ille quem ueniens dom*i*n*us* *eius* *est* i*n*uenerit s*i*c
facientem ⁴⁷ Amen dico uob*is* q*uonia*m su[pr]a omnia bona sua c*on*-
stituet eu*m* ⁴⁸ S*i* *hautem* malus il[le s] e*r*uus d*i*xerit incordesuo mora*m*
facit dom*i*n*us* [me]us uenire adme ⁴⁹ Et incipiet c*on*seruos suos p*er*
cnt*er*e manducet *hautem* et bibet cum ebrios*is* ⁵⁰ Cum *hautem* ueniet
dom*i*n*us* serui illi*us* in die qua n*on*sperat et oraqua ignorat ⁵¹ et
diuidet eum parte*m* q*ue* *eius* ponet cum hypochritis Ibi erit fletus et
XXV. stridor dentium ¹ Tunc simulabitur regnum caelorum ·x· uirginib*us*
quae | acciper*unt* lampadas suas et p*ro*diar*unt* obia*m* sponsi [f. 15 r.
et sponse. ² ·u· *hautem* ex e*is* erant fatuae et ·u· sapientes ³ fatuae
hautem accept*is* lampadibus suis n*on* su*m*pser*unt* oleu*m* secu*m*
⁴ sapientes *hautem* sumpser*unt* oleum secu*m* in nass*is* cum lampadib*us*
suis ⁵ mora*m* *hautem* sponsu*s* faciente domier*unt* ⁶ media *hautem*
nocte clamor factus Ecce sponsu*s* uenit exite obiam ei ⁷ tunc surrexer*unt*
omn*es* ille uirgines acceper*t* lam padas suas ⁸ FAtuae *hautem*
sapientib*us* d*i*xerunt date nob*is* deoleo ue*st*ro q*uia* lampades nostre
extingunt*ur* ⁹ Resp*on*der*unt* prudentes d*i*xer*unt* nonne forte n*on*-
sufficiat nob*is* et uob*is* ite putins ad o*ue*s qui uendunt emite nob*is*
oleu*m* ¹⁰ euntes emere oleu*m* uenit sponsus Et quae parate erant
int*r*auer*unt* cum eo adnuptias et clausa *est* ianna ¹¹ postea ueniar*unt*
reliq*ue* uirgines dicentes dom*i*ne dom*i*ne aperii nob*is* ¹² At ille
res*p*ondiens d*i*cit Amen dico uobis. q*uia* nescio u*os* ¹³ uigilate itaq*ue*
q*uia* nesquitis diem Neque hora*m* ¹⁴ sicut *enim* homo p*er*egre p*ro*fici-
ciens uocauit seruos suos Et tradidit illis Substantia*m* sua*m* ¹⁵ Et
uni quidem dedit ·u· tallenta Alii *hautem* duo. Alii n*er*o unum
unicuiq*ue* *secundum* p*ro*pria*m* uirtutem Et profectus *est* continuo
¹⁶ *hautem* ab hiis ·u· tallenta acceperet et operatus *est* ine*is* Et lucratus

est alia ·u· [17] similit et qui duo tallenta acciperat lucratus *est* alia
duo [18] Qui h*autem* unum acciperit fudit inte*rr*am et abscondit
peccunia*m* domini sui [19] Pumultum^{ot}|tempus uenit d*omi*nus [f. 15 v.
seruorum illoru*m* Et cu*m* possuit rationem eis [20] accessit qui
·u· tallenta accipe*r*at Et obtullit alia ·u· diciens d*omi*ne ·u·
tallenta mihi tradidisti. ecce alia ·u· lucratus su*m* [21] ait illi d*omi*nus
eius euge serue bone et fidelis q*uia* super pauca fidelis fuisti
sup*er* multate constituam intra ingaudiu*m* tuu*m* et d*omi*ni tui
[24] Accedens h*autem* qui unum tallentum acciperat ait illi d*omi*ne
seebam q*uia* homo durus es metis ubi n*on* seminasti [25] Timui ergo
et abii Et abscondi tallentum tuu*m* inte*rr*a ecce habes q*uod* tuum
est [26] et respo*n*diens h*autem* d*omi*nus *eius* d*ixi*t ei serue nequ*am* et
piger scebas q*uia* meto ubi n*on*semino et colligo ubi n*on*sparsi
[27] Oportuit ergo uenundari peccunia*m* mea*m* numularis Et ego ueniens
recipisse*m* cu*m* ussuris q*uod* meu*m* est [28] tollite itaq*ue* abeo tallentum
et dá ei qui habet ·x· tallenta [29] Omni *enim* habenti dabit*ur* ei et
habundabit ei q*ui* n*on* habet q*uod* habet etia*m* auferet*ur* abeo [30] Et
nequam seruu*m* ieccit*ur* foras intenebras exte*r*iores illic erit fletus Et
stridor dentium [31] Cum h*autem* uenerit filius hominis inmaiestate sua
et omn*es* angeli cum eo tunc sedebit sup*er* sede*m* maiestatis suae [32] Et
*con*gregabuntu*r* ante eu*m* omn*es* gentes et sperauit eos abinuice*m*
Sicut pastor segregat eos abedís^{ue} [33] et statuet oues quide*m* adextrís suís
edos h*autem* asenistrís [34] Tunc dicet réx bís q*ui* adextrís su*n*t Uenite
bene*d*icti patris mei possedite|regnu*m* q*uod* nobis paratum [f. 16 r.
est aborigine mundi [35] Essuriui *enim* et dedistis mihi manducare
Sitiui et dedistis mihi bibere ospes eram et suscipistis me
[36] Nudus et co ope*r*uistis me infirmus era*m* et uissitastis me IN
carcere*m* fui et uenistis adme [37] Tu*n*c respondebunt ei dicentes insti
d*omi*ne q*uan*do té uidimus essuriente*m* et pauimus té a*ut*sitiente*m*
et pauimus té [38] a*ut* q*uan*do h*autem* teuidimus hospitem et suscipimus
té a*ut* nudu*m* et co operuimus té [39] *uel* q*uan*do té uidimus infirmu*m*
uel in carcere et uenimus adté [40] Et respo*n*diens rex dicet illís Amen
dico nobís quandiu fecistis uni ex fratrib*us* meís minimís mihi
fecistis [41] Tunc dicet hiís qui asenistrís su*n*t discedite ame maledicti-
sunt in igne*m* ete*r*nu*m* q*uem* p*r*aeparauit pat*er* meus sabulo et angelís
eius [42] Essuriui *enim* et n*on* dedistis mihi manducare sitiui et n*on*dedistis mihi bibere [43] hospis era*m* etn*on* suscipistis me Nudus fui etn*on*
co ope*r*uistis me INfirmus fui et incarcere et n*on* uenistis adme
[44] Tunc respondent ei iniusti dicentes d*omi*ne q*uan*do te uidimu*s*
essuriente*m* etsitiente*m* a*ut* hospitem a*ut* nudum a*ut* infirmum a*ut*
in carcere Et n*on* ministrauim*us* tibi [45] Tunc re̅spondet eís diciens
Amen dico nobís quandiu n*on* fecistis uni ex minimis istís nec
mihi fecistis [46] Et tunc ibn*n*t in insti inigne*m* ete*r*nu*m* iusti h*autem*
inuita*m* pe*r*petuam [1] Et factu*m* *est* cum consu*m*masset ih̅s̅ omnia
nerba h*ae*c d*ixi*t discipulís suís|[2] scitis q*uia* post biduum [f. 16 v.
pascha fiat Et filius hominis tradet*ur* principib*us* sacerdotu*m* et

XVI.

xxvi. 2. The second letter of "cr[ucif]iget*ur*" looks more like "u" than "r."

cr[ucif]igetur ³ Tunc *congregati* sunt principes sacerdotum et seniores
populi in atrium principis sacerdotum qui uocabatur caiphas ⁴ et
consilium fecerunt ut ihm̄ dolo tenerent ⁵ et dicebant non in diem
festum Et tumultus fierit in populo ⁶ Cum *hautem* esset ihs̄ in
bethania in domu simonis leprosi ⁷ accessit adeum mulier habiens
alabastrum ungenti praetiosi Et effudit super capud eius recum
bente ipso ⁸ quod cum uidissent discipuli indignatisunt dicentes
ut quid perditio haec ⁹ potuit haec uenundari praetio magna et
dari pauperibus ¹⁰ quod ut cognouit ihs̄ ait illís quid molesti estis
mulieri Bonum opus operata est in me ¹¹ non semper pauperes habebitis
uobiscum me *hautem* nonsemper habebitis ¹² Ecce enim mittiens in
corpus meum ungentum adsepeliendum mefecit ¹³ Amen dico nobis ubi
cumque praedicatum fuerit hoc euangelium intoto mundo narrabitur
Et quod fecit haec inmemoriam ipsius ¹⁴ Tunc ābiit unus dediscipulís
suís qui dicitur iudas scarioth Et principes sacerdotum ¹⁵ Et ait illis
quid uultis mihi dare etego uobís eum trad[am] at illi constituerunt
ei xxx· staterís ¹⁶ Et ex inde querebant oportunitatem ut eum traderet
eis ¹⁷ prima *hautem* die azemorum accesserunt discipuli ad ihm̄ dicentes
ubi uís paremus tibi comedere phascha ¹⁸ At ille dixit eis

*   *   *   *   *   *   *

│ ad discipulos suos et ait illís dormite iam et requies cite ecce   [f. 18 r.
adpropincauit ora et filius hominis tradetur inmanus peccatorum ⁴⁶ surgite
eamus ecce adpropincauit qui me tradit ⁴⁷ Ad huc eo loquente ecce iudas
unus de xii et cum eo turba multa cum gladís et fustibus misi aprincipibus sacerdotum etsenioribus populi ⁴⁸ qui *hautem* tradet eum dicit
dedit illís signum diciens quem cumque osculatus fuero ipse est tenete
eum ⁴⁹ Et confestim accessit ad ihm̄ et dixit aue rabbi osculatus est
eum ⁵⁰ cui dixit ihs̄ āmice ad quod uenisti fác Tunc accesserunt et
manus inecierunt in ihm̄ et tenuerunt eum ⁵¹ et unus ex hís qui erant
cum ihū Extendiens manum exemit gladium suum et percussit sernum
principis sacerdotum et abscidit auriculam eius ⁵² Tunc ait illi ihs̄
conuerte gladium tuum in locum suum omnes enim qui accipiunt
gladium gladio peribunt ⁵³ aut non putatis possum me modo rogare
patrem meum Et exiberet mihi plus quam xii milia legionis angelorum
⁵⁴ quomodo ergo inplebuntur scripturę quasi oportet fieri ⁵⁵ in il[l]a hora
dixit ihs̄ ad turbas quasi ad latro[nem] uenistis cum gladís et fustibus
conpraechendere me Cotidie apud uos eram intemplo dociens
et nontenuistis me ⁵⁶ Hoc *hautem* totum factum est ut inpleretur
│ scripturae profetarum tunc discipuli eius relicto fugerunt   [f. 18 v.
⁵⁷ illi *hautem* tenentes ihm̄ et perduxerunt eum ad caifán princi pes sacerdotum inquo scribe et sacerdotes conuenerant ⁵⁸ Petrus *hautem* sequebatur eum alonge usque in atrium principis sacerdotum Et ingressus
intus sedebat cum ministrís uideret exitum rei ⁵⁹ principes *hautem*

xxvi. 8.   We should perhaps read " hoc " for " haec."
xxvi. 18.   A misplaced leaf (f. 17) follows this verse in the manuscript.
See note on xxiv. 22.

sacerdotum Et uniuersum concilium querebant falsum testimonium
aduersus ihm ut eum morti traderent ⁶⁰Et non inuenerunt in eum
quiquam nouisse hautem uenerunt duo falsi testes ⁶¹Et dixerunt
Audiuimus hunc dixise possum distruare templum dei hoc etintridum
re dificare illud ⁶²Et surgiens princeps sacerdotum ait illi adiuro té
per deum uiuum ut dicas nobis si tues xp̄s̄ filius dei uiui Et dixit illi
nihil respondis ad ea quae isti aduersus testificantur ⁶³ih̄s̄ hautem
tacebat respondiens principes sacerdotum Ait illi adiuro té per deum
uiuum ut dicas nobis si tu es xp̄s̄ filius dei uiui ⁶⁴Et dixit illi illi
ih̄s̄ tú dixisti Uerumtamen dico uobis amodo uidebitis filius
hominis sedentem adextris uirtutis Et uenientem innubibus caeli
⁶⁵Tunc princeps sacerdotum scidit uestimen|ta sua diciens   [f. 19 r.
scidit blasfemauit quid adhúc opus uobis Ecce audistis blasfemiam
eius ⁶⁶quid uobis uidetur At illi responderunt omnes dixerunt
reus est mortis ⁶⁷tunc expuerunt in faciam eius et colofis cedentes
⁶⁸profetiza nobis xp̄ē quis te percussit ⁶⁹Petrus hautem foris inatrio
sediabat Et accessit ad eum una ancilla dixit ei et tu cum ihū
galilio eras ⁷⁰at ille negauit coram omnibus diciens nescio quid-
dicis neque intellego ⁷¹EXiunte hautem illo ad ianua uidit eum
alia ancilla et ait eis qui erant ibi Et hic erat cum ihū galilio ⁷²Et
iterum negauit eum iuramento diciens nonnoui hominem ⁷³et post
pussillum accipiarunt qui ministrabant et dixerunt petro uere exillis
es tú nam et loquellam tuam manifestaté ⁷⁴Tunc coepit deuotare sé et
iurare quod non nouisset hominem Et continuo gallus cantauit ⁷⁵Et
recordatus est petrus nerbi ihū quod dxerat prius quam gallus cantet
VII. ter me negabis Et egressus foras amarissime fleuit ¹Mane hautem facto
consilium fecerunt principes sacerdotum et seniores plebis aduersus
ihm ut eum morti traderent ²Et uinctum adduxerunt eum et tradidia-
runt pontio pylato praessidi ³Uidiens ih̄s̄ indas qui eum tradidit
quia damnatus esset poenetentia ductus retullit truogenta argenteos
principibus sacerdotum Et senioribus ⁴diciens peccaui quod tradi
|derem sanguinem insti At illi dixerunt quid ad nos tú   [f. 19 v.
uideris ⁵Et piecteis arcadgabuthc intem plo secessit et abit et laqueo
se suspendit ⁶tunc princeps sacerdotum acceptis argenteis dixit non licet
mittere eos in corbán hoc est in locum quia praetium sanguinis est
⁷Consilio hautem accepto emerunt exillis agrum figuli insepulturam
perigrinorum ⁸propter quod uocatus est ager ille acheldemáth quod
est ager sanguinis usque in odiernum diem ⁹Tunc inpletum est quod
dictum erat per heremiam pro featam dicentem et accipert xxx
argenteos praetium quod adpraetiatuerunt filius israhel ¹⁰et dederunt
eos inagrum figuli sicut constituit mihi dominus ¹¹ih̄s̄ hautem stetit
ante praessidem Et interrogauit eum praesses tues réx iudeorum dicit
ei ih̄s̄ tu dicis ¹²Et cum acesit á principibus sacerdotum et senioribus
nihil respondebat ¹³TUNc dicit illi pylatus non audis quanta aduersus
té dicunt testimonia ¹⁴Et non respondit ei ullum uerbum ita miraretur
praesis uechimenter ¹⁵per diem sollem nem CONsuerat praessis dimitere
populum unum uinctum quem uoluisent ¹⁶habebant hautem uinctum

insigne*m* q*ui* d*icitu*r barabbañ ^{17} *congregatis*u*nt* h*autem* illís d*ixit*
pylatus q*uem* uultis dimittañ uobís barabán a*ut* ihm̄ qui d*icitu*r
x̄p̄s̄ ^{18} sciebat h*autem* q*uod* p*er* in uidia*m* tradi | der*u*nteum [f. 20 r.
^{19}sedente h*autem* illo p*r*o tribunali missit ad eu*m* uxor *eius* diciens
nihil sit tibi et iusto illi diciens multa *enim* pasus su*m* hodie p*er*
uisu*m* prop*ter* eu*m* ^{20} Principes h*autem* sacerdotes et seniores populi
p*er*suaser*unt* populo ut peteret barabán ihs̄ h*autem* p*er*dider*unt*
^{21} resp*ondiens* h*autem* p*r*aesis ait illis q*uem* uultis deduobu*s* dimitta*m*
uobis At illi d*ixer*unt*runt* barabbán ^{22} D*ici*t illís pylat*us* q*uid* er*go*
faciem*us* ihū qui d*icitu*r x̄p̄s̄ ^{23} d*icu*nt omnes crucifigat*ur* Ait illís
p*r*aessis q*uid* *enim* mali fecit at illi magis clamabant crucifigat*ur*
^{24} Uidiens h*autem* pylat*us* q*uia* q*uod* fecit nihil s*ed* magis tumult*us* fieri
acepta aqua lauit manu*s* suas coram populo diciens   INnocens ego
sum assanguine huiu*s* iusti uos uideritis ^{25} et resp*ondiens* uniuersa tu*r*ba
d*ixit* sanguis *eius* sup*er* nés et sup*er* filios uestros ^{26} T*unc* dimissit illís
barabbán ihs̄ h*autem* flagillís cesum traditit eís ut crucifigerent illum
^{27} Tunc militis p*r*aesides duxer*unt* eu*m* inpraetorium et *congregau*er*unt*
adeu*m* uniuersu*m* chortem ^{28} et *cum* spoliassent eu*m* uestiar*unt* tonicam
purpureu*m* et clamide*m* cocinia*m* *cum* deder*unt* ei ^{29}et coronam despinís
texer*unt* Et possuer*unt* sup*er* capud *eius* inarundine*m* dexter*am* et ad
genu flexu ante eu*m* delúdentes eu*m* dicentes aue réx iudeorum ^{30} Et
expuer*unt* infacia*m*eius accipiar*unt* infacie*m*eius acciper*unt* arun-
dine*m* et p*er*cutiabant capud *eius* ^{31} et p*ost* q*uam* inluser*unt* eu*m* et
spoliauer*unt* eu*m* calamide*m* ut crucifigeret*ur* induer*unt* | eu*m* [f. 20 v.
uestimente sua ^{32} EXeuntes h*autem* inuenerunt hominem cirinium
uenientem obiam sibi no*m*ine simonem hunc [an]gari auer*unt*
uttollere*nt* crucem ^{33} et uenit inlocu*m* qui d*icitu*r golgoda q*uod* *est*
caluarie locus ^{34} Et deder*unt* ei bibere uinum Et *cum* felle mixtu*m* et
cum gustaret noluit bibere ^{35} P*ost*q*uam* crucifixer*unt* diuisiar*unt*
uestimenta sua miser*unt* sortes ut inpleretu*r* q*uod* dictu*m* *est* per
p*r*ofeata*m* Diuisiar*unt* siui uestimenta mea et sup*er* uestem mea*m*
miser*unt* sorte*m* ^{36} et sedentes seruauear*unt* ^{37} et inposuer*unt* sup*er*
capud*eius* causa*m* scriptu*m* *est* hic *est* ihs̄ x̄p̄s̄ rex iudeor*um* ^{38} t*unc*
crucifixer*unt* cu*m*eo duos latrones unu*m* addexter*am* et unu*m* adsin-
istra*m* ^{39} Transseuntes h*autem* blasfemabant eu*m* mouentes capita sua
^{40} et dxer*unt* ei uá qui distruas te*m*plum dei et intriduo redificabas
illud libera té ipsum si fili*us* dei es Et discende de cruce ^{41} similit*er*
et p*r*incipes sacerdotu*m* deludes eu*m* Et scribís et farisseís dicebant
^{42} alios salnos fecit se ipsum n*on* pot*est* saluu*m* facere sí réx israhel *est*
discendat nunc decruce et credim*us* in eu*m* ^{43} *con*fidet in*deum* libent*er*
n*unc* sí uult eu*m* D*ixit* *enim* q*uia* fili*us* dei sum ^{44} id ipsum h*autem* et
latrones q*ui* crucifixer*unt* *cum* eo inp*r*operabant ei ^{45} et p*ost* qua*m*
crucifixu*s* *est* Asexta h*autem* hora tenebrae factae su*nt* sup*er*
uniuersa*m* te*r*ra*m* in hora*m* nona*m* ^{46}circa ne*r*o hora*m* noua*m* clamauit
ihs̄ uoce magna helii h̀aelii labath sabathani нoc *est* de*us* me*us* de*us*
meus | quid me dereliquisti ^{47} quida*m* h*autem* illic stantes et [f. 21 r.

xxvii. 45. "super" ends a line: "uniuersam" is preceded by a space.

audientes diciabant heliam uocat iste [48] Et continuo surgiens unus
exeis acceptam spongiam inpleuit aceto Et inpossuit arundini et
dabat ei bibere [49] ceteri uero dixerunt sine uidiamus siueniat helias
etliberauit eum Alius hautem accepta lancia pupungit latus eius et
exiit aqua et sanguis [50] ihs hautem iterum exclamans uoce magna
emisit spiritum [51] et ecce uelum templi scisum est in duas partes
assummo usque deorsum Et terra mota est et petrae scisesunt [52] et
monumenta ápertae sunt Et multa corpora sanctorum dormientium
surrexiarunt [53] et exiuntes demonumentis post resurrextionem ipsius
etuenerunt in sanctam ciuitatem et multis apparuit [54] CEntorio
hautem et qui cum eo erant custodientes ihm cum uidissent terre
motum et ea que fiabant timuarunt ualde dicentes uere filius di erat
iste [55] Erant hautem ibi mulieres multae alonge uidentes quae secutac
fuerant ihm agalilia ministrantes illi [56] inter quas erat maria magda-
leana Et maria iacobi et ioseph mater et mater filiorum sebedei [57] Cum
hautem sero factum esset uenit quidam homo dines abarimathia
nomine ioseph qui et ipse discipulus erat ihu [58] hic accessit ad
pylatum et petit corpus ihu tunc pylatus iusit dari cor

---

xxvii. 54. For "timuarunt" possibly "timiiarunt" should be read.
xxvii. 58. The verso of the leaf which ends here is blank.

APPENDIX B.

THE SCRIBES OF THE BOOK OF MULLING.

IN the foregoing pages I have endeavoured to avoid speaking dogmatically as to the number of scribes who were at work upon our book.   The question whether the entire manuscript was penned by a single hand is one which must be left for its final decision to expert palæographers.   I think it well, however, to state here the convictions on this subject which have been produced by a fresh examination of the book, made when this work was already in type.

I believe that I can distinguish the work of four different scribes in its pages.   The Synoptic Gospels appear to have been written throughout, with the exception of a few pages to be mentioned presently, by a scribe whom we may designate by the letter A.   He was assisted or followed by three others:

B, who wrote the first fasciculus, containing Jerome's Prefaces, etc. This scribe seems to have written with the side of his pen, the horizontal strokes being heavier than the vertical.   This peculiarity distinguishes him at the first glance from A.   He further differs from the latter in the form of certain letters.   The letter *a*, for example, is usually open at the top; the horizontal stroke of *g* is written to the right of the vertical stroke, and sometimes resolves itself into a mere curved continuation of the latter; *z* also varies from the norm.   Some of the abbreviations are peculiar, such as p^t, instead of p^o, for *post*, ig^i instead of g', for *igitur* ⌢ instead of ÷, for *est*, at instead of h̄, for *autem*.

C, the writer of the Office for the Visitation of the Sick: see above p. 9.   Like B, this writes p^t for *post*.

D, the scribe of St John's Gospel.   His most prominent characteristic is his frequent use of the double point (..) as a punctuation mark, and his habit of dividing the text into short paragraphs.   His large initials are not usually projected into the margin.   He seldom uses the symbol known as " ceann fa eite " (ff), so frequently found in the Synoptic Gospels.   His *a* and *g* resemble those of B, but he uses also an open *q* and is fond of V and *v* for U and *u*, and (now and then) of N for *n*.   He writes g^o, instead of g̊, for *ergo*.

It has next to be remarked that, supposing the distinction between these scribes to have been made out, it can, if I mistake not, be proved that A B D were contemporary.   A has, in fact, sometimes handed his pen to one of the others.   Thus f. 62 (Luke, vii. 4–viii. 2) has been shown to differ in its script from the pages which precede and follow it.   But the peculiarities which distinguish it are in almost all cases found in the first fasciculus: it has the same forms for *a g z*, while the symbol for *est* differs only by the addition of a mark like a comma below the horizontal line.[1]   We may conclude,

---

[1] This difference is quite consistent with identity of hand. We find a similar

with some probability, that for this leaf B relieved A. When we turn to the first column of the verso of f. 72 (Luke xiv. 28–xv. 7) we find a not less striking difference from the preceding and following writing, and here we recognise at once the hand of D. There is the same fondness for short paragraphs and the double point which we have noticed in St John, the same forms of *a, q* and *n* are found, and the same abbreviation is used for *ergo.*

It is clear that if the conclusion to which we seem now to have been led is correct, some statements made in an earlier part of this volume must be modified. We can no longer (see pp. 8 *sq.,* 72 *sq.*) speak of the entire manuscript as coming from the pen of a single scribe. It was the work of a group of scribes who wrote side by side in the same scriptorium. The corrector, again, is not to be identified with the scribe of the book, but with one of the three A B D, or perhaps with another of the same set of workers. It is worth noting here that the marginal numerator agrees with the writer of the Eusebian Canons, against the text, in representing the number five by *v* rather than by *u.* May we infer that both numbers and corrections were added by B? See above p. 70.

But, again, if we have succeeded in showing that our Book was penned by a group of contemporary scribes, working together, we find at once a strong corroboration of the hypothesis that the colophon is not original (above p. 17). For it is clearly written by D, the scribe, as we have seen, of but one of the five fasciculi. And yet it undoubtedly asserts that the entire manuscript was written by one scribe, and it no less certainly implies that that scribe was the author of the colophon itself. This, if we have argued aright, is untrue in the case of the book now in our hands, though there is no reason why it should not have been true of its archetype.

But on the other hand it is right to state that the unanimity of palæographers as to the date of our manuscript has been somewhat over-stated at p. 15. So competent an authority as Mr W. M. Lindsay wrote on Oct. 24 1896 : "What precise amount of authority the tradition has which connects it [the Book of Mulling] with the end of the seventh century I do not know. But so far as I can see, there is no palæographical counter-evidence. . . . The nearest approach to the Book of Mulling is the Naples Charisius." And again, on Feb. 11, 1897 : "I saw the Naples Charisius at Rome. . . I saw enough to convince me that the writing is Irish pointed minuscule of a style very closely resembling that of the Book of Mulling." And he then proceeds to mention certain authorities who assign the Naples manuscript to the end of the seventh or beginning of the eighth century.

variation in the symbol for *est* in the Rosslyn Missal, an Irish MS in the Advocates' Library, Edinburgh, in passages undoubtedly written by the same scribe. The word *dixit* does not occur in the first fasciculus, nor do *post, igitur,* in f. 62. It is therefore impossible to argue from the peculiar abbreviations used for these words.

INDEX.

NEILL AND COMPANY, PRINTERS, EDINBURGH.

CPSIA information can be obtained at www.ICGtesting.com
Printed in the USA
BVOW06s2056200516

448935BV00021B/168/P